TEACHING LITERATURE IN THE REAL WORLD

TEACHING LITERATURE IN THE REAL WORLD

A Practical Guide

Patrick Collier

BLOOMSBURY ACADEMIC
LONDON • NEW YORK • OXFORD • NEW DELHI • SYDNEY

BLOOMSBURY ACADEMIC
Bloomsbury Publishing Plc
50 Bedford Square, London, WC1B 3DP, UK
1385 Broadway, New York, NY 10018, USA
29 Earlsfort Terrace, Dublin 2, Ireland

BLOOMSBURY, BLOOMSBURY ACADEMIC and the Diana logo are trademarks of Bloomsbury Publishing Plc

First published in Great Britain 2021

Copyright © Patrick Collier, 2021

Patrick Collier has asserted his right under the Copyright, Designs and Patents Act, 1988, to be identified as Author of this work.

For legal purposes, the Acknowledgments on pp. viii–ix constitute an extension of this copyright page.

Cover design by Eleanor Rose
Cover images © Getty Images

All rights reserved. No part of this publication may be reproduced or transmitted in any form or by any means, electronic or mechanical, including photocopying, recording, or any information storage or retrieval system, without prior permission in writing from the publishers.

Bloomsbury Publishing Plc does not have any control over, or responsibility for, any third-party websites referred to or in this book. All internet addresses given in this book were correct at the time of going to press. The author and publisher regret any inconvenience caused if addresses have changed or sites have ceased to exist, but can accept no responsibility for any such changes.

A catalogue record for this book is available from the British Library.

A catalog record for this book is available from the Library of Congress.

ISBN: HB: 978-1-3501-9505-9
PB: 978-1-3501-9506-6
ePDF: 978-1-3501-9508-0
eBook: 978-1-3501-9507-3

Typeset by Deanta Global Publishing Services, Chennai, India

To find out more about our authors and books visit www.bloomsbury.com and sign up for our newsletters.

To my students and colleagues, and especially my greatest teachers: Bonnie Kime Scott and Ann Ardis

CONTENTS

Acknowledgments viii
Preface x

1 Why Teach Literature? Or, What Exactly Are We Doing? 1

2 Teaching Advanced Reading Comprehension 25

3 Teaching Advanced Literacy 59

4 Articulating Goals and Designing Integrated Courses 97

5 Managing Relationships 119

Appendix 1: Engaging Students in Criticism and Theory 131
Appendix 2: Grading and Feedback in Literature Classes 141
Notes 150
Bibliography 158
Index 161

ACKNOWLEDGMENTS

In 2002, in my third year on tenure track, a colleague unexpectedly asked me to teach a class I had never dreamed of teaching: a graduate course on literary pedagogy called "Teaching Literature in Higher Education." Another colleague had been pulled into an administrative role, leaving the course open and needing to be assigned on relatively short notice.

At the time, I was very much struggling to figure out effective pedagogical practices, even to understand what I was trying to do in the literature classroom. My own training in pedagogy amounted to an informal, one-credit class in graduate school that took place on some couches arranged in a faculty lounge. The course I was being asked to teach was a full, three-credit class and a requirement for our literature PhD students.

I was nervous, but I was also pretenure; I didn't feel like I could say no. And I thought, "Well, I'll figure out what on earth I'm trying to do by teaching this class."

This late assignment was the first of many minor career twists and turns that led me toward this book. Others included being called upon to lead the committee devising a program assessment system for my department, witnessing the creation of a new core curriculum designed around the then-striking concept of "cognitive transformations" (and, as an administrator, helping populate it with English courses), and serving as a member of my university's New Faculty Academy—a robust on-boarding program for new tenure-track hires.

I am in debt to everyone who helped me at each of these stages, but none so much as the students that took "Teaching Literature in Higher Education" that year and in subsequent years, as I became the course's main instructor. Year after year, students in that class have been willing to investigate the existential questions about the teaching of literature: Why do we do it? What are its politics? How does it benefit students to study literature in college? What exactly is the nature of their learning? Their answers have consistently surprised and enriched me, prodding me to a cycle of new classroom experiments, more reading, and more trial and error—all of which provided grist for the next iteration of "Teaching Literature in Higher Education."

The immediate spark to write this book came in lunch conversations with Sreyoshi Sarkar, a new faculty member in 2017 and my mentee. We talked pleasurably and at length about the problems and joys of teaching literature. At one of these meetings, she said, "You should write a book about this stuff." So thanks, Sreyoshi.

Thanks are due also to the many innovative teachers I have had as colleagues, including Amit Baishya, Melissa Adams-Campbell, Joyce Huff, Vanessa Rapatz, Adam Beach, and Emily Rutter. Add to these Lauren Onkey, whose section of "Teaching Literature in Higher Education" I took over in 2002 and who held my hand and passed a brilliant syllabus to me that year. Suzanne Churchill and Helen Sword, colleagues from other universities, helped me to make the course mine over the ensuing years, both through their published writing about their pedagogical experiments and with suggestions for reading. Thanks also to Annette Biesecker, who came to the rescue, with *pro bono* administrative assistance, when I had emergency eye surgery near the end of this project.

Finally, huge thanks to two more brilliant teachers and colleagues, Molly Ferguson and Deborah Mix, resourceful and original teachers who provided feedback on draft versions of this book—friends to whom I go often with teaching conundrums.

PREFACE

Teaching literature in college is difficult, and doing it successfully over the long term requires an ability to walk away from unsuccessful classes, student conferences, even entire semesters, without giving in to self-doubt, cynicism, or burnout. Successful literature teachers accept the messy, inconsistent results that can follow even the best planning and intentions. Then, with care and deliberation, successful literature teachers reflect on what went wrong in that classroom (or in that conference, or with that assignment) and discern where the problem lay and what they could have done differently (sometimes, though rarely, the answer is "nothing"). In doing so, they deliberately transform a single, contingent, and unpleasant event into knowledge: it becomes part of their bank of teaching experience, producing at minimum a memory they can draw on when a similar situation arises again, at best a new strategy that becomes part of their repertoire.

The emotional results of this process are as important as any concrete strategies that emerge. Successful teachers have to walk a narrow path between caring too much and numbing themselves to the inevitable feelings of disappointment and inadequacy that go with the territory of teaching. Teaching literature can be amazingly rewarding. How many jobs can you name which entail—even enforce—a lifelong process of learning, growth, and self-knowledge, a lifetime of grappling with important ideas and working to give others access to them? Experiencing the joy of a successful career as a literature professor, though, means doing it with absorption and intensity. It requires enough commitment that the small failures—the class period badly spent, the look of boredom on a student's face, the recalcitrant learner, unreached in a conference—are going to hurt. If you don't feel anything at moments like these, you are not putting enough of yourself into the work of teaching. However, there is a difference between experiencing disappointment and allowing it to undermine your confidence. Successful literature teachers know that their work is difficult; they accept the inevitability of small failures, feel the short-lived pain they bring, and then integrate them into their knowledge and experience, turning them into strengths.

This book is designed to help people who teach literature in college to succeed—to experience and enjoy the absorption, commitment, and passion of a professional life spent engaging with imaginative texts and helping students develop the capacities and dispositions to do the same. It does so by offering an unvarnished description of what teaching literature is really like for me and, I believe, for many professors like me, teaching in ordinary, nonelite colleges and universities with substantial teaching and service loads. I start from the premise that successful teaching begins with acceptance of the conditions you find yourself in—from your work demands, to the preparation of your students and the challenges they face, to the eccentricities of your institutional culture. (Acceptance does not mean approval, and working to change adverse conditions is also part of your job.) But I have called this book *Teaching Literature in the Real World* in part to underscore the reality that teaching necessarily takes place among, and has to work with, a steady stream of frustrations and small failures. On this basis I hope that this book will speak to literature teachers everywhere, regardless of the kinds of students they teach or the specific obstacles they face, though the book's insights are drawn from my experience, at a second-tier state university serving a mostly traditionally college-aged student body.

From that basis it goes on to offer thoughts about what we can and should try to achieve in literature classes and what strategies are best suited to these goals. If a clear-eyed acceptance of the joys and frustrations of teaching literature in the real world is the foundation of success in this field, it is just as essential that we understand and can articulate—in the greatest detail possible—what we think the goals of literary study in college are: otherwise, how can we pursue them?

The core of my argument here is that teaching literature means teaching *methods*: methods of reading and writing, interpretive and analytical methods, most crucially methods of *learning*. It names the concrete benefits, for students, of this approach as *advanced reading comprehension* and *advanced literacy*. It explains these concepts and argues for their utility as a framework for understanding what we are trying to do—and how we might go about doing it—in the literature classroom. And it offers advice—from how to adjust psychologically to the realities of teaching literature in the real world to specific classroom strategies for leading students toward these goals.

My own acceptance of realities has been a slow process and is ongoing. I teach at a successful and dynamic second-tier state school that morphed fifty years ago from a "normal school" (teaching college) and has been in a long transition to becoming a true university. It has a distinctly bureaucratic culture—historically generating and rewarding a lot of administrative and service work, and its flagship programs (which naturally receive a lot of attention and resources) are not the old, traditional liberal arts disciplines. I work in a small, rust-belt city, far, in all imaginable ways, from the teeming, culture-drenched East Coast cities in which my teen-aged and young-adult dreams were set. I teach students of widely varying abilities and levels of preparation for college, a vast majority of whom view college mainly as a means to good work and economic security or mobility.

And yet in important ways my work conditions are ideal. I teach three sections per semester of literature and film studies courses to groups of twenty-five or fewer students, a setting perfect for the discussion-driven class sessions and writing- and project-intensive work I favor. I have the luxury of knowing students pretty well and being able to give them extra attention when they want it (although balancing their needs against the other demands of my job is a constant, ongoing negotiation). I give a great deal of feedback on student writing and thinking. Much of this is possible because I have not, on the one hand, had to struggle with an outrageous teaching load or a heavy component of first-year writing or, on the other hand, faced excessive scholarship expectations for tenure and promotion. My department does not run large lecture classes with cohorts of graduate assistants who do the work of leading discussion and engaging with student writing (or, as I like to call these activities, the teaching!).

My place in the middle of the higher-education pecking order has thus given me a very close look at the kinds of learning that do (and do not) happen in literature classrooms, to see students grow and change across multiple classes and to know what many of them end up doing afterward. This experience has shaped the evolving positions I take in this book about such matters as the canon, the politics of teaching literature, and the relative value and relations of empirical knowledge and skills, among many other issues. I believe that this point of view reveals some fundamentals of teaching literature in higher education that, when foregrounded, will benefit teachers in any institutional setting.

At all times, this book acknowledges the inevitability of difficulty, even failure, and the need for both students and teachers to transform the frustration of small failures into the impetus for learning and growth.

1 WHY TEACH LITERATURE?

OR, WHAT EXACTLY ARE WE DOING?

In Praise of Small Failures

With this credo on the record, then, permit me to offer a personal story of teaching failure.

The text is an old warhorse, William Wordsworth's "Lines Written a Few Miles above Tintern Abbey," and the lines

> These beauteous forms,
> Through a long absence, have not been to me
> As is a landscape to a blind man's eye:
> But oft, in lonely rooms, and 'mid the din
> Of towns and cities, I have owed to them,
> In hours of weariness, sensations sweet,
> Felt in the blood, and felt along the heart;
> And passing even into my purer mind
> With tranquil restoration:—feelings too
> Of unremembered pleasure: such, perhaps,
> As have no slight or trivial influence
> On that best portion of a good man's life,
> His little, nameless, unremembered, acts
> Of kindness and of love. Nor less, I trust,
> To them I may have owed another gift,
> Of aspect more sublime; that blessed mood,

> In which the burthen of the mystery,
> In which the heavy and the weary weight
> Of all this unintelligible world,
> Is lightened:—that serene and blessed mood,
> In which the affections gently lead us on,—
> Until, the breath of this corporeal frame
> And even the motion of our human blood
> Almost suspended, we are laid asleep
> In body, and become a living soul:
> While with an eye made quiet by the power
> Of harmony, and the deep power of joy,
> We see into the life of things.

I'm in my second week on tenure-track, teaching British Literature 2. "Tintern Abbey" had been a formative poem in my education. I read it as a nontraditional, returning junior at the age of twenty-nine, from a photocopied handout in a class called "Intellectual Heritage." I remember vividly my astonishment that poetry could do this kind of thing. (I liked poetry in theory, which meant that I wanted to be someone who likes poetry. And I had had a similar "I didn't know poetry could do that" moment at age seventeen, reading Blake's "A Poison Tree.") But here was something new to me; poetry that seemed to be addressed confidentially to the reader, in language that seemed to me straightforward (despite its complex syntax), poetry that traced thought in detail and thus revealed the mind at work. Later in courses on Romanticism, I came to recognize "Tintern Abbey" as definitive of a scrum between competing visions of the world: a defense of the inspired and imaginative *contra* the rationalist, mechanistic, and scientific, yes, but more than that: a poem committed both to concrete details of the real world and to the mind's response to them—an attempt at a reconciled vision of humanity that both validated this life and its particularity and hoped to see through it to something eternal. These issues seemed then (and, "though changed, no doubt," still seem to me now) absolutely vital questions about what it means to be human. What is more, one of my greatest teaching moments of my young career had come a year earlier, when I subbed for my dissertation director in British Literature 2 and led a successful class on the poem. Afterward, two students approached me and asked, "What other classes do you teach?"

So here I was, walking students through a poem I loved, beginning with what I thought of as a fairly basic schematization of its time frame. The students had on their docket this week a take-home quiz that asked the question, "In 'Lines Written a Few Miles above Tintern Abbey . . .' ll. 23-50, Wordsworth mentions *three* ways in which the scenes at Tintern Abbey (these forms of beauty of l. 24) have affected him *while he has been away*. What are the three ways?" My thinking was that poetry reading is a skill that can be learned, and one important element of learning it is to pay close heed to details and stay with the speaker's voice line by line, building up a straightforward, denotative sense of what is being said. I envisioned the students having these quiz questions at their side as they read, which would prepare them to talk about the key passages (or, rather, what I took to be the key passages). So, at the start of class, I posed the quiz question to the students: What effect had the memory of Tintern Abbey had on the speaker while he was away?

You know what's coming next. Students could not come up with an answer that did justice to the complexity of the lines. They could not identify three ways. Some students could come up merely with "he really loves nature" but did not articulate any of its influences. Most could come up with one: it made him feel better when he was feeling down. A few glimpsed a second: it played an unconscious role in his behavior, sparking his "nameless, unremembered acts of kindness." (Over long experience teaching this poem, it is clear that this phrase hits home with students, where phrases like "tranquil restoration" do not.) To my astonishment, no one in the room even seemed to have looked at the last half of the passage, where the speaker describes the most important influence on his life—the exalted state of consciousness in which he can "see into the life of things."

In those days I was nothing if not committed, so I took pains to lead the class line by line through this section of the poem, picking out syntactic units: "[F]elt in the blood, and felt along the heart; and passing even into my purer mind" I read, gesturing toward my heart and my head. Looking around the room (twenty-five desks, approximately twenty occupied), I saw that most of the students were listening, attentive. But in my mind that edge of frustration that all teachers will know had wormed its way into my consciousness, that edge that threatens to show in your affect and to drive a wedge between you and the students. I could feel it in my chest, and in the slight flush in my face. A few minutes later and a few lines down, I glanced at the clock, to find that there were three minutes left in class. "You know what?" I said. "Read this poem again for next time, and we'll pick up from there."

Things did not go better, or much differently, in the next class. We trudged our way through more sets of lines, snagging this time on Wordsworth's next set of temporal markers: his "coarser" love of nature as a boy; youthful adulation of nature as a young man, when running free in the woods was a physical and spiritual joy free of thought, with "no need of a remoter charm / By thought supplied, nor any interest / Unborrowed from the eye"; mature love of nature, informed by knowledge of human suffering and producing a vision of divinity, a "sense sublime / Of something far more deeply interfused." Things played out similarly, with me pulling out phrases and asking students what they meant, often to increasingly embarrassed silence. Again, the clock ran short. Again, I said, "Ok, we'll finish up on this next time."

At the start of the next class, a young woman named Jane raised her hand before we started. She asked, "Why are we spending so much time on this poem?"

Already flustered and struggling, I came up with something like, "Because this is an important poem for laying out the fundamental issues in Romanticism." (Let's be honest here: in the defensive crouch this unfolding failure was producing, what I was thinking was: "Because I say so.") Jane did not ask the crucial next question, and it took me a few years to ask it to myself: "Why are 'the fundamental issues in Romanticism' important?" Only now am I ready to ask, more scandalously, "How important are they?"

In retrospect, the dynamics at work in this classroom, muddy at the time, are clear to me. I walked into that classroom carrying some baggage I needed to lose and lacking the one thing I needed. What I had, and needed to jettison, were a fully articulated reading of the poem that I wanted students to share, and an unexamined belief that an understanding of Romanticism's agon with modernity and the Enlightenment was indispensable equipment for living. What I lacked was a philosophy of teaching, grounded in the realities of teaching literature in the real world, that could articulate the purposes of a class like British Literature 2, serve as the grounding for reasonable objectives and methods for such a class, and thereby allow me to put in perspective and work with the relative (un)importance of a poem like "Tintern Abbey" to a college junior in Indiana in September 2000.

Twenty years later, I still teach "Tintern Abbey" when I get a crack at British Literature 2, which I share with two other professors. But much has changed: I no longer expect students to emerge from one evening's engagement with "Tintern Abbey" armed to build up an interpretation that closely parallels mine, keen to parse out the poem's engagement in epistemological questions about the nature of knowledge or political questions about the validity of individual vision. I have ceded substantial power and initiative to students, letting them identify what (if anything) speaks to them in an individual day's or week's reading and to write about it on a public discussion board. Based substantially on the week's student writing, I decide which poems to focus on in class. My preparation involves grading and giving feedback on this writing and—in an internal compromise among their ideas and interests and my own priorities—deciding which issues and questions to pursue when we meet as a group. The class being a survey, I cannot give "Tintern Abbey" the space for thorough interpretation and contextualization—not remotely so. It now shares a two-day unit called "The Conversation Poem," alongside Shelley's "Mont Blanc," Coleridge's "Eolian Harp," and short excerpts from Shelley and Wordsworth's defenses of poetry. I know that we are not going to do what feels to me like justice to these two poems in 100 minutes. But I know what I can do: first, give students incentives to read with attention. There are many ways to do this, and I discuss them at greater length later. Most often I do so through the discussion board posts, which I insist should represent the best possible writing students can manage given deadline constraints, and which I grade promptly and with high standards and substantive, if concise, feedback. Then, I can set up a fruitful group discussion or set of activities each day that draws on the students' interests, questions, and perplexities but also works toward a clarification and foregrounding of issues I think are important.

And this shift in objectives, from having students "understand Romanticism's ripostes to the enlightenment" to having them take part in a multiple-stage process of interpretation, beginning alone in their rooms but continuing into the classroom and then into more formal and ambitious writing, embodies a change in my approach that is also part of a larger transformation in the teaching of literature in the United States in the last decade or so. To use broad, layman's terms, I (and many other literature professors) have come to think that what students *can do* is more important than what they *know*.[1] I and much of the profession have moved from an emphasis on content knowledge to an emphasis on method, on what has variously been called "strategic knowledge," "procedural knowledge," "textual power," and "textual literacy."[2] As Sherry Lee Linkon has pointed out, our curriculum designs have not caught up with this change: undergraduate literature majors are typically designed not around these skills but around literary history: movements, periods, and so on.[3] This creates a situation in which individual teachers find ways of foregrounding methods within courses, like historical surveys, that were designed, many decades ago, to convey the old canon of masterworks. But most of us would agree that the methods we teach are the most valuable things we offer students.[4] And, as I show in Chapter 3, these are methods not only of reading, interpretation, and critical writing but also of learning—means for discerning what you need to learn and figuring out how to learn it. If we succeed, what we do in college, regardless of major or field of expertise, is develop in students the capacities, strategies, and dispositions needed to learn.

Every college literature teacher needs to come to his/her/their own accommodation of the relative importance of knowledge and method. Some of us teach Shakespeare to young people who are studying to be schoolteachers, and our society, via its accrediting agencies, has decided that those students need to have content knowledge about Shakespeare. The hearty Renaissance experts and generalists in our ranks must balance the competing values of a student's ability to parse lines of Renaissance English, or to read *Hamlet* with comprehension and pleasure, against the student's knowledge of Shakespeare's biography and his world. Myself, I still want students to finish my class knowing roughly what the Enlightenment was and how not only Romanticism but also Victorian sentimentalism, modernist anxiety, postmodern radical skepticism, and postcolonial critique grappled differently with its legacies. I do some of this work through brief lectures, but most of it by placing students in positions where careful reading, which is clearly valued and rewarded, will put them in position to seize upon such questions when they arise. And I recognize that not everyone will finish my class knowing these things, and that only those who reactivate that knowledge later—through continued reading, or careers (like teaching or law or politics) that entail ongoing questions about history, knowledge, authority, and liberty—will remember it ten or twenty years hence. Thus, though I still personally value content knowledge and what one might call cultural literacy, I ultimately value intellectual methods above all. I design my teaching to encourage and reward the development, practice, and improvement of intellectual methods.

Here then is the central premise of my teaching philosophy, and the central premise of this book: that "teaching literature" means, above all, teaching *methods*: teaching students to do things, putting them in the position to develop and improve at a repertoire of perspectives, moves, and activities that will allow them to read literature (and other complex texts) for the rest of their lives. Other things we value will happen, for some, perhaps many, students as we do this: some, perhaps many, will become more compassionate human beings, or come to appreciate and respect diverse kinds of people; some will come to love some of the same things we love; some will become knowledgeable about literary history or history proper. But *long-term* success in these latter outcomes—the only success that matters—is not something we can measure in individual students, nor is it something we are likely to achieve by going at them directly.

In contrast, if we are deliberate and nuanced enough in our teaching of methods, we and our students will be able to see concrete results. Learning is, by definition, a process of change in which learners gain new knowledge or capacities, and teaching is the attempt to place the learner in position to undergo desired change and assist him/her/them as the change unfolds.[5] And the many individuals and agencies who pay us to do our work—the students themselves, their parents, the government agencies that (sometimes) subsidize a (decreasing) amount of the expense, the accreditors who underwrite our authority—want evidence that the change is really happening. We tread on perilous ground if we feel superior to their desire for us to show results. (Among many other things, what I mean by "teaching literature in the real world" is working within the institutions that employ and regulate us and working with the interests—often different from ours—of the students we teach.) And while studies have shown convincingly that reading imaginative works increases compassion, it is difficult to show that an individual person (or a class of thirty people) has become more compassionate or less self-centered because of fifteen weeks of directed reading and writing.[6] But with the proper set of well-designed assignments and frequent feedback, we *can* demonstrate improvement in methods.

The emphasis on method has another happy side effect: it puts to rest any need to grapple with the question of what has been for decades vacuously called the "student-centered classroom." For if your objective is to teach your students methods, the only legitimate way to do so is to demonstrate the methods to them and then have them practice them, over and over again, to give them copious feedback, and to assess them by requiring performances of those methods. There is little place for being the "sage on the stage" in this understanding of teaching literature. Even if some lecturing is called for (and that's a legitimate method, though more difficult than it looks), everything needs to be deliberately subordinated to the goal of empowering students with method. A sort of politics of pedagogy is thus implied in the emphasis on method. But what are the broader politics of teaching in this way?

The Politics of Teaching Literature in the Real World

I do not mean to minimize the possibility (or the importance) of teaching literature for the purposes of social justice: this is not a "Save the world on your own time" argument, as one well-known dismissal of the liberatory politics of teaching would have it.[7] Indeed, an emphasis on method is not politically neutral or agnostic. It is, first, a more egalitarian engagement in the politics of education itself, one that honors the student's right to pursue her or his own answers to vexing political questions, trusting the student to use the tools we offer as he or she sees fit. What is more, even in terms of politics per se, developing interpretive and critical methods is not politically neutral: the skills involved in parsing out denotative and connotative meanings in cultural texts, in producing a defensible argument about how they functioned in their historical context, in gathering and evaluating evidence to support that argument—these are the skills necessary to understand and evaluate conflicting information and to frame arguments contextually in political and professional life. In terms of the painful historical moment in which I am writing this, these skills enable people to discern fake news, including that species of fake news that involves politically self-serving claims that actual facts are fake news. If our teaching succeeds in helping students to recognize propaganda, even as it teaches students to recognize the (usually) more benign rhetorical designs of novels and films, we will be helping to build a society not in thrall to such symbols and sacred texts at the US flag and the Constitution, as Robert Scholes advocated two decades ago. If, as Scholes suggested, the decline of a New Critical literary education practiced upon a narrow canon of great works can be perceived as a "fall," it is a fall that left in its wake a practical emphasis on methods—and a fortunate fall, at that.[8]

The shift from knowledge to method is not new; but it bears restating now precisely because literary scholarship and the culture of graduate schools (which remain, with few exceptions, primarily training grounds for scholarship, not teaching) have moved the study of literature so profoundly toward questions of power, oppression, and social justice. This is all to the good, in my view: in the mid-twentieth century, the emphasis on aesthetic values and formal complexity in isolation threatened to turn the study of literature into sophomore-level "art appreciation." But literature is vital because it matters to people's lives, and the best literature has always raised questions about power, liberty, belonging, and their lack. Even Oscar Wilde's aestheticism is illegible without the context of a deadening, mechanistic modernity and a restrictive culture of gender norms that it rejected, with a stunning combination of secrecy and cheek. Naturally, the regime of class-gender-race as lenses for literary study, augmented more recently with inquiries into the Anthropocene and the post-human, has shifted the discussion about teaching literature and its purposes, a discussion injected with urgency by the parallel discourse of "crisis in the humanities." So how do we accommodate our desire to make our teaching matter in urgent political times with my insistence that method is the core of what we offer students?

I want to begin answering this question by suggesting that the ways we've framed the politics of teaching literature to date have mostly been unrealistic and unhelpful. Old-fashioned or nostalgic approaches that want to return to the canon and cultural literacy—which enjoy much more currency in the popular media than they do among educators—are virtually always written or informed by people with elite school backgrounds and assume a student body and an educational setting utterly alien to most US college students. And they fail to address the alienating effects of a "Great Tradition"-style education on a student body of diverse demographics and abilities; such arguments amount to an endorsement of exclusionary education operating under cover of a sort of nationalistic moralism. The supposed neutrality of Stanley Fish's relentlessly eccentric *Save the World on Your Own Time*—a methods-based argument for an entirely depoliticized pedagogy—is similarly founded on elite school experience and amounts to a thorough capitulation to the political and cultural status quo, despite an emphasis on skills of analysis that I share.

More progressive visions of the purpose of teaching literature offer a more complicated mix, combining an understanding of the power dynamics of the classroom (i.e., the relative power of teachers and students) with a sense of how those relations are connected to broader social relations. Literature teachers of my generation tend to think (1) that practices of collaboration and open discussion in the classroom model respectful discussion and exchange of ideas upon which democratic theory is based and which are essential to a democratic polity; (2) that reading literature makes students more compassionate, and that reading literature about social groups *unlike* them makes them more tolerant; and (3) that, conversely, reading books about social groups *like* them makes minority students see their experience as valid and themselves as having a place in American society. As I've made clear earlier, this all may be true, but certainly not for everyone, or in every setting, and it is difficult to document.

Still, these beliefs powerfully inform most of our defenses of the humanities generally and the teaching of literature specifically—defenses that feel more urgent because of the so-called crisis in the humanities. In contemporary defenses, two threads predominate: one a resurgence of claims about the moral, ethical, and political good of reading, learning, and teaching literature and the other a pragmatic, institutionally savvy argument that humanities education develops skills that are valued in the workplace. I do not disagree with either of these sets of claims, but I would add in each case: "sometimes." Sometimes, perhaps even a lot of the time, studying African American literature sensitizes white students to their privilege, causes them to acknowledge and recognize structural racism—in short, makes them better people. Sometimes, perhaps even a lot of the time, studying African American literature helps black students access their own history and arms them with understanding and arguments to help them pursue social justice. Other times, undoubtedly, studying African American literature causes small-minded white students to roll their eyes at what they've learned to perceive as hyper-liberal, propagandistic institutions of higher education, and to use their developing cynical reason to use the sorts of language and make the basic intellectual moves they think their teachers want to see. (Given the urgent need today for new, anti-racist policies at all levels of society, humanists are going to have to spend some time in serious thought and doing hard research on how our professions can contribute more practically and demonstrably to social equality. But that's a topic for a different book.)

Similarly, sometimes, maybe even a lot of the time, students develop marketable and transferable skills by studying literature. Obviously this speaks to my emphasis on methods, and, as will become clear, I think much of the methodological toolkit we can offer students can be covered in the term "advanced literacy"—a major but largely unacknowledged part of which is best described as "advanced reading comprehension." I have absolute faith that the abilities to decode (construct basic denotative meaning) and interpret (contextualize, analyze, and evaluate) complicated written texts are extremely valuable skills in most workplaces and for life in general; likewise, the ability to write clearly and well under firm but negotiable deadlines, collecting evidence cannily and marshalling it effectively; likewise the ability to think on one's feet and take part in extemporaneous conversation that ranges over a shared set of texts and contexts. But again, "sometimes." Anecdotally, I have taught English majors who have done extraordinary things: published popular and celebrated nonfiction works of social critique, started successful arts-oriented businesses, become publishers and agents, developed content for Hollywood films, and more. And I also know of English majors who, more than five years after graduating, were working in the university cafeteria or behind the meat counter at a grocery store.

This is why, to my mind, teaching literature in the real world requires a clear-eyed look at the functions our individual institutions actually perform, and how our work and our students' desires, dispositions, and practices fit into them. In many institutional settings, a credulous embrace of liberatory pedagogy is mainly a salve to conscience, as no amount of good will and teaching commitment will ever counteract the gravitational pull of a consumer-driven, capitalist society and its ability to co-opt the work we do to the larger project of re-producing a professional middle class, of sorting and credentialing students for professional life. Most students are thoroughly interpellated into this value system by the time they get to us: the annual Survey of Student Engagement confirms that a vast majority of students enter college with the primary goal of having it increase their earning ability and career success, and this is true for a higher percentage of students in the lower echelons of higher education than in the elite schools. And sociologists have shown that family and social background are much more powerful influences on political opinion than college education. I was faced with this reality in a painful manner when a student I taught in an upper-level seminar on Virginia Woolf—a student who seemed genuinely turned on by ideas and saw himself as a creative and sharply critical thinker—graduated to writing blog posts for David Horowitz's *Front Page* and other right-wing outlets.

These dynamics are complicated and unique to virtually every teaching situation. The social purpose of teaching literature at a historically black college is different from that at a white-majority, mid-sized state school, like the one where I teach. Even within the same institution, these dynamics function and are arrayed differently: say, when I teach British modernism to twenty white, midwestern students, ten of whom want to be high school teachers, versus when my colleague Emily Rutter teaches a core curriculum class in African American literature to a black-majority classroom within our white-majority institution.

There is, then, no blanket prescription for how to teach literature in a way that makes people more compassionate, or makes them better citizens, or offers specific promises for social reconstruction. Personally, I steer my students' learning in the direction of the political by approaching literary texts as arenas in which conflicting values (and their locations and power relations) contend and are adjudicated (or, more rarely, fail to be adjudicated). I use analogies to contemporary life and contemporary clashes of value and power relations steadily, both to show what is at stake in the primary texts and to illustrate their relevance to contemporary life. I don't presume that my classes will inspire students to overthrow capitalist society, but I do seek to empower students to think critically about it and to recognize the "symbolization of power"—the way power is exercised symbolically in cultural texts.

Such strategies need to proceed from a specific understanding of the power dynamics not only of the classroom but of the institution and its economic functions—an understanding in which our students should also be involved. I spend a good deal of time (more than my students like) talking about and returning to my teaching philosophy and objectives in any particular class and engaging students in the questions and conflicts involved in it. For me, a democratic classroom is not one in which students make pedagogical decisions (though that is sometimes an appropriate strategy), but one in which we all recognize that multiple, often conflicting interests flow through all of the activity that takes place there: the students have their interests (grades, credentialing, upward mobility, learning, and personal growth); I have mine (I want you to know what the Enlightenment is, damnit!); the institution has its own (mine particularly wants students out in four years), and outward in widening circles. Henry Giroux's recent comments on "critical pedagogy" are apposite here: critical pedagogy, he writes, "is not about an a priori method that can be applied regardless of context." He continues:

> It is the outcome of particular struggles and is always related to the specificity of particular contexts, students, communities, available resources, the histories that students bring with them to the classroom, and the diverse experiences and identities they inhabit.[9]

All this is a lot to concern yourself with, but for me the buoy in this roiling sea of conflicting interests is method. And the foundation for successful teaching of method is acceptance of the conditions of teaching literature in the real world. If our teaching will help a student become a politically aware citizen, or help that student find a good job, our influence will come in the day-to-day realities of teaching. Which brings me back to my Wordsworth episode.

Leading Real-World Discussions

I want to return to this teaching failure for a moment because it raises the most fundamental and the most practical questions about what we do in a discussion-based literature classroom. I emphasize this teaching mode because the class discussion is, for a large majority of college literature teachers, the core of the enterprise. Even in large land-grant schools, where intro classes or surveys are taught in large-lecture formats, the existence of teaching-assistant-led discussion sections nods to the centrality of extemporaneous, live discussion to literary pedagogy in the United States. And like any powerful paradigm, its premises are rarely questioned. For me the basics questions are: What are we seeking when we lead discussion on a literary text? What is this activity's value for students? What do we expect them to take away from it? To frame it more pedagogically: What change or changes in the students are we hoping to enable? And how does fifty minutes of talk about "Tintern Abbey" contribute to that change?

Let us set aside the big picture and the longer time frame of a whole undergraduate experience for now and think in terms of day-to-day realities. What do we want students to take away from a class focusing on a single literary text? There are many possible answers, and each entails its own corresponding methods. For instance we might, as was the norm in the canonical days, want them to leave knowing that Wordsworth was an important poet and "Tintern Abbey" an important poem and having a viable interpretation of it. These were the objectives (not explicit, even to myself) in my ill-starred week of flailing away at the poem, and they were problematic for multiple reasons. For one, all of these goals could be accomplished via lecture. It would have been simpler, and a great deal more efficient, for me to talk through the interpretation I brought into the room rather than try to draw it painstakingly out of the students. Not least of the problems with this approach is the fact that the interpretation will not be the student's—it will be the teacher's, or the teacher's teachers, handed down over the generations via what Paolo Friere has called the "banking model of education"—in which students are conceived of as passive containers into whom teachers "deposit" information.[10] I can attest, from having taught some brilliant graduate students from the Middle East, that this method of instruction—in which a teacher provides both literary-historical context and specific exegesis, via lecture, to large groups of students, who then write papers that reproduce that context and that exegesis—is very much alive and well in various parts of the globe.

Another downside of this method is that it does not even succeed on its own, highly questionable terms: students will forget who Wordsworth is and what his important poem was called shortly after the exam, if not before, unless they have repeated occasions to reactivate that knowledge. Minimally capable students can memorize facts such as a definition of Romanticism or a knowledge of the titles of Wordsworth's major works—the so-called declarative knowledge—but this knowledge is simply stored and will evaporate unless students have the occasion to reactivate it repeatedly. In a brilliant essay for the MLA's *Profession* annual, Marshall Gregory distinguished between such "stored" knowledge and knowledge that is "absorbed":

> We only remember stored knowledge when we continue to use it and thus reinforce it. We remember absorbed information all our lives because what gets absorbed does not have to be recalled. Instead of being carried about as part of the mind's burden, it changes the interior architecture of thinking itself, which means that it becomes part of the mind's structure.[11]

Because they have studied a narrow canon (and because they are graduate students), the Middle Eastern students I teach have had occasion to reactivate such knowledge and can do so quite well. My job as a teacher—a difficult one—in their cases is to get the students to work away from such declarative knowledge and toward original thought of their own.

But if what I was doing in the failed "Tintern Abbey" classes was not lecturing, it was also not terribly far from what students sometimes perceive, with reason, as playing "guess what the teacher thinks."[12] I had an interpretation (true, a capacious one, sensitive to nuances, tensions, and contradictions—I came of age in the years of deconstruction, after all!), and my aim was to draw something approximating that interpretation from the students, quilting it together out of scraps of line-and phrase-readings they provided. The students were more active when I tried to get them to build the interpretation than they would have been listening to a lecture—they did have to parse and interpret individual lines and phrases, and skilled ones offered moments of synthesis and consolidation—but the resulting interpretation was still going to be largely mine, not theirs.

Indeed there is a kind of intellectual dishonesty about this procedure, which purports to be a process of discovery, while in reality the "discovery" has already been predetermined by the teacher and the series of leading questions are designed to push the students toward that outcome. Experienced college students know this process, which is why it is so common for a student to preface a comment with the qualification, "I don't know if this is what you're looking for, but . . . ." If we're honest, we will admit that we have all lead "discussions" like this one and that it is easy and natural to fall into this mode, even if we start with better intentions. When we teach a text that we know well, it is impossible not to feel somewhat committed to an interpretation (or, at best, a range of overall interpretations) as well as a multitude of readings of individual details. It takes restraint to really let students build their own, collaborative interpretation in real time. (And it also opens up the possibility that the resulting interpretation will not be viable or coherent, a problem I will address later on.)

If class discussion of a literary text is not directed toward an accurate, consensus or professionally sanctioned reading, what is it directed toward? In answering this question we might be tempted to abandon the notion of accurate reading altogether, and put our chips entirely on class discussion as a process. We might, in other words, invest entirely in the value of class discussion per se to the extent that the content of discussion seems beside the point. I remember being in this position in graduate school—being so nervous that my students would be bored and disengaged that I mistook any class discussion for quality class discussion, any session in which students opened their mouths as a success. And we agree, certainly, that the ability to speak extemporaneously and smartly in front of others is a pure good and should be fostered in all students. In an ideal world, all college students would become highly skilled in thinking and verbalizing on their feet.

But this understanding of the value of class discussion, though valid, is not enough, because it goes so far to the edge of the continuum between content and method that it's entirely content neutral. This is a problem not merely because of institutional politics: if the ability to speak extemporaneously is the only value inherent in a discussion-based pedagogy, why should a student pursue it specifically in the English major? Any field that can be taught successfully in a discussion-based manner—from political science to business administration—would be equally, even indistinguishably, valid for that purpose. For that matter, if verbal acuity is the sole value in discussion-based pedagogy, shouldn't everyone major in communications—where verbal presentation skill is not only among the primary learning objectives but also the subject of study? Moreover, though verbal quickness may be a value in its own right, there is a profound difference between class discussion that is directed toward the discovery of insights and class discussion without such direction. I trust that I am not alone in having led discussions whose aim seemed mainly to fill the available time and, at best, give students the opportunity to display their knowledge and ability. The problem with such an approach is that it mistakes a method—class discussion—for an objective, or, at best, settles for a general objective (verbal skill) in the absence of any discipline-specific ones.

So what are we looking for in a class discussion of a literary text? If denotative knowledge of literary history (Wordsworth is a Romantic poet) is at best secondary, and our goal is not to disseminate consensus readings of the texts we study, and not merely to give students practice in speaking ex tempore, what are we after, exactly? As my declarations above imply, I understand class discussion as a forum in which students practice intellectual methods: not verbal quickness generally but the practice of discipline-specific intellectual moves in real time. This orientation means that our discussions will occupy a middle ground between undirected class discussion for its own sake and the kind of overdirected, overdetermined "group" interpretation I was trying to lead on "Tintern Abbey." It means we have to relinquish control of the end point of discussion—the actual insights about and meanings for the text that the class constructs—in order to focus instead on helping students develop and practice interpretive methods. Instead of leading toward dramatic interpretive revelations (though, on our best days, these will come, and be new and fresh not only to students but to us), we act as coaches on method, and our work gets done in the small moments, as we help our students hone and specify their claims, marshal and explain their evidence, consider countervailing data, express their ideas more clearly. It does not mean, for me, accepting any reading of any line, figure, or word, no matter how wild or idiosyncratic—say, with a shrug of the shoulders and a half-hearted nod or an equivocal "perhaps," or a generous reframing in an attempt to spin dross into gold. We are working, after all, to help our students develop interpretive skills. Accurate decoding of denotative meanings is foundational to this work; and a reader's willingness to reconsider errant or questionable decodings or ill-advised interpretive leaps is an indispensable disposition for intellectual growth—one that is both discipline specific and generalizable, and one that does not come naturally, that needs to be developed with practice.

This method of leading class discussion draws on research findings that are so strong that they are virtual premises of learning theory. If you want to teach someone to do something—and the basic orientation I am urging for literature teachers is to imagine their mission as *to teach students to do things*—the consensus goes something like this: make them do it, repeatedly; give them frequent and useful feedback; then assess their progress. Who could argue with this approach? Yet while we are often, I suspect, quite rigorous with our students (and ourselves) in applying these precepts to written work, we often abandon them in leading discussion, settling for a vague and self-confirming sense that the interchange of ideas is a pure good, or a democratic practice, or that trying out ideas in discussion necessarily leads to better ideas, absent any rigor or assessment.

Granted, assessing class participation is tricky and, like so many other teaching tasks, requires careful balancing between maintaining rigor and developing an open, participatory atmosphere. But I am advocating for a vision of a semester's work that takes as its main objective the development and improvement of skills, and is integrated around this goal, with readings, class discussion, and writing all designed to maximize skill-building and assessed with varying stakes but always with high standards. This skill-building may be conducted within a framework of concepts drawn from literary or cultural history or contemporary preoccupations and controversies, all of which is perfectly legitimate; and may also work alongside objectives involving such declarative knowledge as definitions of movements, landmarks of historical context, biographical background, and so on. I do not mean to suggest that for every professor developing interpretive skills should be the only or even the ultimate goal, though it is the primary goal for me. But I do believe it is a goal virtually all of us share—whether we see our mission as preparing workers or fomenting skeptical citizenship or saving souls—and thus an appropriate foundation for teaching literature.

None of this is easy: leading directed, quality discussions requires from teachers, among other things, intense attention (leading class discussion requires world-class listening skills) and a willingness to withstand the discomfort of pushing students, some of whom are unused to being pushed, particularly in front of peers, toward better interpretations and more solid intellectual moves. Sometimes it requires, after the fact, the smoothing of feelings, apologies, explanations, meetings of the mind tête-à-tête. And it requires student consent to our methods and thus requires that we make clear to them, early and often, where we are coming from in our philosophy of teaching and how our methods fit into it. And, again, it requires that we give up control of the readings and interpretations our class discussions produce, leaving open what they will ultimately reveal about the texts we study, so long as they generate quality intellectual labor. Sometimes this mode will produce classes that conclude not with a ringing moment of shared, interpretive insight or consensus but with a mess of unresolved questions on the table. (Again, uncomfortable, but all to the good: comfort with ambiguity is a high-order intellectual skill and a marker of personal maturity.) On the most satisfying days, it will generate striking new discoveries for everyone. Almost always, if pursued in good faith, it will produce genuine discovery and interpretive work that is the common product, and thus the common property, of everyone in the room.

Discipline and Practice

In suggesting that part of our job is to help our students increase their tolerance for discomfort, I am in part arguing for a revalidation of "discipline" as something to be pursued in education. "Discipline" is of course a complicated and contentious term, not least because Michel Foucault's persistent currency in academia has given it a bad name. Not that Foucault's persistence is inappropriate: his razor-sharp anatomy of how institutions and daily practices shape us into self-policing subjects makes profound intuitive sense, which is why his work remains current while many other voices of the theory revolution have receded from the foreground. And the discipline Foucault outlines—the internalized sense of being perpetually surveilled by a wide range of institutions (as well as one's fellow subjects, and one's self)—is a painful and lamentable condition that has only become more tenacious as social media has transformed its workings. Thus we may feel queasy when we invoke discipline as a learning goal in our course designs, and even more so if we invoke it as a value in talking to our students. As someone who completed grades one through ten in the 1970s, the word "discipline" invokes for me the archetypal metal ruler and the paddle, both of which were not infrequently applied in the Catholic and public schools I attended.

I want to suggest, though, that we re-inflect "discipline" by combining and emphasizing its academic connotations—of a discipline as a body of knowledge and set of methods that one pursues through education—along with its connotations in both pop-Buddhist mindfulness practice and athletics: the sense that frequent and committed practice results in strengthened and expanded competencies and consciousness, in the ability to go deeper, longer, and further in activities that expand the self. A literature course is a perfect setting for such practice, if you accept my premise that the first thing we teach when we teach literature is advanced reading comprehension. As Sheridan Blau has pointed out, reading research shows that the primary difference between strong readers and weak readers is that the former persevere when they cannot immediately decode what they are reading; they are willing to entertain and test several hypotheses and to look elsewhere in the text to test them, whereas weak readers either try to read around the gap in their comprehension or give up on the text entirely. Strong readers view texts that are not instantly consumable as challenges; weak readers read them as failures on the writer's part or evidence of their own inability.[13] If we view ourselves as coaches—the loving, encouraging kind rather than the barking, abusive kind—then a substantial part of our job is to help our students to practice effectively; and class discussion is part of this practice.

"Practice," too, is a word that we could use more advisedly, deemphasizing its connotation as preparation for a performance that comes later. This speaks to my rejection of the college/real-world binary, a damaging ideological construct whose major effects have been to trivialize education and underpay educators while also, paradoxically, masking the economic exchanges upon which education is founded. The fact that students are not getting paid for the intellectual work they do under our guidance—that they are, rather, paying for the experience—does not mean that their performances are not valuable, nor that they are not taking place in the "real world." All practice *is* performance, and all practice, if undertaken with consciousness and intention, has inherent value, not merely as preparation for something else. (Granted, some performances are higher stakes than others.) We will do well if we envision "practice"—and encourage students to envision it—in two other senses: that of the attempt to improve in an activity by doing it but also the sense, straddling the religious and professional realms, that combines "perform" with "observe the traditions of"—as in "practice medicine" or "practice Buddhism." The intellectual habits we teach, in other words, are both arenas for continuous growth—practice may not make perfect, but it does create improvement—and observances that contribute to an intellectual way of being in the world, elements of a "practice" in a quasi-religious sense. By helping our students develop and strengthen their dispositions toward practice, which asks that they push through moments of difficulty and discomfort, we mentor them into an understanding of reading and writing as disciplines in the best senses—as areas of continuous growth requiring perseverance and committed ways of living.

Teaching Literature in a Postcanonical World

If the raison d'être for literary study in college is method—practice and discipline—then, what of content? Does it not matter at all which texts students practice upon? Few literature professors today believe that there is a central set of writers that everyone, or even all English majors, should read, much less what that central set of writers should be.[14] As with the shift from content to method, the shift away from a (relatively) well-defined canon is a fact of life. My intention here is not to relitigate this shift but rather to point us toward the best ways to work in this landscape as teachers committed to method. But a very brief discussion of how we got here will be useful.

New Criticism, that former hegemon that enshrined close reading at the heart of literary study—and is thus foundational to my (and the profession's) emphasis on method—took much of its initial energy from pursuing a fundamental question: What is the subject of literary study?[15] New Criticism's explicit answer, in short, was "language, at the furthest frontiers of its powers of precision, resonance, and suggestiveness." But it also—more or less implicitly—enshrined a narrow, traditional set of texts as the canon in which such language was embodied. I came of age amid the ruins of the New Critical regime. My generation of literature professors, whose mentors unleashed the canon-busting energies of feminist and postcolonial criticism and critical race studies, takes as articles of faith the need for literary study to represent diverse experiences and the fundamental conservatism (which we rejected) of the New Critical aesthetic values of compression, ambiguity, tension, and paradox.

Our students, we believe, should be able to recognize themselves in the literature they read; and, they should imaginatively undergo the experiences of others quite different from them; literary study, too, should expose students to the struggles of oppressed peoples and their efforts to use writing to document their experience and demand their freedom. Working-class students, students of color, students of other marginalized communities should not have the experience of Irie Jones in Zadie Smith's *White Teeth*, who, upon suggesting in a high school class discussion that Shakespeare's "dark lady" might be black, is scolded, by a narrowly intentionalist teacher, for finding personal and contemporary relevance in Shakespeare's words:

> She had thought, just then, that she had seen something like a reflection; but it was receding; . . .
>
> "No, dear, you're reading it with a modern ear. Never read what is old with a modern ear. In fact, that will serve as today's principle—can you all write that down please."
>
> [The class] wrote that down. And the reflection that Irie had glimpsed slunk back into the familiar darkness.[16]

Opening the canon meant some chipping away at the old, New Critical aesthetic standards of compression, paradox, ambiguity, and so on. While some writers of color and from other marginalized groups have sought the formal complexity the New Critics valued—think of Ralph Ellison and Toni Morrison—many have not. The syllabus would thus not consist solely of works of apparent formal complexity. This change in values—really a change in the purpose of teaching literature, but one played out around the subject of literature—also meant that writing with strident rhetorical or political aims (the essays of James Baldwin, say) and literature that aspired to popularity by speaking plainly to the experience of people without elite educations (the conventional fiction of Jesse Fauset or Harriet Beecher Stowe) were also appropriate grist for scholarship and the classroom.

In practice this change has had profound results. It has shown that the maneuvers of close reading can be practiced with equal success—though with different results—on "popular" and middlebrow texts whose creators were not seeking immortality or even ingenuity. Sometimes formal complexity *is* what close reading such texts reveals; almost always, close reading reveals texts to be more complicated than we expected. At the same time, the close reading of less aesthetically ambitious texts helped to normalize so-called "symptomatic" reading—close reading that reveals not highly articulated aesthetic form but a complex interweaving of ideological and cultural discourses, operating to some extent—often to a great extent—independent of the creators' intentions.[17]

Take *Casablanca*—one of the most beloved of classical Hollywood films, and a superbly realized product of the Hollywood machine—but no one's example of a formally avant-garde or intellectually challenging artifact. Nonetheless, it is one of my favorite texts to teach, precisely because some deliberate, genre-specific close reading—that is, the application of some basic methods of film analysis that students can master—reveals how the film's form (camera angles and movements, sequencing of takes, bravura use of classical cutting techniques in the "La Marseilles" scene) secures the viewer's identification and harnesses her emotion in service of a propagandistic message. A little historicization also reveals the film's use of stock footage provided by the US military and the story's utter ordinariness within the film market of 1943 (it was one of literally scores of films with a virtually identical message: that profound personal sacrifice was needed in the service of a greater cause). Form is part of what this close reading reveals, but so is ideology and the interweaving of ambient discourses, as is the relative crudeness of its emotional appeal. And, in context, I use this analysis to help students identify how classical Hollywood filmmaking manipulates our emotions and reiterates consensus values. Rather than a text of unquestioned value, which we read carefully to unfold its complexities, the film is a text whose functioning as a symptom of larger historical and ideological rhetorics can be revealed through analysis.

By my lights this is all to the good. Literary study will be doing better social work if it is designed to create awareness of historical power relations and compassion for the oppressed, rather than to provide social currency and exclusive cultural codes to the children of the haute bourgeoisie—children who can afford to major in noninstrumental subjects because they trust that their Ivy League classmates, and their fathers, and their Ivy League classmates' fathers will set them up with jobs and law school recommendations.[18] So, yes, please: heterogeneous literature: popular and avant-garde, written from the center and written from the margins, literature that conveys conservative mainstream values, literature where the cracks in those values can be discerned through symptomatic reading, literature that lampoons, eviscerates, and spits upon mainstream values. Our young people will be all the better for learning deeply that the world is full of a dizzying variety of expression—a thousand times too much for anyone to master—and for learning, under our leadership, how to bite off manageable chunks of this universe and find ways to discern meaning in it. In all of this I agree substantially with the late Robert Scholes, who named the set of methods, competencies, and dispositions I am articulating here "textual power" and called for a shift from literature to textuality—the interpretation, evaluation, and creation of texts—as the subject matter of the English major.[19]

But it is also helpful, I think, to acknowledge that something was lost with the passing of the "Beowulf to Virginia Woolf" years—the age when reading early-nineteenth-century British literature meant the Big Six Romantic Poets and undergraduates never troubled with Robert Southey, to say nothing of Felicia Hemans. That something was coherence. It is possible, over the course of a semester, to tell a coherent story of the last two centuries of British literature if you have students read texts by only ten or twelve big names, and if you lecture a good deal and test students on their recall of these names and texts and the keywords of your lectures. More broadly, it's possible to tell a coherent story if you design highly directive literature majors composed of classes that take this approach. And there are some benefits to such an education: as a BA graduate from such a program, you would have read a lot of complex works that people throughout the past few centuries have also read, giving you storehouse of images, metaphors, tropes, narratives, characters, and settings that you share with thousands of people, living and dead, who've read a similar set of works. Also, you'll be likely to recognize allusions to *The Tempest* or *The Scarlet Letter* or "The Love Song of J. Alfred Prufrock" when later writers with literary aims invoke them, as they do. There's a chance you'll be able to name William Wordsworth as Samuel Taylor Coleridge's erstwhile bestie and the author of "Tintern Abbey" when the question is asked on Jeopardy.

Even these benefits, though, are far from assured: as I've noted, content knowledge sticks in your head in the long run only when you've reactivated and used it repeatedly. This surely explains the striking prevalence of people with advanced degrees in humanities subjects as contestants on Jeopardy. And—less beneficially—you'll be given the sense that you understand the broad outlines of something called "literature" or "literary history"; this sense would be harmless if it were accompanied by a sense that any such history is absurdly reductive, filtering out not only hundreds of authors who were admired by their discerning contemporaries but also hundreds more who may have something to say to our, later era but whose obscurity, marginal social location, lack of access to publishers and evaluators of literature, or preference for devalued genres has prevented their works from getting to you.

More profound, though, than such narrow cultural literacy (and any cultural literacy is going to be narrow in a culture as heterogeneous and text-saturated as ours) is the benefit of learning a coherent tradition, even though that tradition is reductive. This benefit lies in a "tradition's" status as a way of ordering and structuring information. Students need to learn to recognize such structures and to construct such hierarchies of information for themselves.[20] When students have had a coherent tradition constructed for them (or, more accurately, when students have developed a sense of a coherent tradition, in dialogue with their teachers, their syllabi, and the texts they've read), they probably have a considerably better chance of being able to construct and organize an alternate tradition of their own. A canon of texts is constructed around a schema or a set of schema: poets in column A, fiction writers in column B; or Cavalier poets in column A, Puritan writers in column B, restoration figures in column C, or; the sixteenth and seventeenth centuries as one large cluster; the eighteenth as a second; the nineteenth as a third. It probably helps to have experienced such a "tradition"—or witnessed one being built—in order to build a well-organized one, with well-conceived categories and hierarchies, for oneself. I have continually found it surprising over the years to learn, from students and colleagues educated under a banking model in places like India, Saudi Arabia, and Iraq, how strong their knowledge of canonical traditions is and how grateful they are to have it. Professor Amit Baishya, a star of zombie studies and certainly one of the most edgy and original thinkers I've ever had the pleasure of working with, put it simply in a conversation with me some years ago: what you get in a canon-based, banking model is "a coherent narrative."[21] There's no doubt that Amit's facility for efficiently limning the history of the zombie figure in Western culture, its multiple, incommensurate cultural work, and the vast, intertextual network of zombie narratives owes something to the coherent set of schemata he had spoon-fed to him as an undergraduate in India.

Organizing and hierarchizing information—constructing what Linkon aptly describes as "webs of related information . . . organized into clusters"—is a high-order intellectual skill that should be an explicit goal of higher education; if students choose to major in our subject, we need to make this one of our goals and build it into our curriculum deliberately.[22] But this does not mean that we should be teaching a narrow canon, or that simply being taught from a narrow canon necessarily means that you will be able to schematize information successfully.[23] My undergraduate education was quite canonical but virtually devoid of any discussion of what makes a canon; an education that more consciously foregrounds issues of canonicity and requires students to build up their own structures of information would be far superior to the passive exposure I got to a set of schema that were never explicitly recognized as such. I mean to urge us, as teachers, to deliberately design assignments that speak to this higher-order intellectual function. A simple way to do this would be as a capstone activity in which literature students need to construct, explain, and defend a list of the thirty literary texts that are most important to their education. I talk about ways of helping students learn to build up strong and resilient knowledge structures in Chapter 3.

Realistically, though, I believe today's students in the postcanonical English major are not graduating with the texts they've consumed, or the knowledge or capacities they've built, arrayed in a well-conceived, robust hierarchy of knowledge. When I was a new professor, I believed, naively, that undergraduate students exposed to a heterogeneous (bordering on random) collection of texts would construct their own sense of literary history. This was before my years as an adviser and department administrator taught me that most students do not think beyond the end of the semester, and choose classes based not on a plan to cover an adequate variety of literature but, mainly, on how well they fit into their schedules.

Still, I don't pine for the days of the Six Romantic Poets. Exposing students to a diverse, even an incoherent, collection of literary texts more closely parallels what their adult lives will be like, indeed what their lives are like now, with cultural texts in multiple, new, and constantly transforming media competing for their attention. I hold with Scholes, who urged us two decades ago to build our majors (and indeed, to build liberal arts education as a whole) around a canon of methods.[24] In practice, I think, we have taken partial, halting, and in most cases half-conscious steps in this direction. I believe one of the methods in this canon should be the ability to hierarchize information—to construct schema that organize our reading experience in multiple categories that represent and embody clear and sensible relations among texts.

But the design of an undergraduate major is beyond the power of new professors, and the design of an overarching undergraduate curriculum is beyond the reach of all but a few. Most of us face the daily challenge of teaching students how to build their own schema of knowledge when even the best and most advanced of them are unlikely to be familiar with a large, shared body of literary texts. What is more, texts, authors, movements, and other such traditional literary knowledge are not the only information students need to accumulate and schematize in order to achieve the kind of advanced literacy that I advocate in this book. Teachers of postcolonial literature will bear me out that, just as passing knowledge of *Hamlet* is necessary for a robust reading of "The Love Song of J. Alfred Prufrock," an at-least sketchy knowledge of the ethnic make-up of India and the partition is essential to an even basic comprehension of scores of texts. But none of us is going to provide students with all of this declarative knowledge in fifteen weeks; indeed, even four years of humanities education will not equip readers with everything they need to know to interpret the complex texts they'll encounter in their lives: far better for students to graduate with a sharpened awareness of what they don't know, and a repertoire of strategies for finding it out.

So what is the literature teacher in the real world to do? I argue that the answer to this problem—the way to turn it into an asset—is, as with so many other problems, consciousness. Or, to use a more precise and pedagogical term: "metacognition." I think we should put this problem right in front of students and work through it with them, in the full light of day. We should help students become conscious of the ways in which their reading is made possible and hindered by their prior knowledge of contexts—contexts ranging from historically bound words and usages to basic historical facts to the intertextual networks in which texts situate themselves. We cannot hope to provide them with the expansive literacy, including a sense of world history, that would enable a single reader to decode *The Odyssey*, *Crime and Punishment*, and *The Jew of Malta*. We can, however, sensitize students to the cognitive process of making meaning from literary texts and its reliance on contextual information. This is one of the many kinds of metacognition that, I will argue in this book, English majors develop, and whose development they ought to seek consciously and actively.

As with many of the other reorientations I am calling for in this book, the one I'm calling for is already underway. We have had no choice but to adapt to a postcanonical world—to adjust our teaching, from week to week and moment to moment, to the obvious reality that only a few students in any given classroom recognize a lot of literary allusions, or could summarize, even broadly, the differences that drove Protestant and Catholic monarchs to send their subjects into battle against each other for three centuries, or could piece out a useful, working definition of "The Enlightenment." But our adaptations have been piecemeal, arrived at in relative isolation and without shared deliberation. The tack most of us have taken shares something with Scholes's notion of a canon of methods and is anchored in close reading, that central value bequeathed by the New Critics: we have, in practice, committed ourselves to teaching methods. While our public statements pay service to the notion of exposing students to varied human expressions and experiences, we have chosen not to agree about what specific expressions these should be. This has left us with method as, to use a commercial phrase, the "value added" we bring to students. We may not graduate students who have internalized a shared body of texts; virtually all of us hope, however, that we are graduating students equipped to contend with texts (and, beyond them, problems and situations) that tax their analytical, interpretive, and synthetic abilities. We believe, fervently, that the skills and dispositions that are called upon when a person confronts a text that demands focused cognition, resourcefulness, hypothesis testing, and patience are the skills we teach, and that these skills will stand our students in good stead when they graduate and set out to make their way in the marketplace and the world.

What We Teach: Advanced Literacy and Advanced Reading Comprehension

It would be disingenuous not to add that the economic uncertainty our students will face—and the political pressure humanities departments feel in this setting—has helped to push us in this direction. We may have come to teaching literature out of love; we may have come to it out of a desire to foster compassion and fuel social justice. But we teach in societies in which—though many of our students share these dreams—they have to go out and earn a living in a marketplace that values compassion, justice, and beauty less than it values efficiency, productivity, and salability: a world where some people manage to make a living through humanistic creativity but many others wish to but cannot. It would be a huge mistake for us to feel superior to our students' (and their parents' and spouses') anxieties about how their college education will prove to have paid for itself. These tensions bring us back to method: you can do anything with an English major we say (I've said it myself, scores of times), because we teach you how to think analytically, read, write, and communicate, and you need to be able to do all these things in any job you'll ever have. If we really believe these things—or if we benefit from the efforts of our administrators to say them to parents, deans, legislators, and donors—then we had better be doing our best to strategize consciously about how to inculcate the skills we're claiming to teach.

I would not be writing this book if I did not believe these things to be true. What I hope to accomplish is to make them more specific, to push our thinking beyond that all-purpose platitude "critical thinking" to more precise learning goals, such as metacognition and hypothesis testing and schematizing knowledge, to key into and address the precise hindrances and solutions to high-level reading and interpretation. I want to dig into the realities of classrooms in the real world and help us identify what exactly our students can (and should) learn to do, how we can get them to do those things successfully, and how we can know that it's working.

This brings me to my central claim in this book, the one of which the others are consequences and articulations: in literature classes, what we teach is *advanced literacy*, and its foundation is *advanced reading comprehension*. In the next two chapters, I will define each of these terms, sketch out what I see as the challenges to helping students develop them, and offer methods and examples of teaching strategies and learning activities designed around them. After that, I shift gears and, in a set of shorter chapters and appendices geared to practical, day-to-day strategies, address various fundamental practices. In Chapter 4, I discuss course design, arguing the benefits of specific objectives and course designs that are fully integrated to those objectives. At all stages I will be emphasizing teaching that activates consciousness and metacognition—that makes visible the learning problems that are at work in the classroom and enlist the students in forming deliberate strategies for their solution. In Chapter 5, I return to the psychology of teaching literature and offer advice for managing your expectations and weathering disappointments in order to survive and thrive in our difficult but fulfilling profession. Central to this effort is managing your relationships with students; this involves soliciting and using feedback from students and learning to relativize and, when necessary, ignore the less useful feedback that often comes in the form of student teaching evaluations. Finally, short appendices offer discussions of grading and the use of literary criticism and theory in the classroom, with sample assignments and methods.

2 TEACHING ADVANCED READING COMPREHENSION

If we are doing our jobs well, our undergraduates will graduate with one concrete, demonstrable, and unquestionably valuable skill: advanced reading comprehension. It's not for nothing that young people who want to go to law school have often majored in English: the Law School Admission Test (LSAT) is essentially a reading comprehension test, and all of the sophisticated issue-framing, rhetoric, and analysis of complex legal tangles and overlapping regimes that effective attorneys practice is founded on advanced reading comprehension. We have done a poor job of emphasizing this in the copious public discourse about the value of the humanities, perhaps because "reading comprehension" sounds like the stuff of primary school, an elementary skill, in more than one sense. But think for a moment how much effort is involved—even for a literature PhD who doesn't study Shakespeare—in parsing out the basic meaning of lines like these:

> You shall mark
> Many a duteous and knee-crooking knave,
> That, doting on his own obsequious bondage,
> Wears out his time, much like his master's ass,
> For nought but provender, and when he's old, cashier'd:
> Whip me such honest knaves.
>
> (OTHELLO I IV)

Many of us, I am sure, spend copious time in class and in one-on-one conversations helping students work out the meanings of passages like this one. I suspect I am not the only teacher who has found myself prodding students toward a reading of *Othello* that sizes up the play's racial politics, or its anatomization of political hierarchies, or (more modestly) its metaphorics around the human/animal distinction, only to have to pause for a prolonged, phrase-by-phrase translation of a passage simply to piece out the denotative meaning. I would never attempt to use *Othello* in class without asking students to confront its racial and gender politics. All the same, I think the work we do to model and compel students to paraphrase difficult passages is as important as these cultural discussions. Historical and political readings are, in most cases, the work we do in our scholarship, so it is natural and appropriate that training students in such readings is one of the endgames of our pedagogy. But we should not underestimate the value, or the difficulty, of helping students to advance their ability to decode increasingly difficult texts. The cultural/historical/political readings they generate will always be thin if they're based on vague comprehension of the text: they may learn to phrase claims about patriarchy or heteronormativity or the racial Other that sound something like ours, and there is value in trying these out—of dwelling in the "zone of proximal development" in which students mimic their teacher's ways of thinking and speaking as they take steps toward doing it independently.[1] But that value is severely compromised if those claims are not based in vigorous grappling with the basic difficulties of the text and earned—even if partially errant—decoding.

In Praise of Confusion

For our students to become more adept at decoding complex texts, they must learn to recognize when they are losing track of the main sense of the words they are reading or when they have encountered something unfamiliar or ambiguous; they must train themselves first to recognize when this is happening and second to pause and allow themselves to formulate the problem, the difficulty, or the question begged by the text. For many students this is a profound change in orientation, a counterintuitive stance with emotional consequences, because most students (indeed, most human beings) become uncomfortable—insecure, nervous, or angry—when a task becomes difficult. And this is particularly the case when they think of the task as something that they or most intelligent, educated people should have mastered. (Psychologists have noted that when humans experience difficulty in intellectual tasks, the body cues its "freezing or flight" response, and that anger is an ordinary reaction when one encounters an impediment to one's goals.)[2] So it is not surprising that students often fail to even register, much less reveal out loud, the micro-errors in their decoding that can launch errant readings of texts. Indeed, as Sheridan Blau has pointed out, it is often the stronger readers in a classroom who will express their confusion at an interpretive crux, because their greater reading skill includes a metacognitive capacity for "paying attention to the state of one's understanding while one is reading so we can catch problems and solve them when they arise" (57). While some other students will be quietly secure in errant readings, and others will be aware of their incomprehension, but will not speak up because they are ashamed at their perceived inability, students who actively voice confusion will actually be at a position of relatively advanced comprehension. "The student who is confused," Blau writes, "is frequently the one who understands enough to see a problem" (21).

This tolerance for confusion and difficulty is perhaps the most crucial disposition required for students to develop advanced reading comprehension. People who study reading have noted that what differentiates strong from weak readers is not an ability to instantly decode most texts: rather, it is the strong reader's willingness to stay with a text that presents difficulties. Indeed, this tolerance is perhaps better described as a disposition than a skill, but dispositions, like skills, can be learned. (Ask anyone who used to hate exercise but now doesn't feel right unless they go for a run five mornings a week.) Indeed, transformed dispositions interweave with newly acquired skills: skills foment changed dispositions and changed dispositions fuel desire for new skills. Weak readers either give up on a difficult text or arrive quickly at an errant reading and keep going, intent on getting the reading task off their plate. Strong readers recognize their confusion, try to dispel it and—crucially, and this is a mark of advanced reading comprehension—suspend their decoding until they have gathered more information, from the text or from context. They then revisit the confusing word or phrase and try out hypotheses until they arrive at a strong hypothesis for the word or phrase's meaning or meanings. We must teach in ways that open up a path for students to reorient themselves toward tolerating difficulty and confusion, helping them to recognize confusion in reading as a sign of learning as surely as an itch is a sign that a wound is healing.

This reorientation on the part of our students requires a reorientation on our part, as well: an acceptance of and sympathy for our student's interpretive struggles and their natural, human tendencies to gloss over them or to hide them from us. Ultimately, the solution to this problem—which I will begin to exemplify later in this chapter and pursue further in later chapters—will be to make problems of interpretation a recurring, standard focus of our interactions with students and thus to normalize the process of grappling collaboratively for meaning. In doing so, we can bring to consciousness the obstacles to decoding and interpretation in the texts before us. In other words, we need to help students feel safe expressing their intellectual vulnerability and taking risks, and we will do this by placing interpretive difficulties at the center of our assignments and discussions, by making it ordinary to own up to confusion and work it out together.

In order to do this in a good-natured and compassionate way, we would do well to remember our own reading challenges—the hands thrown up in frustration at Baudrillard, the awkward muddling-through of the literature of a disfavored period. (I swear a CAT scan of my brain would show injuries from the afternoon I spent reading Dryden's *Annus Mirabilis*.) To establish a tone in which confusion is seen as an opportunity, showing our own difficulties with texts is essential, so that we don't reenforce students' belief that we are congenitally skilled readers with talents they can never share. For this reason it is crucial, in every semester, to work periodically with students on texts that you have not mastered (and without preclass help from Google!), so that they can see you struggle with details and puzzle over them alongside you. Bonding with students over shared difficulties is especially important because otherwise our greater fluency in straightforward decoding can become a wedge between us. When we encounter difficulty with a text, Blau writes,

> we assume that the text must be very difficult and therefore one requiring our concentrated effort and long attention. Our students, however, assume that the same difficulty, when they encounter it, is evidence of their insufficiency as readers. . . . When it comes to the reading of difficult texts, the difference between us and our students is that we have a much higher tolerance for failure. (30)

Neither remaining ignorant of student struggles, nor growing frustrated and allowing it to show, is a promising teacherly response to this difference.

But, as I have implied, charity begins at home, and I want to suggest that, as teachers, we take our first steps along this road by recalling and resensitizing ourselves to our own interpretive difficulties. One of the best and most sympathetic scholars of pedagogy in higher education, Stephen D. Brookfield, has emphasized the need for teachers to practice intensive self-awareness of their own history of learning. In that spirit, I want to indulge in three anecdotes about my own learning.

Tales of Textual Confusion

Anecdote 1: Pattee Library, Penn State University, September or October 1983. That uncomfortable-looking student, red-faced with frustration, sitting at a study carrel crammed between the tightly spaced stacks is me. I'm "reading" a recommended article for a general education, political science class called "International Relations." I am doing so because, as a conscientious and somewhat prideful student, carrying a 4.0 average into my third semester in college, I am following the instructions on the syllabus, which straightforwardly advised that one difference between A students and B students in this class is "knowledge of recommended readings." This is probably my first exposure to academic prose, and after perhaps forty-five minutes (perhaps less, though it felt like two hours) I have determined that I am incapable of gleaning anything from this text. I leave the library, a welter of discomfiting thoughts and emotions contending in my mind. I'm angry and mystified at a world in which texts are written that someone as smart as I am is unable to read; at the same time, I'm semi-consciously holding at bay a more upsetting notion: that I'm not smart enough to understand something that at least some other people (at least the professor!), apparently, can. Above all, I leave resigned to the notion that even getting a B in this class might be a stretch.

Anecdote 2: A small two-bedroom apartment near Bethlehem, PA, several years later. That uncomfortable-looking, "non-traditional" student, red-faced with frustration, in the old-fashioned, red easy chair is me. I'm reading Francoise Meltzer's chapter on the "Unconscious" from Lentricchia and McLaughlin's *Critical Terms for Literary Study*, an introductory theory textbook for a sophomore-level class, required of English majors, called "Literary Theory."[3] I am doing so because, as a conscientious but insecure young adult who fantastically flamed out at his first attempt at college, I am determined to establish that I really am smart and that my first couple semesters at Penn State are more representative of my intellectual abilities than were the following semesters, beset by excessive partying, absenteeism, and acute mental health problems. I sit, attention fixed on the fifteen-page chapter, jotting down notes and questions in the margins, following the tortuous syntax of long, compound/complex sentences, writing unfamiliar words and their definitions, culled from a big red *American Heritage Dictionary*, which sits on a footstool nearby. After close to two hours (I was working twenty hours a week and commuting more than an hour to school, so I was acutely aware of how I was spending my hours), I finish with perhaps 40 percent comprehension of the article and with a set of questions and perplexities that I am hoping to have cleared up in class.

Anecdote 3: Cut forward eighteen months. I am now in graduate school and am, along with my cohort of first-year MAs, struggling through Jacques Lacan's "The Mirror Stage." Having determined that I am incapable of gleaning anything from this text, I return to Meltzer's "Unconscious" chapter. I find, to my shock and delight, that I can now read this chapter in under a half-hour. More striking still, I see that, eighteen months ago, I had to write the words "ineluctable" and "topographic" in the margins, with short definitions beneath them—words familiar enough to me now that I can't believe I didn't know them so recently.

The messages of these anecdotes—that one's ability to comprehend difficult texts is comprised of skills and practices that can be learned, and that one's reading comprehension can improve throughout adulthood—may seem obvious. But this truth is not obvious to many undergraduate students, who, like the nineteen-year-old me in Anecdote 1, take the impenetrability of texts that are beyond their present reach to represent either (1) their own inadequacy or (2) the failure of the author or (3) a social injustice or hoax perpetrated by academics on nonexperts in order to maintain their power and status. It is also a truth that many of us can forget and others among us—possessed of preternatural intelligence that made us especially precocious young readers—may never have been conscious of; the sort of cognitive moves that comprise advanced reading comprehension seem to come natural to us either because we have forgotten learning them or because we were never—as adults or near-adults—conscious that they were cognitive moves at all.⁴ Such "unconscious competence" on the part of teachers creates what learning scholars call "expert blind spot"—a blindness to the "learning needs of novice students."⁵ And it is a truth that has incompletely informed our teaching in literature classes, where our eagerness to lead students to ways of reading that historicize texts and problematize power relations often skips over our more fundamental duty to teach advanced reading comprehension. This oversight is understandable, mainly because literature PhD programs typically pay little or no attention to teaching literary pedagogy. But I fear it deprives many students of one of the most valuable and tangible things we can offer them.

Several more specific insights that now inform my teaching are visible in these anecdotes as well. For instance, the difference between me in Anecdote 1 and me in Anecdote 2 lies not in motivation—I was highly motivated in both cases—but in tolerance for confusion and partial failure. This probably stems from the fact that I was older and had been working full time for a number of years, increasing my experience of learning to do new things, my tolerance for frustration, and my capacity to complete tasks that are not instantly or inherently pleasant. And, perhaps most crucially, in Anecdote 2, I had developed the capacity to discern when and why I was getting confused. In some cases, as my use of the dictionary indicates, the problem was that the essay's vocabulary was slightly beyond me. In other cases it was the length and complexity of sentences; in Blau's terms I had become capable of "paying attention to the state of [my] understanding" so I could "catch problems and solve them when they arise." Whereas in Anecdote 1 the entirety of the text, in my memory at least, was an alien, impenetrable monolith, in Anecdote 2, I was differentiating the bits I did understand from those I did not. In other words, I was practicing metacognition, which, as I argue later, should be central to our objectives in teaching literature classes.

A further challenge, which continues to present itself in Anecdote 2 and which I could not have articulated at the time, lay in the fact that I was not yet integrated into the audience or interpretive community for which the chapter was written and therefore did not recognize the conversations in which it was taking part. By the time of Anecdote 3, the early years of graduate school, I had taken steps toward integration in this community and was developing the awareness that identifying the conversations and the critical tradition in which an essay situates itself are among the higher-order skills necessary to comprehend academic prose. As a strategy to widen the context and thereby facilitate my (to this day, minimal) comprehension of Lacan, I returned to an essay that helps to reconstruct the critical history and the conceptual landscape in which Lacan was writing—a resourcefulness which I lacked entirely in Anecdote 1 and substantially in Anecdote 2. Anecdote 3 in effect marks the early stages of expertise, which consists rarely, if ever, of encyclopedic knowledge but rather of tolerance for difficulty, a growing array of strategies, an increasingly complex set of schema through which knowledge can be organized, and knowledge of appropriate resources for solving intellectual problems.⁶

As this and the following chapters will show, my pedagogy seeks to act on all of these insights: I design class activities to help students discern when and why their reading comprehension of a given text is incomplete, and to encourage them to pause at that moment and think about solutions. I foreground the skills and strategies that can help students solve comprehension problems and thus help them to become resourceful readers. I talk to them, as a class and individually, about the specific capacities that specific texts call upon, and I emphasize to them that these skills can be developed and strengthened. (Indeed, I share Anecdotes 1–3 frequently.) When I assign literary criticism or theory, I add activities that prompt students to work on identifying the critical context—the preexisting conversation—that the text enters into.

But First: Students Need to Read

My sense that awareness of our own ways of learning is essential to pedagogy comes in part from the helpful work of Stephen D. Brookfield, who argued in an early edition of *The Skillful Teacher* that all professors ought to take a class every few years to resensitize ourselves to what learning feels like.[7] But while this self-awareness is important, the applicability of my anecdotes—and the narrative of growth that they sketch out—only go so far. Maturing as a teacher in the real world entails a series of disillusionments, and one of the most profound is realizing how few of your students share your intellectual hunger and drive, which were strong enough to propel you through years of virtual poverty and the inevitable setbacks and chastenings of graduate school, onward through the terrors of the job market, to become a PhD and a college literature teacher. Most of our students are not like us in this way, and many who do share similar dispositions (or could share them, under the right circumstances) are, in addition to attending your class and three, four, or five others, working full time or more, commuting, caring for children or other relatives, and dealing with many other contingencies of life. Thus even a student who truly wants to do so may not have the luxury of puzzling for two hours over Francois Meltzer's "Unconscious" chapter; and for every student who wants to do so and cannot, you are apt to encounter twenty-five for whom the notion of puzzling over a difficult essay for two hours is entirely alien. (Take it from me: I was that student, in Anecdote 1.) Teaching literature in the real world means discerning and entirely accepting the students and the teaching situations we find ourselves in, and building our strategies from there; accepting, also, the fact that our efforts will not infrequently fall short.

This brings us to the question of how to get students to do their reading. The most obvious and common response to this problem is to quiz students on details of the primary texts—most often plot developments or character details in narratives. (Multiple choice: which major character remains alive at the end of *Hamlet*? Trick question!) But I am not a fan of fact-based quizzes, particularly pop quizzes assigned with a strategic, seeming randomness designed to keep students doing the primary reading in fear of the quiz's looming threat. There are at least three problems with this strategy. First, it communicates to students that we value factual knowledge of texts very highly, when in fact most of us care about recall of textual details only to the extent that it serves the higher value of literary interpretation. (Louise Rosenblatt noted as far back as 1938 the irony in testing students on their recall of textual details, as if what were important to us in literature were the "information" it contained.)[8] Second, it adds to our schedules the empty calories of time spent grading fact-based quizzes—a condition that is likely to mean that we assign quizzes less frequently at the busier times of the semester, when the disincentives to student reading are also at their strongest.

Third, and most profoundly, unannounced quizzes are incompatible with the atmosphere of trust and collaboration needed to make students feel safe enough to take risks and expose their vulnerabilities—emotional/intellectual transitions essential to growth in advanced reading comprehension. Students perceive unannounced quizzes, not wrongly, as a "gotcha" practice. In constitutionally anxious students they provoke actual fear; in those who tend toward a cynical, transactional view of college, they will encourage a defensive disengagement. (The negative impacts of fear on learning are so profound and varied that the education journal *Learning and Memory* recently dedicated an issue to it.)[9] While pop-quizzes may be well-intentioned, motivated by a desire to set the stage for good work in the classroom, there is no escaping their punitive nature or the degree to which students experience them *as* punitive. If we are honest, I believe we teachers will recognize at least a faint desire for the pop-quiz's punitive force.

Still, we undoubtedly have to do something to encourage students to complete reading assignments, tempting as it may be to move entirely in the opposite direction, placing the responsibility entirely in the students' hands and saying, "It's their loss if they don't read." Such an approach may even seem democratic or student-centered—a ceding of teacherly authority to the students. But remember that our job is to facilitate learning—to put students in positions to learn and provide them with the materials most likely to facilitate and stimulate learning. No one will make progress in developing advanced reading comprehension if they don't read a good deal. In practice, few literature teachers pass entirely on holding students accountable for reading: the experience of attempting to lead a class discussion in a room where a small minority of students have done the reading will have cured many of us of any idealistic notions about student's class preparation practices, or their inherent motivation, or the leveling of power relations in the classroom.

Any attachment we have to such idealistic notions can be cured with a good, stiff dose of the reality of students' lives. Rebekah Nathan provides this tonic in her extraordinary book *My Freshman Year: What a Professor Learned by Becoming a Student*, which recounts her experience of enrolling as a freshman at the

University of Northern Arizona, where she was an anthropology professor, and studying the lives of herself and her fellow students through one academic year. Nathan's book ought to be required reading for any college professor who wants to teach literature in the real world (though I promise I will not quiz you on it), as it portrays in exquisite detail the complex of incommensurable imperatives that contend for the attention of ordinary college students. Her account documents the astonishing complexity of student schedules and the vigorous juggling they do to get everything done. The book was published in 2005, and these contending imperatives have only increased since then.

As an anthropologist, Nathan views student life through a lens of cultural relativism that allows her to describe student coping strategies analytically but without judgment. Thus she recounts how successful college students master a continuous practice of "strategic corner cutting" that allows them to manage the competing demands of four to six classes per semester, university activities, paid work on or off campus, and socialization.[10] In deciding which corners to cut, class reading (and class preparation in general) are among the most tempting targets, as students make rational decisions about what absolutely must be done immediately, what can be pushed back until later, and what can be faked. Nathan interviewed a set of highly successful juniors and seniors about how they make decisions about class preparation. She found that such students

> do not casually or lightly discard assignments. Rather, they mentally ask themselves a series of questions:
> "Will there be a test or quiz on the material?"
> "Is the reading something that I will need in order to be able to do the homework?"
> "Will we directly discuss this in class in such a way that I am likely to have to personally and publicly respond or otherwise 'perform' in relation to this reading?"[11]

Nathan's own epiphany came when a teacher in one of her lecture classes remarked, at the end of a class meeting, that he was putting an extra article on the web that "would amplify the subject of his next lecture"; she found herself "chuckling, realizing that I had no intention of doing this reading and would not even copy down the information." Later, bringing these insights to bear on her own teaching, Nathan determined that she needed to trim the readings she assigned for her courses while creating "new classroom forums for making direct and immediate use of the readings I seriously want my students to prepare."[12]

A quick glance at the most recent data from the National Survey on Student Engagement (NSSE) suggests that student practices have changed only slightly since Nathan's book was published in 2005. In 2018, 73 percent of students reported that they come to class unprepared very often (6 percent), often (15 percent), or sometimes (52 percent). In the same year, 37 percent reported spending between one and ten hours per week preparing for class and 57 percent reported spending fifteen hours per week or fewer. (Consider this the next time you're breaking up *David Copperfield* into daily reading assignments!) All of these numbers have actually improved a bit since 2003, the NSSE year Nathan used in her book.[13]

Nathan's experience offers a number of insights, but I want to emphasize the way in which putting herself in students' shoes revealed that student behaviors that we sometimes take personally, and frequently respond to with annoyance or anger, have nothing to do with us but, rather, arise out of students' entirely rational attempts to manage their time. It will be a boon to our mental health if we can accept that corner-cutting is an ordinary, and even appropriate, student behavior. This will enable us to do two things: to effectively (and calmly) strategize means to encourage and reward reading throughout a semester and to shrug off the inevitable, occasional class period to which a majority of students come without having read completely, or well, or at all. As I have said, my understanding of the politics of the classroom entails acknowledging explicitly that multiple, in some cases conflicting, interests are at work in the classroom and negotiating those interests openly as the semester goes along. I believe it is fine to acknowledge that students have understandable, even rational reasons for not doing their reading for your class and to discuss with them directly how your class design is set up to push back on these impulses. Having slowly and often painfully come to this position, I now not only assign what I think are reasonable amounts of reading; I actively plan for days when the number of students who have read carefully will be down.

The Reading Schedule, and How to Talk About It

I pay particular attention to the number of pages I assign over the course of the semester and in individual weeks and consider carefully the time it will take students to read. Since graduate school, I have been taking note of how long it takes me to read certain things (I can read forty to forty-five pages of a contemporary novel in an hour; thirty to forty pages of Dickens; twenty to twenty-five pages of George Eliot; fifteen to twenty pages of the late Henry James novels; two sentences of *Finnegans Wake*. If they're short sentences.) Recognizing that some students will read more quickly than I (but with less attention and comprehension) and some will read more slowly, I estimate how long individual reading assignments may take. At the undergraduate level, I teach a cohort that is composed of 90 percent English majors, so I assume somewhat higher tolerance for reading than in the general student population; and because of the reading-intensive nature of the major, I assume that students are spending more than the national average of ten to fifteen hours on class preparation per week. (No doubt, *some* students in my class are spending only that much time.) Obviously, if you teach your literature classes to mixed populations or mainly in general education classes, your calculus on this will be different. Amid these calculations I also bear in mind the old common wisdom, taught to incoming students since my days as an undergraduate, that you should plan for two-to-three hours of work outside the class for each hour spent in the classroom. I assign longer chunks of reading over the weekend and ease up as the busy week goes along. Inevitably, I have to overload students now and then: otherwise I could only assign short novels. In cases like this, I flag these heavy-reading periods for students early in the semester and ask them to plan for them; keep reminding them that they are coming up; and jovially browbeat them as the assignments approach. (I also urge them to track their own pages per hour and to plan accordingly.) Here is an example of a heavy-reading period in my British literature survey class. I shall return several times to this section of syllabus in this chapter.

September 23—**Essay #1 due. Intro to Victorian Literature:** Longman Victorian intro 1044–74; Arnold, "Dover Beach" 1562–63, *Culture and Anarchy* excerpts 1595–1604.

September 25—**Victorian mindsets (1: Gender and Sexuality):** Tennyson, "Mariana," "The Lady of Shalott" 1179–85; Christina Rossetti, "Goblin Market" 1650–63, "Winter: My Secret" 1649–50; Longman intro to "Victorian Ladies and Gentlemen" 1520–22 and excerpts from Ellis 1525–28, Beeton 1542–44, Victoria 1547–52, Grand 1552–3.

September 27—Victorian mindsets 1, continued. Read first four chapters of *Great Expectations*.

September 30—*Great Expectations*

October 2—*Great Expectations*

October 4—*Great Expectations*

October 7—*Great Expectations*

October 9—**Victorian mindsets (2: work):** *Longman:* "Perspectives: Industrialization" 1088–1113; working-class poetry (handout), Tennyson, "Ulysses" and "The Lotos Eaters" 1185–91; Carlyle from *Past and Present* 1076–83.

October 11—**Catch-up day.**

October 14—**Midterm Exam.**

This is a Monday-Wednesday-Friday fifty-minute class. The weekends of September 28–29 and October 5–6 are going to be heavy-reading weekends, and I will tell students to make note of it on the first day of the semester and do so again, numerous times, in class, via email, and over whatever course management program we're using, as these weeks approach. Weekend reading assignments during this stretch of the semester will be around 150 pages (5 hours of reading at 30 pages per hour) to allow for shorter reading assignments on the other days (75 pages between Monday and Wednesday and 50 or fewer between Wednesday and Friday would be average). That gets us about 475 pages over 5 class periods. The current Penguin edition of *Great Expectations* weighs in at 489 pages, so some minor tweaking will get us there—in this case a slightly longer-than-usual assignment for the first Friday: four chapters or about sixty-five pages. This being the real world, I recognize that many of the students—including, experience suggests, some very good students—will fall a bit behind in the reading while doing their best to keep up. I talk about all this openly and in a friendly, supportive manner in class. As we get toward the middle of the second week I may check in by doing a quick, informal poll to see how far people are, and sometimes I will adjust the day's discussion so that major spoilers (OMG Orlick clobbered Pip!) don't get revealed in class. As you can see I have also built a safety valve—a "catch-up day"—into the schedule for this part of the semester, so that if students are really struggling to keep up I can add another day on *Great Expectations*; if not I can use this day to review for the midterm. All of this, of course, requires good communication practices on both sides—students have to be tuning in to your messages (whether you send them on Canvas or Blackboard, via Twitter, or on old-fashioned email), so you have to establish a culture in which students understand the flexibility in your schedule and know to keep up with changes.

Some teachers, I know, will say that I am coddling students and encouraging a "customer-service" mindset by being flexible and by condoning students' "failure" to keep up with the reading. To that I have two responses: (1) while I do think instilling good work habits is one of the aims of college education, I think enabling learning is more important. Yes, I seek to teach and live in the real world, and I recognize that, regardless of what I do, one of the most profound effects college has on students is that it teaches them to be overscheduled adults. But turning students into grinds is not one of *my* teaching objectives, and, in fact, negotiation of workloads and deadlines are as much part of many real workplaces as stress and hyper-competitive compulsion are of many others. (2) Real students, even real English majors, sometimes cannot read a 500-page novel in three or five or even seven days; if we force them to be accountable for assignments they cannot complete, we are forcing them into the waiting arms of the internet, where they can access more free cheater's guides to *Great Expectations* than you could reasonably count. My job is to put students into situations where they will develop advanced reading comprehension and advanced literacy. In the instant case, my job is to get them to read as much of a thick Victorian novel as they can with care and critical acumen, and to practice their budding advanced literacy skills on this novel. I have no doubt that my chances of success will be better if I'm reasonable about the reading load, engage with students constantly on how it's going for them, and accept the fact that not every student will read every word.

What to Do When No One Has Read

So much for arranging reading to maximize the number of students who engage with it seriously. But what of those days—I'm sorry, they're inevitable—when a majority of the students have not read? On my syllabus above, the first day—September 23—is worth our attention, as it is a classic nonreading day. Students have a formal essay that counts as 20 percent of the course grade due on this Monday morning. My experience tells me that the chances are almost nil that more than two or three out of twenty-five students will read forty pages of literary-historical introduction to the Victorian period and nine pages of Matthew Arnold's dilatory, nineteenth-century prose in *Culture and Anarchy*. Indeed, the most tactically savvy students—successful juniors and seniors—will have planned their schedules to allow them to do most of the work of writing their essays on Sunday evening. The most Type A may have written opening paragraphs, theses, and outlines (at my prompting) in advance and shared them with me, but a large majority will do the entirety of their work on the paper on Sunday night and the small hours of Monday morning. Still, I want to get moving on the Victorian section of our class; and I don't want to spend the 50 minutes lecturing. (It's almost mid-semester; some of these students will have deprived themselves of sleep to get the paper done; they are not apt to be primed to glean useful and durable information by listening to me talk for fifty minutes, either.)

My strategy in this case is simple: I plan a class period that can be successful—that can meet its specific objectives—regardless of whether the students have read or not. This is a strategy I use often. As I've made clear, I talk with students about how they're doing in keeping up, so I can usually tell when they're starting to sag. In busy times of the semester, I often enter the room with two plans—one for if a majority has read, one for if a majority hasn't, and I begin by asking them how prepared they are. Doing so begins with advance deliberation about objectives and methods. As you know, my philosophy emphasizes skills over content, which makes the survey class itself a somewhat uneasy fit for me, based as it is on an older model of a literary education weighted more toward declarative knowledge. Still, for this particular class, content objectives step to the fore a bit: I want introduce students to the idea that the Victorian era was one riven by conflict and anxiety, fueled by an acceleration of the changes—technological, economic, social, political, and so on—that we group together under the term "modernity"; and I want them to begin recognizing which particular historical developments are producing specific anxieties. But, in keeping with my own philosophy, I want to move us there by having students practice their interpretive methods. So, here's the plan:

> 10–10:15: (1) In a short intro, I reinvoke "modernity" and posit that the Victorians are grappling with the continued escalation of the forces of modernity; (2) read "Dover Beach" aloud; (3) have students individually reread the poem silently and pick a short passage—sentence, line, phrase—that strikes them. (For any reason: they like it, they don't understand it, they don't like it, etc.) Have each student write about the line, in freewriting style, for five to seven minutes.
>
> 10:15–10:35: All-group discussion of Dover Beach; the objective here is to identify the conflicts that actuate the poem—the speaker's sense that the "sea of faith" has receded, leaving us "naked," and that the society around him is devolving into "ignorant armies" locked in "confused alarms of struggle and flight." Allow student-chosen lines to lead us in this direction; parse out lines carefully when appropriate; if time allows, work through some of the metaphors; leave loose ends ungathered at the end of twenty minutes, if necessary.
>
> 10:35–10:50: In mixed lecture/discussion, project quotations from the Longman introduction to Victorianism and quotations from the *Culture and Anarchy* excerpt that express Arnold's concern about working-class restiveness, middle-class complacency and lack of moral leadership, and the threat of anarchy. Conclude the class by clarifying that class tensions, exacerbated by industrialism and the rise of a middle class that does not have the cultural authority once granted to the crown and the aristocracy, are among the major cultural conflicts that will inform the texts we read for the next couple of weeks.

As you will see, though this class is tailored to a day on the schedule when I expect sparse class preparation from students, it begins in the way that most of my classes do: with activities that get students' brains working on the texts or issues that we shall be working on that day. I began starting virtually all of my literature class periods with active-learning set pieces like this one several years ago, after reading Blau's *The Literature Workshop*. Blau's approach in total is even more methods-driven than mine, and therefore best suited to introductory classes and even to high school teaching. But spending frequent and ample time in class having students do things makes unexceptionable sense if we agree that the main objectives of a literary education have to do with helping students develop skills and dispositions rather than having them "learn" texts, authors, and historical periods.

And it has further advantages: for one, it freshens students' recall of the texts on the table—even if they *have* read thoroughly—and generates material for ensuing discussion; students who take part in starter activities with some gusto will have built up some intellectual momentum that can then energize the discussion that follows. In situations where a class has a reticent dynamic—where, via the luck of the draw and other mysteries of the universe, you've assembled a group dominated by introverts and shy people—a starter activity ensures that everyone will have generated something to contribute to discussion and have it on a piece of paper or a computer screen in front of them—a fact you can point out to them, with gentle good humor, in the rare cases where the activity does not quickly transition to discussion. Finally, as my planning for this class shows, making students do something vigorous with a text in class is a virtually foolproof way of running a meaningful session on a day when a majority of students have not read.

There are few experiences in a literature teacher's professional life that are more unpleasant than trying to lead discussion in a classroom where no one, or almost no one, has done the reading. Like every literature teacher ever, I have had this experience, many times. In the past, I am chastened to say, I have gotten angry and shamed my students, with raised voice. Or I have dismissed classes early, with a tone of (faked, and probably unconvincing) emotional neutrality. I decided some years ago that I am not going to do any of these things any more. If students haven't read, I am going to find out, and I am not going to judge them, and we are going to do something else that day—something that gives them practice or instruction in the skills of advanced reading comprehension.

One further point about the "Dover Beach" class begs explanation. I have said that I know from experience that this class day is going to be a no- or low-reading day. Why, then, assign any reading at all? That's a fair question, and perhaps it *would* be better not to assign any reading. In some cases of nonreading days I might do just that. But there are problems with that, as well. By this time in the semester we have established a practice in which materials from the reading schedule constitute the agenda for the day. If there is no reading assigned, students might assume that nothing important is happening and—now that we are in the age of Canvas and Blackboard, and they do not have to be physically present to hand in their papers—think that this would be a great day to skip, that they deserve a break anyway, having just finished a major assignment, and so on.

But in fact, in the arc of the class's central narrative about literary responses to modernity, this would not be a good day to miss; as a group, I want the students to share the intellectual reorientation toward the new material, and today's activities are aimed to allow us to look back, to our earlier discussions of modernity, and forward, to the particular form anxieties about modernity are going to take in the texts we read for the next set of weeks. In other words, it's more important for me that students come to class on this particular day than it is that they have read thoroughly. And students are less likely to skip class if there is material on the syllabus that they are responsible for, in one way or another. Frankly, given my sense of the reality of student schedules, I would rather have them spending time putting their best effort into their papers than reading Matthew Arnold on Sunday, September 22; but I also want them in the room on Monday, September 23. And, as I hope I've convinced you, it is entirely possible to get good work done, both in continuing to build the literary-historical framework for the class and in the more crucial objective of helping students develop advanced reading comprehension, regardless of whether they spent time reading before class or not.

This day is a case of a nonreading day that is evident on paper, before the semester even begins. (Other such days include class periods right around midterm exams, and just before holidays and breaks.) It is relatively easy to schedule light reading or to prepare yourself for an underprepared group, well in advance, for days like this. More challenging is keeping tabs on the ebbs and flows of student energy and preparedness as the semester moves along. But this is possible with good communication. Depending on your personal style and the particular dynamic that develops in an individual class (all happy classes are alike; every unhappy class is unhappy in its own way), you can do this in casual chat in the five minutes before class starts or the first couple moments of class; or you could use more formal methods, such as frequent student response questionnaires that engage students on what and how they're learning. (I discuss student response questionnaires in Chapter 5.) In this way you can have a sense of whether students are keeping up with a long novel and identify unpredictable points in the semester when a great number of your students are badly overscheduled. Having a sense of all this will let you know when you need to enter the room with a Plan A (students have read) and a Plan B (most students have not.) But even when you are completely blindsided by an underprepared group of students, it is still possible to make productive use of the class period. All you need is a set of well-chosen, rich passages prepared in advance, along with a set of specific, objective-oriented questions or activities to have them apply to the passages. Then you can set students to work, alone or in groups, to produce interpretive material out of those passages.

This is how such episodes typically go in my classes: Ten minutes or so into class, discussion is lagging or almost stopped, and/or more than one student has said something that indicates that he or she hasn't read ("I love Mr. Rochester! He seems totally honest to me!"). At that point I'll stop and, in a firm but friendly manner, ask how many people have read. Hopefully we're at a point in the semester where students know that this sort of thing doesn't make me angry—that I'm not looking to catch anyone out. I'll say, "Honestly, who has done the reading? How far are you?" Once a show of hands has shown me where we are, I'll say, "Alright, let's change tactics so that we can do something more productive," and set up the activity.

Taking this approach clearly has benefits beyond making productive class periods possible when students are underprepared. More profoundly, operating in this fashion puts into action aspects of my understanding of a democratic classroom, in that I recognize the conflicting interests in the room and the obstacles to pursuing those interests; I engage with students to figure out where we are and, with their knowledge and understanding, adapt the day's structure to those facts. This does not mean that I am relinquishing my authority in the classroom: I am still setting the objectives and substantially devising the structure of how we reach them, though I am doing so somewhat improvisationally at the moment. But I am exercising that authority in what I see as a legitimate way, one that acknowledges the power dynamics and the economic decisions at work (managing a student schedule is a series of economic decisions about the scarce resource of time) and that makes transparent the actual conditions under which we are working.

And more importantly, students are likely to see this way of operating as legitimate: they know that I am not overworking them because of some arcane "no pain/no gain" ideology, nor am I adopting a punitive relationship with them, nor am I behaving it in ways designed to bolster my own self-image or express my own power. When I let students know that I have a sense of their struggles to get everything done and adapt my use of class time to where they actually are, I am, finally, communicating two things to them: that their learning is the most important thing to me—much more important than disciplining them in the scary, capitalist way—and that I see class time as extremely valuable to that effort, too valuable to waste in a charade in which I know they didn't read, and they know that I know, but we all fake it in the interest of decorum.

Homework and Advanced Reading Comprehension

This brings me to my own practices for encouraging students to read, which are time consuming for me but extremely productive of learning, as they double as student practice in advanced reading comprehension. In my career I have relied heavily on various forms of homework, including targeted, very short writing assignments, take-home quizzes, and discussion board posts, each of which I discuss separately in this section. All, if designed deliberately, are effective in encouraging reading and helping students develop advanced reading comprehension, in large part because I grade them promptly and give specific feedback. Course management platforms have made giving this sort of very frequent, targeted feedback easier, doing away with those manila folders full of papers and the time spent shuffling them and making sure students who were absent get their old assignments back. (I have also found that, after a relatively short period of adjustment, my grading speed increased appreciably when my classes went paperless.)

Frequent feedback on low-stakes, high-standards assignments constitutes, in effect, an ongoing, mediated tutorial between me and each student. If a student seems to me to be applying inappropriate questions to a text or has flatly misread a keyword or phrase, I will discuss that in my comment. If a student is not generating truly interpretive claims or using evidence, I will explain that. If a student is doing everything well except for writing clear, concise, and grammatical sentences, I will explain specific error patterns. If a student's work is showing evidence of very weak language skills, I will invite the student to meet with me to strategize for the semester.

This approach proceeds from the unexceptionable (I believe) logic, which I discussed in the introduction, that if you want students to learn to do something, you make them do it, repeatedly; give them prompt and frequent feedback; and assess them on it. What is more, this frequent feedback allows you to set specific agendas with specific students. If a student needs particular work in using evidentiary reasoning, you can explain that and keep coming back to it in subsequent weeks. If a student is not making the leap from close reading of details to overall interpretive claims, you can talk to the student about that. If a student writes well but has a penchant for repeating one higher-order error—such as parallel structure problems—you can explain this briefly, save it as a macro, and repeat as necessary. With discussion board posts, which I discuss later, such frequent feedback is particularly effective in upper-level classes, where you may not want to spend as much class time on fundamentals of interpretation as you would in an intro class: you can do the necessary extra, tailored instruction in making good interpretive claims, marshaling and reasoning from evidence, and so on in concise, targeted feedback on homework.

Yes, all of this grading is time consuming, but for me it is possible (I set aside sections of each week where this work, and only this work, gets done), and with practice, it goes more quickly. I make the usual economic decisions: I limit myself, except in unusual cases, to three to four meaty sentences of feedback; I write very little about excellent work or completely careless work, particularly later in the semester; I write less in the final quarter of the semester, where I am appropriately moving from formative assessment to summative assessment. (I recognize that a more targeted use of such low-stakes writing—or some other approach entirely—might be necessary where teaching load or other contingencies require it. I know of teachers who require students to post tweets about overnight reading assignments on Twitter, for example.) When using my approach it is very important to stay on top of providing weekly feedback in the early and middle parts of the semester, when students still have time to act on insights about their interpretive and writing skill and to schedule appointments with you. While it remains important not to get behind on this work later in the semester, for your own mental health, it becomes less important for students, who in the last three or so weeks of the semester are scrambling so much to manage their stress and workload that they are less likely to come to any new insights or practices in terms of their reading comprehension.

Take-Home Quizzes

Over the years I have shifted from relying mainly on the take-home quizzes to emphasizing discussion board posts, though I still use both of them strategically, for reasons I address later. But take-home quizzes remain effective for a number of functions, including steering students to difficult and important passages, pushing students to read material that provides declarative knowledge (introductions to writers or periods, literary or critical terms or concepts), and prompting them to put concepts into use. A sample quiz question of this type might look like this: having assigned a short reading defining "imagery," or having introduced the topic in class, I ask the following question:

1. Describe the imagery in Elizabeth Bishop's "The Fish," watching for changes in the imagery and contrasting the images in the second half of the poem from those in the first half.

This exercise nudges students toward an active reading that will move them past surface readings of Bishop's notoriously reticent poem, offering data for a discussion that seeks to explain the surprising evocation of "victory" at the poem's conclusion. And it prompts students to exercise a fundamental skill in literary analysis that will be easy and familiar for some but new to others.

I teach an introductory Film Studies class, and the take-home quiz works extremely well in that setting. Students need to learn the elements of film form in order to recognize and analyze them in scenes, films, and directorial styles, so they must quickly develop a sizable vocabulary of things such as shot types (angle, distance, duration), editing techniques, sound devices, and so on. During the part of the semester where this work gets done, students read a textbook that explains and exemplifies these fundamentals. I assign take-home quizzes with listing and fill-in-the-blank questions that push students to transcribe basic definitions, followed by questions that ask them to apply them to concrete settings. In subsequent classes, we will watch multiple clips and have open discussion, during which I prompt students to use the terms to analyze the formal properties of scenes. In this way the students will have begun by assembling the requisite declarative knowledge, used it procedurally on the quiz, then had a forum in which to apply it further—and see it applied by other students—in class.

Here are two questions from a quiz covering the chapter on shot angles and distances.

1. Camera angles

_____ tend to slow down movement and increase the importance of setting or environment; the importance of the subject is reduced.

_____ are often point-of-view shots which suggest tension, transition, and visual anxiety; they are used infrequently.

_____ are the most unusual and disorienting shots because they flatten perspective; they are photographed from directly above the object.

_____ tend to minimize environment, heighten the importance of the subject, and speed up motion.

_____ are the most commonly used angles in American cinema.

2. Re-watch the first two takes of the "crop-duster scene" from North by Northwest.

   a. Describe the camera angle in the first take and the effects it has in that context.
   b. Describe the camera angle in the second take.

The first question takes students directly to the parts of the reading that are essential to their success in this unit of the class and makes assembling the proper terms and definitions *their* work. This means that rather than ploddingly lecturing my way through these terms in chalk-talk fashion, I can rely on them to gather the vocabulary and spend class, instead, developing the larger contexts from which these cinematic conventions emerge and in which they take on meaning, and giving the students practice in recalling the terms and applying them appropriately, a cognitive move that they will have practiced initially in the second question. In subsequent quizzes I can craft questions that repeat these applications of the vocabulary and synthesize them with other ones; and in class I can repeatedly ask students to identify increasing numbers of elements from longer and more complex scenes, so that their toolkit of terms and concepts is building and being reinforced all along. Here is a question from a take-home quiz later in the semester that prompts recall of terms relating to multiple elements of film form, a question I frequently use, as well, on the midterm exam.

Rewatch the "fireplace scene" in Citizen Kane, and answer the following questions:

a. Describe the camera distance and angle in the first take.
b. In terms of Classical Hollywood editing, what is unusual about the first take?
c. How does the clip use sound to enhance dramatic effect or characterization?

Of course, the reading comprehension at stake in these instances is very basic. But later on in the film class, or in literature classes, I will use quiz questions to prompt close attention to more challenging language, both to get students to practice basic decoding and to prompt them toward more advanced interpretive work. The following two questions come from a quiz that covers two short but challenging readings: an introductory chapter on cultural theory and Brian Gallagher's critical essay on the film "Double Indemnity."[14]

> Briefly sketch out the similarities and differences in attitudes toward popular culture between the (1) Frankfurt School, (2) American mid-twentieth-century critics such as Dwight McDonald, and (3) the Birmingham school of cultural studies.
>
> "The battle over Walter is, at base, a sexual battle," Gallagher writes. Who is battling over Walter, and why is this battle sexual, according to the article?

In literature classes, quiz questions can prompt and measure basic decoding by forcing attention to difficult and important passages and by asking students to recognize straightforward implications that nonetheless require some basic inference-making and are essential to literal understanding:

> In line 43 of "Ulysses," Ulysses says that his son Telemachus "works his work, I mine." What is Telemachus's work, and what is Ulysses'?

This question prompts recognition of a contrast that clarifies the central values of the poem—effort, exploit, discovery—and can lead productively into the gendered nature of the work the poem celebrates. But it begins with basic decoding—understanding what are the two different kinds of work evoked in the line. Other questions urge students to tune in to the syntax—to note the relations of the parts of complex sentences. This is particularly useful in helping students become better readers of poetry, because the tension between poetic line and sentence structure is often a source of confusion for students, who will unconsciously treat the poetic line as a unit of sense, when often it is mainly or entirely a unit of sound. One remedy for this problem is sensitizing students to the fact that, when they are beginning to get confused about the plain sense of a poem, it is helpful to figure out where they are in the sentence, where the sentence begins and ends, and what its parts are. This can be particularly challenging in pre-twentieth-century poetry, where poetic diction replete with archaisms and inversions is at work. So questions like the following ones can be helpful:

> In the clause that takes up most of lines 17 and 18 of "The Lotos-Eaters"—
> ... and, dew'd with showery drops
> Up-clomb the shadowy pine above the woven copse.
> What is the subject of the clause?
>
> In line 5 of "Ulysses," who "hoard(s), and sleep(s), and feed(s)"?
>
> In "Adam's Curse," the section beginning, "And thereupon" is all one sentence. What is its main verb?

These questions are unlikely to come up specifically in class, but they prompt students to focus on difficult passages carefully. They speak to basic decoding, which is often more of a challenge for our students than we expect, and particularly so when standard literary difficulty of one kind or another—conventional poetic diction of previous eras, or avant-garde practices of modern and contemporary poetry—are at work. Even nineteenth-century prose, with its expansive sentence structures, can be an obstacle to basic decoding for our students. Indeed, prompting students to tune in closely to particular, challenging sentences may be even more important in the case of fiction, because students are more apt to assume a norm of transparency for fictional prose and therefore not even realize it when they are missing something important in a novel, whereas most students already assume that poetry will be difficult and thus expect a text that resists their efforts.

Homework Assignments and Interpretive Methods

Beyond basic decoding lie analysis, interpretation, and contextualization, the higher-order elements of advanced reading comprehension. A good introductory class in literary analysis should be designed to introduce students to the purpose and practice of literary analysis and the fundamental cognitive moves involved in doing it. And it should be sequenced to move from fundamental to advanced analytical methods. In the midst of all this the teacher should be working to suss out problems in basic decoding and to address them—in class when they are widespread and one-on-one (efficiently done through feedback on quizzes) when they are more eccentric. In such introductory classes, instead of quizzes I prefer to use homework assignments targeted to specific methods. Since, in essence, an introduction to literary analysis is already a methods class, the methods are the class's primary content, so homework assignments that foreground them are more in step with the class objectives than quizzes that are tied to the content of literary texts.

In my literary analysis class, texts are the vehicles for students to develop and practice methods—something I make clear to them verbally and through class materials—and homework assignments treat literary texts in this fashion. I use Rosenwasser and Stephen's *Writing Analytically* as a textbook for introduction to literary analysis, because it breaks analysis down into a host of specific moves and activities. These lead students from the most basic moves (noticing striking details, finding patterns) to the more risky and tentative moves of positing a detail's significance and making interpretive leaps about the significance of patterns. Here is a homework for early in the semester, drawing on Rosenwasser and Stephen's assertion that interpretation begins with noticing significant details:

> Do a "Notice and Focus" (WA 35–36) on one of the poems we have read so far this semester. Then write one paragraph interpreting several of the key details that you listed in your "notice and focus" exercise.

Here is one from a week or so later, drawing on Rosenwasser and Stephen's typology of "the Five Analytical Moves": suspend judgment; define parts and how they are related; look for patterns of repetition and contrast; make the implicit explicit; keep reformulating questions and explanations.[15]

> Without consulting any sources, write a paragraph analyzing some aspect of one of the Dickinson poems. Then go back to *Writing Analytically* pp. 4–10 and (1) identify which of the analytic moves you used in your paragraph, and (2) rewrite the paragraph, using at least one more of the analytic moves than you used the first time around. Add a sentence at the bottom of the page that explains which analytical moves informed each version.

A bit later, I am prompting students to take the risk of positing significance for patterns of details—talking about what they mean in context, reading them as metaphors or symbols, linking them to larger patterns, making claims as to why they are there or why they are important. First, I provide a list of detail-clusters to choose from, in James Joyce's "The Sisters":

> Pick *two* of the following details of Joyce's "The Sisters" and *brainstorm* on the implications of their use in the text. You don't need to write in complete sentences or edit yourself—brainstorm freely. Do your best, however, to interpret in context (You'll have to read the story in full first before you do this assignment).
>
> - The chalice (p. 11, lines 282–6 and 303)
> - "smile/smiling/laughing" (p. 5 lines 80–83, p. 7 139–42, p.8 177–183, p. 11 297–307)
> - The ellipses ("...") in the story: p. 3 lines 18–20, p. 4 27–28, 50–60, p. 4–5 66–68, p. 7 153–55, p. 8 203–207, p. 10 243–46, 265–67, p. 11 281–299.
> - The boy's dream (p. 5 lines 71–83, p. 7 150–156)
> - The physical descriptions of the priest (p. 5–6 lines 98–113, p. 7 139–49. p. 8 180–85).

The emphasis here is on brainstorming—on generating a lot of material, which can then be reexamined for the initial interpretations that seem most solid, persuasive, or promising. For that reason I have done the work of gathering the details into patterns, so as not to overload the students and to have them recognize that there are distinct, often sequenced cognitive moves involved in literary interpretation.

Another homework assignment, slightly later in this sequence, seeks to help students recognize the benefit of generating a lot of interpretive claims, of varying quality, so that they can then pick and choose the best claims and the ones that can cohere into an argument. Again drawing on Rosenwasser and Stephen's methods, the assignment attempts to move students away from the notion that texts—and their significant details—each have one correct reading. The assignment also introduces students to the fact that writing a good essay means generating a lot more interpretive raw material than you will actually end up using—a fundamental practice of rich humanities research and expository writing which, if we are successful, will become a disposition in our students. The assignment works on the fundamentals that will lay the groundwork for rich, nuanced interpretations that, by finding multiple suggestions, echoes, and connotations, recognize the multivoiced nature of complicated text and begin to steer a path through it. Rosenwasser and Stephens call this exercise a "10-on-1"—students posit ten analytical claims about a single detail, thus "drawing as much meaning as possible from your best example."[16] This contrasts with the archetypal student essay, which is more like a "1-on-10": students come up with one basic analytical claim ("Victor Frankenstein's foundational sin lies in his disregard for family and the domestic life") and offers ten examples to support it, resulting in a flat argument that, while it may assert a provable claim, uses an additive structure rather than logical argumentation. A homework that prompts students to keep working over a key example looks like this:

> Do a "10-on-1" on a detail you find to be significant from *one* of the following stories: "Grace," "Ivy Day in the Committee Room," "The Dead." In essence, a 10-on-1 is a brainstorming exercise in which you try to come up with ten interpretations of a single piece of evidence. Start by reading *Writing Analytically*, pages 211–220, which explains the concept.

Metacognition and Demystifying Interpretation

In addition to focusing on specific interpretive methods, these assignments, which come early in my literary analysis class, put into action my understanding of advanced reading comprehension as a set of skills and dispositions that students can develop. Most crucially, they make clear to students that literary interpretation is not an innate talent which their teachers possess in Olympian measure. They demystify literary interpretation by breaking it down into its component parts—many of which even less advanced students will already have, to some degree, put into practice—and allows students to recognize the cognitive moves they are already making. Thus chief among the skills called upon in the homework assignments are various forms of metacognition: moments when we, as readers, recognize what our minds are doing and are thus able to do so more thoroughly and consciously. Anyone who likes to read, for example, is struck by certain details, descriptions, plot developments, bits of dialogue, turns of phrase, or instances of figurative language: for reasons that may be opaque, and which we usually do not query, certain details stand out. The "Notice and Focus" exercise raises to consciousness this experience of "being struck" and uses it as grist for initial interpretive brainstorming. At every level of skill in literary analysis, powerful interpretations are born in that moment of being struck, which therefore forms the launching point for many activities I use to seed class discussion, as we saw in the "Dover Beach" class plan I described earlier.

Just as basic is the cognitive move of forming binaries—breaking subjects of analysis into opposing elements and/or recognizing existing binary oppositions evident in texts and other objects of study. Because these cognitive moves are virtually universal and indispensable (even if ultimately limiting) my literary analysis class begins there. An early homework assignment will choose a poem that divides nicely into binaries with a sufficiently rich trail of details that can be organized around them. Blake's "The Clod and the Pebble" works well, with a five-minute setup in class to ensure that students have succeeded, through basic decoding, in recognizing that the poem is structured into two voices.

"Love seeketh not itself to please
Nor for itself hath any care,
But for another gives its ease,
And builds a heaven in hell's despair."

So sang a little clod of clay
Trodden with the cattle's feet
But a Pebble of the Brook
Warbled out these meters meet:

"Love seeketh only self to please
To bind another to its delight
Joys in another's loss of ease
And builds a hell in heaven's despite."

The prompt is simple: ask students to recognize the central binary (some will be literal and concrete, heading the columns "clod" and "pebble"; others more abstract, using something like "generous" and "selfish"), and list details under each column. The assignment can then provide grist for discussion in the next class, or can be set aside and revisited later, for brainstorming of interpretations of details (a 10-on-1, for instance) or for some practice coming to larger interpretive leaps and thus forming a hypothesis for a potential essay.

In my literary analysis class, this comes after a first-day activity centering on Wallace Stevens's "Anecdote of the Jar," which provides a splendid entree to literary analysis: my experience suggests that this short lyric appears to many students strange and intractable on a first reading but opens up quickly to even relatively inexpert close reading. And it is a perfect text for introducing the concept of metacognition, because students, virtually without fail, succeed in dividing the poem into binaries without prompting. This allows you to foreground: (1) the fact that students are already using interpretive methods—making the cognitive moves on which literary interpretation is based, and (2) the fact that advancing one's skills of literary interpretation (and thereby one's advanced reading comprehension) requires such metacognition—recognition of how your mind is working on a text, along with assessment of what you are understanding and what you are not, where the text's (and your own) interpretive questions, mysteries, and problems lie—followed by a resolution to set out deliberately to explore them. I want to walk through this opening-day class activity because it so fully embodies my approach to demystifying interpretation and helping students develop metacognition as a disposition.

I start this assignment in the very first moments of the semester, before I go over the syllabus and class policies. I do so as a sort of estranging mechanism, throwing students into working on a text before we have performed the conventional rituals of the new semester. This proceeds from my intuition that students' minds might be a bit clearer and sharper when they haven't settled into the familiar, first-day-of-class mode of sitting and listening; students often have difficulty with dramatic changes of mode in mid-class-period (for instance, doing active reading or discussion after they've listened to a thirty-minute lecture); I suspect that trying to get them to work with the requisite energy might be difficult if I've started the period with twenty minutes of jokey self-introductions and recitation of class policies. I hand out the poem on a half-sheet, read it aloud, and then give them a solid ten minutes to mark it up as vigorously as they can. "Do what you do with poems," I say. (This is an introduction to literary analysis class, so the prompt is appropriate. In a general education intro to literature, a different prompt might be required, but I believe the poem would still work.) Then students get to work on "Anecdote of the Jar." (You can read the poem at https://www.poetryfoundation.org/poetrymagazine/poems/14575/anecdote-of-the-jar.)

Once students have scribbled in their margins for ten minutes, I start our discussion by introducing the concept of metacognition: our objective, I say, will be not just to register our responses to the poem but to understand where those responses came from. I linger on this point, making sure students understand, providing a definition of metacognition and some examples, if necessary. (Example: when you have a song stuck in your head, and you can't remember why, then you trace your thoughts back to the thought or stimulus that reminded you of the song: metacognition—thinking about what's been going on in your mind.)

When students have finished marking up their sheets, I open the floor, pointedly asking *not* for overall interpretations of the poem but for responses to details. I will write down a few keywords from each student comment on the board. I have used this opening activity more than 10 times, and it has never failed that someone very early on, perhaps even first, invokes a binary in response to the poem (the jar and the wilderness, wild/not wild, etc.). I seize on this point and enunciate, clearly and loudly, what has just happened—we have divided the poem into constitutive, binary oppositions as a way of understanding it. I say that this is a valid, fundamental interpretive strategy. I reiterate: metacognition: we're not just interpreting, we're paying heed to the cognitive moves we're making as we interpret. Then I talk briefly about what binaries are, how central they are to human thought (gesturing with my hands and pointing to my eyes to indicate the bilateral symmetry of the human body), and pausing to ask whether everyone is with us and whether anyone has questions. In a typical group of students in this class at my university, there will be some reasonably skilled and confident readers, some who are less so. The benefit of this metacognitive moment is that even many unskilled readers will have made this basic move, and more skilled students will have done it unconsciously, seeing it not *as* a cognitive move but as a natural response to what is on the page. Less confident students get to see that they are capable of an important analytical skill. And, should there be anyone in the room who did not engage in any binary thinking in analyzing the poem, our work so far will have shown them this basic move in action and emphasized that literary interpretation is not an innate talent but a set of discrete moves that can be identified and practiced.

At this point I turn our attention back to the poem, and ask, "What do you think is the central or most important binary in the poem?" Answers will vary: some students will go concrete (the jar and the wilderness, or the jar and Tennessee, or verdant vs. "gray and bare"); some (precocious!) will go abstract and want to leap to overarching interpretations ("order/chaos" or "civilization/nature"). It doesn't matter what we ultimately choose as the governing binary: whatever we decide, as we talk I will sketch out two columns on the board in which we array the connected elements in each category. Along the way, students will voice interpretations that illustrate other interpretive moves. For instance, someone is sure to point to imagery patterns (such as wilderness/wild/bird/bush/hill, though they may not call it an "imagery pattern.") This is another opportunity to pause and have a "metacognitive moment." "Look," I'll say, "[Student A] has just made another fundamental cognitive move: she has recognized a pattern in the details and grouped like details together. Later this week you will be reading a book called *Writing Analytically*, which identifies this as one of the basic moves to interpretive thinking." Depending on the time and how tuned in and up-to-speed the students seem, I may introduce briefly the word "imagery" here. As we have been working through all this, something like the following will have developed on the board at the front of the room:

Jar	wilderness
Round	wild
Tall	slovenly
"made... surround."	"rose up"
"took dominion"	"ceased to sprawl"
"of a port"	
"did not give"	(implicitly) gave "of bird or bush"
Manmade	natural
Order	chaos?

Depending on how much time is left, I may, if the leap to implications and abstraction has occurred—"manmade/natural" and "order/chaos?"—pause for another "metacognitive moment" (sharp students are now recognizing that this phrase is one of my things, and that they're going to be hearing it a lot). I will note that we are now reading implications out of the details rather than merely arranging the details in categories and that—finally—we are beginning to construct an interpretation, which is a narrative separate from the words in the poem but shaped in response to them, one that functions at a higher level of abstraction and which posits a general insight or set of suggestions which, while not explicitly stated in the words of the poem, can be posited from them and defended with reference to its details.[17] (Even if we do make it to this point, this later, more complicated concept—the nature and status of interpretive generalizations—will need to be returned to and lingered over, carefully and repeatedly.)

The next stage is to allow individual students to take some interpretive leaps based on the material we have generated through close reading. Some will be tentative, some obtuse, some overly confident, but at this point it's all good. So I now get students to write—in a freewriting mode—for five to seven minutes, positing an interpretation of the poem. The results are less important than the fact that we've broken the interpretive process down into component parts and made clear that distinct cognitive moves, which can be recognized as such, learned, and practiced, underlie it. Indeed they are, hopefully, now practicing further instances of cognitive work—the stating of a hypothesis and the gathering of evidence, which I can mention as we are wrapping up. I will usually conclude the class with a few complicating questions (it's not at all unusual that no one has addressed the matter of "Tennessee"), and I may ask a question that I don't want an answer to—"Which does the poem prefer: the jar or the wilderness?"—and end the discussion there. Consistent with the approach I've been describing in this book, I am not interested in closing down discussion of that question, which is to me the shaping ambiguity of the poem. I am specifically disinterested in the class ending with a consensus, hypothesis-driven reading of the poem. So I do not ask students to share their hypotheses or read their freewriting. This class has been about introducing and practicing metacognition on fundamental interpretive practices. It has only been about "Anecdote of the Jar" inasmuch as the poem works supremely well for these purposes.

Later, when students have practiced a number of interpretive moves and some are gaining confidence, I often introduce an exercise meant to create awareness of the hermeneutic circle, the interpretive dynamic in which, having interpreted small details, we make an interpretive leap to more general and abstract interpretive insights, then shift our attention back to details, bringing the larger hypothesis to bear as we interpret further particulars and using them to sharpen, adapt, or correct the hypothesis. In the introduction to literary analysis class this activity works well around the time we move from poetry to drama, as plays require us to create order out of a much larger range of details than short lyric poems do. In our first class on drama I introduce the concept of the hermeneutic circle in a ten-minute mini-lecture, with examples from a familiar text; have them do an exercise in small groups; then individually do something similar as a homework assignment. In the small-group assignment, a group is given a vague, draft student thesis and asked to complete two full loops of the hermeneutic circle: first go to details and find evidence for and against the thesis, or details that can sharpen it; then return to the thesis and reshape it based on the details; then repeat the entire process again, ultimately ending with a thesis that has been revised twice in dialogue with specific details.

In the mini-lecture that introduces this activity, I call back "Anecdote of the Jar." I project the poem on the wall, alongside a thesis arguing that the speaker of "Anecdote of the Jar" values order and embodies it in the symbol of the jar. I then complicate this reading with reference to the descriptions of the jar as "grey and bare" and as something that "did not give"; and I raise the ambiguous question of whether "Tennessee" is an instance of order/civilization or chaos/wilderness. I finally adapt the draft thesis to describe the poem as ambivalent about the jar's role and argue that this ambivalence is embodied in the unaddressed question of "Tennessee's" status. Students would then get similarly vague prompts to work the hermeneutic circle on, then report out by showing the two subsequent theses they drafted and displaying the details that got them there. Even if the results are rough or even unconvincing, students will have walked through the process and will recognize it—or can activate it consciously—in building their own interpretations. In the next essay assignment, which comes up a week or so after the class exercise, I require students to submit draft theses about a week before the essay is due, then give a homework assignment on which they have to perform the hermeneutic circle exercise on their draft thesis. I have also used a shorter version of this sequence—just the mini-lecture and the group work—in upper-level classes when paper assignments are coming up or in cases when I feel like the interpretive richness of discussions or low-stakes writing needs work.

Low-Stakes Writing: Continuous Practice and Improvement

The methods I have outlined thus far—take-home quizzes, homework assignments, and the metacognition activities around "Anecdote of the Jar"—are all aimed at fundamental skill-building and initial, formative assessment of student skills. Take-home quizzes prompt students to assemble and apply declarative knowledge and push them toward difficult sections for basic decoding, allowing me to identify the skill levels in the class and giving well-prepared students practice in working with difficult texts. These activities all prompt students in the practice of specific skills of analysis and interpretation and foster metacognitive awareness of when they are succeeding (or not) at these skills. But despite the fact that the students are generating the interpretive material, these activities are very teacher-driven—with texts, primary questions, and specific objectives all outlined in advance. In advanced classes—and later on in introductory classes, where most students will have experience of the fundamentals of interpretation—we need to give students greater power in setting the agenda for discussion; we need to recalibrate the balance of contending interests in the classroom further toward those of the students. Yes, we should do so for reasons of the micro-politics of the classroom—because the classroom is a laboratory for the practice of citizenship and negotiation in a democracy. More pragmatically, we should also do so because defining intellectual problems (and taking initial steps in pursuing them) and articulating an agenda for discussion are advanced skills—and crucial ones at that, skills that make studying English appropriate preparation for a great many paths in life. For that matter, so is writing well, with clarity, logic, argumentative force, and sound evidentiary reasoning. At all levels of the curriculum, we should be explicit in making students aware that these are the skills they are practicing, advocating for their value, and promoting metacognition in their practice.

For these purposes, in advanced classes I favor weekly writing in the form of discussion board posts and the high-standards, low-stakes mode. Indeed, in recent years I have largely stopped using take-home reading quizzes in literature classes in favor of discussion board posts, though occasionally I repurpose old questions into prompts, in cases where a particular class (or a small cohort of students) is having difficulty generating good discussions on their own. But my preference is for a standing, open prompt that urges students to identify for themselves the themes, problems, patterns, or details in the text that speak to them and to either frame a path of inquiry that examines them or work out some initial hypotheses. Used as I propose here, this method cedes a considerable measure of agenda-setting about individual texts to the students, and it prompts me to act as a colearner and coinvestigator, frequently requiring me to work without a net (or with a smaller one than I am used to). Here is how it works:

Students are asked to submit weekly posts of 250 to 500 words (depending on the content and other, local objectives, I will adapt the length one way or another). I state plainly, and repeat frequently, my objectives in this assignment: I want the students to have a strong voice in how we approach texts, what we focus on when we explore them; and, I want to look at their writing early and often, so that I can, through my weekly comments, suggest ways of strengthening their writing and their interpretive skill; and, I want to encourage them to keep up with the reading, and I hate pop quizzes. In early weeks, I project exemplary posts (either written by them or culled from previous classes). I emphasize repeatedly that I am looking for the best writing they can manage given the time constraints. My syllabus contains the basic prompt for the assignment; here is one from a recent class in early-twentieth-century British literature:

> **Weekly discussion board posts.** Each week you will write about 500 words of analysis on the common texts we're reading at that time. You may write two posts of 250 words or one post of 500 words, or some similar combination. They should represent careful thought and careful writing. I will occasionally post prompts to stimulate your thinking; otherwise write about what interests, provokes, or perplexes you.
>
> These mini-essays should be posted to the discussion board by 10 a.m. the morning before we discuss the texts you're writing about. (In other words, posts about "A Prayer for My Daughter"—see the reading schedule for January 10 below—should be posted by 10 a.m. January 10).

I keep the prompt short because I will be spending further time in class projecting successful posts and leading short discussions on their particular strengths, and because I want all of this writing to constitute a multiplex dialogue—between me and the individual students and between me and the class as a whole. I don't, incidentally, require students to respond to each other's posts, though some will do so. In this sense calling these "discussion board posts" is a bit of a misnomer: they are short essays, available to all to read. In this sense they are public, which helps the students frame and recognize an audience for their writing. And students who are struggling can refer to strong ones, which I point out to them. Claims, provocations, insights, and details from these posts inform our discussions and class activities in almost every class. The prompt also makes clear that, while an individual post counts for a tiny percentage of the final grade, the activity as a whole is quite important, constituting 25 percent of the grade, in this case. Thus the writing week-to-week is low-stakes, and someone who is in a slump cannot sink their grade by phoning in one discussion board post. But the weekly writing overall is central to their work and will be held to high standards.

These posts then become primary raw material for class discussion and in-class activities. By having the posts due three or more hours before class meets, I allow myself time to read and grade them before we meet. As I grade, I take quick, concise notes on the issues they are raising. If four of five students raise the same question, focus on the same passage, or identify the same theme, that goes to the top of our agenda for discussion. On days when there is less consensus of interest, I will look for subtler themes that link a set of posts and draft some questions that speak to the issues they raise. On days where student interests are widely scattered, I will choose among the most interesting ones and draft a class plan that orchestrates these diverse interests toward one or more themes that seem evident or important to me. Sometimes I will try to synthesize diverse threads into a single interpretive question; sometimes I will list three themes, drawn from the discussion board, that we will attempt to work our way through, either in a single class or over a set of classes, noting that it will be our collaborative task to forge links between these themes and thus move toward one or more coherent readings of the text. These class plans are usually not very detailed—they may contain a list of potential passages to look at along with a list of interpretive questions to ask, roughly sequenced. Usually I will have previously articulated larger objectives for the unit we are in (and which may stretch over a week or more), but even these tend to be pretty general, allowing for lots of student voice in the particular directions our mutual learning will take.

Here are my notes from weekly student writing on Tennyson's "The Lady of Shalott" and Christina Rosetti's "Goblin Market," followed by my class plans for the two, consecutive fifty-minute periods dedicated to these texts. (See the syllabus excerpt in the "Reading Schedule" section of this chapter.)

Discussion Board notes

Goblin Market

- Lizzie follows gender norms; Laura doesn't. Examples re: domesticity (Hannah)
- "Men, like goblins, can be beaten" (Mika)
- Goblin Market: a metaphor for staying virtuous in the face of temptations. (Abbie)

    Q: What's up with the juice?

Lady of Shalott:

- What Victorian notions come into play? (Alexis)
    - The temptation of Lancelot's beauty. "Cause them to stray from what they are supposed to be doing."
- What's up with the curse?
    - She's cursed "because she wanted to be free to make her own choices"; (Cullen)
    - "grey walls and towers" symbolize "gender discrimination." she remains innocent (Marielle)
    - "If you stray, you put yourself at stake" "steering away from temptation will leave you more powerful" (Ashley)

Goblin Market class plan

Write themes on the board

- Gender norms and domesticity
- Equation of men and goblins, moral message?
- Virtue/temptation
- Question: How do we read the fruit imagery?

Passages

- Jeannie's story p. 1654 + 1657 l. 311–15
- Laura pays with her hair—significance?
- Attack of the goblins, p. 1659
- What's up with the juice? 1660–62 l. 446–542

Lady of Shalott class plan

- What's significant about her work?
    - Read aloud from the point of her change in attitude down to the end of section 3
        → Study imagery through which Lancelot is described, and imagery in Part 3 generally
    - What's significant about the curse? What is she specifically punished for?

As you can see, drawing on the weekly student writing allows me to create simple, flexible class plans that are nonetheless thematically coherent, oriented toward exploring identified themes and answering specific interpretive questions. It marks a considerable reallocation of class preparation time and effort from what I did as a younger professor, when I had specific interpretive destinations in mind and spent a great deal of effort constructing a sequence of passages to examine and a long list of questions designed to get students to see the text more or less as I did. Now the work of structuring the class meeting is radically simplified (the "Lady of Shalott" class is built entirely around two interpretive questions and one activity—a short imagery study). And while the path of interpretation is shaped, its results are left open. The time I used to spend devising byzantine close reading "discussions" is now spent grading and taking notes on the discussion board posts—where I also accomplish much of the semester's work of mentoring students in writing, making interpretive moves, and developing metacognition. During the discussions themselves I can prompt, evaluate, and praise good interpretive practices (finding evidence, reading closely, framing good interpretive questions, defending interpretations of details logically) as we move toward answering the questions we've set out. If appropriate, when a compelling interpretive hypothesis is raised, I will write it on the board and ask for evidence, both supporting and countervailing. Once this structure is established, much of the actual work is improvisational. And in a class of students who have prepared well, it is enormously fun.

My emphasis in this chapter has been on methods that help students develop advanced reading comprehension, which starts with the ability to decode the denotative meaning of difficult texts and proceeds to the work of analysis—recognizing patterns, positing significance, considering multiple nuances of meaning, using evidentiary reasoning to support interpretive assertions. I do not mean to suggest that my devices are the only or the best ways to do this. Rather, I offer my assignments and activities to illustrate how my broader understanding of teaching literature in the real world can be translated into action. You can devise your own activities for reaching these goals, and I will continue to come up with new ones, I am sure. But all of these activities (and all that follows in this book) are founded on my sense that the most important thing we can do for our students is put them in position to develop skills and methods that will make them stronger readers and writers; my belief that doing so starts with accepting the students we teach for who and where they are and planning a program of activities for them that they are actually likely to do; and my understanding that teaching students to read and write in advanced ways requires that we make them do it over and over again and give them frequent feedback, nudging them constantly toward the metacognition that will allow them to be their own best critics.

In the next chapter I move from advanced reading comprehension to advanced literacy, which entails the more advanced skills of seeing literary and other imaginative works in their cultural and historical contexts, and the difficult work of teaching students to do so.

3 TEACHING ADVANCED LITERACY

On Being Clueless

This chapter addresses one of the most consistent sources of frustration for literature teachers—students' lack of knowledge of what seem to us basic, essential literary and historical contexts—and the difficulty of addressing it pedagogically. Frustrating as it is, this problem is a fixed feature of the landscape in which we work. Leading discussion on "The Love Song of J. Alfred Prufrock," we find that students don't recognize "to have squeezed the universe into a ball" as a reference to Andrew Marvell's "To His Coy Mistress," which invokes the framework of the seduction poem as an ironic contrast to the speaker's inability to pose his question. Or we find that they don't recognize "I have seen my head (grown slightly bald) brought in upon a platter" as a reference to John the Baptist—a reference that underscores, clarifies, and gives weight to the following assertion, "I am no prophet." (We may breathe a sigh of relief when they recognize an allusion to a guy named Hamlet later on.) These are actually fairly high-level examples. More dispiriting still, while teaching a sonnet, we may find that a stunning percentage of our students do not recognize the sonnet form; or, in American Literature II, we may find that not all students can name the years of the US Civil War.

This lack of requisite prior knowledge (to use a term from learning research) does not merely limit the sophistication and nuance of student's literary interpretations: it poses an obstacle to what I referred to in Chapter 2 as basic decoding.[1] As reading research has demonstrated, the act of reading does not divide neatly into separate skills that are deployed sequentially—recognizing words, combining them into sentences, combining those into chunks of plot or argument and adding them all up into an understanding of a text: readers are never simply decoding and stringing together words but are also providing the contexts not explicitly present in the text but essential to its understanding. To return to my example from *Othello*:

> You shall mark
> Many a duteous and knee-crooking knave,
> That, doting on his own obsequious bondage,
> Wears out his time, much like his master's ass,
> For nought but provender, and when he's old, cashier'd:
> Whip me such honest knaves.
>
> (OTHELLO I IV)

In addition to its unusual syntax ("much like his master's ass" is a bit of a misplaced modifier, or at best an unclear one) and some potential vocabulary issues ("provender" and "obsequious" are probably not in the average undergraduate's lexicon), the passage also requires of its reader a general sense that the society depicted in the play is highly hierarchical—which gives meaning and weight to the repeated term "knave"—and know that kneeling to someone was an ordinary mark of deference and obedience in early modern cultures and that an "ass" is a beast of burden, much used for transportation and hauling in premodern times, as well as a mildly crude term for a human body part. All of this information is supplied by the reader (or it isn't), and is not a matter of simple decoding, though its lack will show up as incomprehension.

We can be frustrated about this, and rail about our school systems or our own thematically random or incoherent curricula, and we may be tempted by conservative solutions—a more lockstep and canonically based curriculum, for instance. I have conversed with creative writers in my department who, frustrated by their students' in ability to recognize allusions, have entertained the notion of a single class that teaches an agreed-upon body of texts. That's not a terrible idea, and it would be fascinating to be involved in the conversations about what those texts should be. But I suspect they would quickly run into the problem that the list would be too short to make a significant dent in the students' canon of texts and would end up looking fairly arbitrary to boot.

Thirty years ago, E. D. Hirsch caused a significant cultural splash with *Cultural Literacy: What Every American Needs to Know*, an extended argument that American schools needed to adopt standard curricula meant to convey a large body of declarative knowledge—ranging from such fundamentals as the planets of the solar system to belles lettres nuggets such as Montaigne's status as creator of the modern personal essay. Such a curriculum would promote "cultural literacy," defined as "the network of information that all competent readers possess" (2). Hirsch's argument was attractive to many readers in part because it makes intuitive, experiential sense that if students have a shared body of declarative knowledge, their reading comprehension will improve, and teachers will not need to constantly re-cover fundamentals or tailor instruction to varied levels of familiarity; teachers could assume that everyone (or almost everyone) in the room has a broad common grounding.

Hirsch was right to argue that reading comprehension depends to a significant degree on declarative cultural knowledge: someone who has never heard of baseball is not going to get a great deal out of Marianne Moore's "Baseball and Writing." As an example of the quandary caused by inadequate cultural literacy, Hirsch asks readers to imagine a classroom in which an elementary school teacher is trying to explain the structure of atoms by making an analogy to the solar system. The teacher knows that the lesson only works if students already know very generally about the shape and movement of the solar system; so she asks how many students are familiar with it. Fifteen students do; five don't. Now, what is the teacher to do? Spend the next twenty minutes explaining the solar system, boring the fifteen, or plunge ahead, confusing the five?

Hirsch's argument hit a nerve because of the seemingly irrefutable simplicity of anecdotes like this. There is no doubt that this class goes better if all the students know about the solar system, just as there's no doubt that students will not understand Iago's animal metaphor if they don't know that an ass is a donkey or that a discussion of Prufrock will be richer if students recognize the allusions. And few moves are more deadening to a discussion of a literary work than an improvised, interrupting mini-lecture that explains an allusion: this is the equivalent of explaining what is funny about a joke, which (as someone who teaches James Joyce, I can attest) is in fact one form of this pedagogical pall-caster. On a second look, though, Hirsch's anecdote also reveals some of the fatal weaknesses of his argument, beginning with its hypothetical, anecdotal nature (Hirsch's argument relies heavily on such illustrative hypotheticals, along with selectively assembled education research). The argument also relies on a fanciful, if extensively worked-out, belief in the power of declarative knowledge both to stick in people's minds and to form itself into schemata for the accumulation of further knowledge.[2]

Hirsch's thinking runs counter to then-current and subsequent learning research in multiple ways. These include the consensus that declarative knowledge evaporates if it is not consistently used (I remember the structure of the solar system because it was taught to me repeatedly, because I've read the science section of the *New York Times* for decades, and because of Jeopardy and its analogues; but if I had to take an introductory class on macroeconomics, I would have to relearn all the terminology and fundamentals I learned when I took it in Penn State's core curriculum in 1983.)[3] Hirsch also ignores (and in a subsequent book discounts) the importance of metacognition, which is essential to higher-order intellectual functions such as defining research questions, making a project plan, monitoring progress, and changing tactics if they are not leading to appropriate results. Hirsch approvingly quotes Alfred North Whitehead, who calls the emphasis on metacognition "a profoundly erroneous truism . . . . The precise opposite is the case. Civilization advances by extending the number of operations which we can perform without thinking about them."[4]

But my point here is not mainly to rehash or refute Hirsch but rather to start by acknowledging his basic insight—that, yes, prior knowledge is important to reading comprehension, and that its lack can produce the sorts of errant or shallow readings we often see from students.[5] Beyond basic comprehension, it would be easier to push our students to more profound insights and nuanced interpretive achievements if they all had instant, if basic, recognition of Andrew Marvell, *The Tempest*, *The Divine Comedy*, *The Waste Land*, *Song of Solomon* and "The Song of Solomon" and a thousand other things. But moving forward as teachers of literature in the real world requires that we accept the reality that the world E. D. Hirsch was trying to create—regardless of whether we share his belief in the fundamental inclusiveness of a "national culture"—does not exist: only a handful of (mostly elite, private) American primary schools have adopted Hirsch's recipe for "Cultural Literacy" and, what is more, our culture has become dramatically *more* segmented since 1988, when most cable packages still had few enough channels to make "channel surfing" viable, and the internet was a utopian prospect that a few of us had read about in scientific magazines. We and the students we teach now live in a culture of narrow-casting, perhaps better described not as a single "national culture" but as a very large and diverse collection of distinct, if sometimes overlapping, subcultures, some of them also quite large in their own right.

In this setting, each successful, individual human being is going to develop his or her own version of cultural literacy that includes the declarative knowledge he or she needs for the functions—in work, leisure, and life—that he or she pursues. I play racquetball in a morning league with a group consisting mostly of highly successful businessmen. And I admit that, in inchoate ways, it depresses me slightly to find out how little they know or care about the cultural artifacts—art, film, books—that are so important to me. But it would be narrow and judgmental to say that their lives are impoverished because they're not into what I am into. (And I highly doubt that their careers have been held back by an inability to quote Shakespeare to knowing colleagues in board meetings.) Do I think that some of these highly capable men would have their lives enriched if they read serious imaginative literature? I do. It is even possible that they would pursue market share in a more humane fashion if they read good books. But that's all hypothetical. I do not envision a world in which every professional adult is going to have read widely in a canon of serious literature, and I cannot discount the evidence that my racquetball pals have flourished without it.

More crucially, it would be erroneous to suggest that these men do not have cultural literacy: they just don't have the same cultural literacy that I have (and that Hirsch desired). They have the declarative and the strategic knowledge they need to function in the vocational and avocational worlds they occupy—to decode the communications they receive and to communicate effectively from their own side. When, in the hallway between games, we engage in small talk, it often focuses on sports, and thankfully I have the minimum background in that area to signal my belonging in this group and hold my own in the social ritual of small talk. When talk turns to business, which in this particular group tends to mean discussions of logistics and markets, I find myself more at a loss. It's worth noting, though, that I don't find myself nearly as clueless in this setting as I do when English majors start talking about the universe of Harry Potter and their upcoming quidditch match or trade anecdotes about their favorite role-playing games. Perhaps I am begging the question by calling these cultural competencies "literacies"; but consider the degree to which communication in any of these spheres takes place through writing and reading—of online journalism, of social media posts, of emails, and so on.

The point is that we live in an extremely diverse culture, composed of countless sub- and microcultures that each have their own, continuously evolving cultural competencies, most of them verbal. In scores of these microcultures we are *all* clueless, and even the most versatile Sir or Madam Philip Sidney among us is going to be clueless *somewhere*. We have all had the experience of feeling lost and unhip when colleagues are talking about the latest must-see TV series or when everyone in our social circle has seen a movie that we have not gotten to. This feeling is one of the engines through which such cultures function and continually reconstitute themselves, and the same process plays out locally in each workplace, profession, discipline, fan base, and so on. Indeed, isn't a culture consisting of multiple, overlapping and distinct spheres of cultural competency, each with its own continuously evolving canon of experiences and declarative knowledge, a more democratic or pluralistic society than one in which every educated person is expected to know and have read the same things? We are more apt to help students develop an aptitude for cultural analysis if we practice it on a broad range of cultural artifacts, including the ones they themselves value. And students will be more apt to value the process of building up cultural literacy when they see that they have been doing so all along, and that we value the literacy they bring into the room.

Even if you don't like it, this landscape of multiple and multiplying sub- and microcultures is in fact what we have, and so the question becomes: how can an education in literary study best empower students to thrive in this setting? The answer cannot be to turn back the clock to the days of the canon, to decide on a set of texts and a body of declarative knowledge and establish that as what constitutes cultural literacy for English majors, because, *pace* Hirsch, that body of knowledge would be just one version of cultural literacy, in most cases not a version that will be relevant to the vocational and avocational settings in which our graduates will find themselves.[6] Our culture has become so diverse that there is no discrete set of declarative knowledge that will provide "cultural literacy" for all people, no "network of information that all competent readers possess." And, as I've noted, the declarative knowledge involved—in the case of college literature, the names of writers and texts, periods, movements, major contexts—will evaporate unless students keep reactivating it frequently. They may not have the opportunity to do so in their workplaces and among their social cohorts, which is where, if they are successful, they will continue to develop the effective, provisional, and constantly reforming and refreshing cultural literacies that will carry them through life.

Many will not be reactivating their knowledge of the literary canon precisely because it will no longer be the canon of declarative knowledge required for cultural competency in their new spheres. (The exception would be graduate programs in English which, in the real world, few students pursue and which even fewer *should* pursue.) In these conditions, our duty to our students is not to give them a canon of declarative knowledge but to teach them how to build one, and to make the building of cultural competency something they consciously strive for. We will want to spur metacognition that gets our students to recognize when they are evoking cultural knowledge in a way that demonstrates and underlies cultural competency. And, perhaps more crucially, we want this metacognition to enable students to register when a lack of cultural knowledge is causing a problem of comprehension, so they can recognize the problem and seek out the requisite knowledge they lack.

In place of Hirsch's "cultural literacy," then, I am proposing that we help students to develop what I am calling "advanced literacy"—a set of skills and a condition of metacognitive awareness that positions a person to continuously build up the local cultural literacies he or she needs. My sense of advanced literacy shares affinities with Scholes's formulation of "textual power"—an acknowledgment of the worldly power of written texts and a methods-based pedagogy oriented to giving students access to that power, a pedagogy "organized in terms of the enhanced capabilities that students will take away from their studies."[7] As with advanced reading comprehension, advanced literacy is a set of methods and competencies rather than a canon of texts or declarative knowledge. Developing advanced literacy means developing strategies for collecting and using the knowledge you need to be culturally competent in the settings in which you seek to function. As human beings, we do this naturally and automatically. But higher education means building these methods and competencies consciously and practicing them deliberately.

Fortunately, we are well-placed to help students develop advanced literacy, whose skills work hand-in-hand with teaching and learning advanced reading comprehension. Developing a broadening canon of texts and references aids comprehension—again, we're at a more advanced reading stage in encountering "Prufrock" if we get the John the Baptist reference—and comprehension of more and richer texts helps to build a more robust set of references to draw from—a set that will be reinforced as we encounter new texts that resonate with the others. As with advanced reading comprehension, the importance lies not in the specific set of texts and references the student builds up but in the student's recognition of how cultural competency works, the student's consciousness that he/she/they are practicing and improving in the functions it requires. So, the good news is that, if we can't make every English major someone who can effortlessly quote canonical texts, we can help them equip themselves to keep developing the distinct sub- and microcultural literacies they will need to build. The less good news is that this is difficult work, that our success will be partial, and that individual teachers' power to effect it will be limited, unless curricular reform thoroughly integrates this skill-building.

Prior Knowledge in Literature Classes

Another anecdote of personal teaching failure will illuminate these dynamics. I teach a four-week unit on postcolonial literature in my British literature survey class, and I am constantly looking for texts that illustrate fundamental concepts of postcolonial critique (such as hybridity, mimicry, and wealth transfer) and are relatively accessible to students. Postcolonial literature is rife with texts that require, for basic comprehension, prior knowledge that most American students lack. While many canonical postcolonial texts were written mainly with Western audiences in mind, and thus artfully make unshared, basic cultural knowledge legible (think of Chinua Achebe's *Things Fall Apart*, where characters' free indirect speech walks through customary practices in detail), others do not, relying on knowledge of national and world histories that would be beyond many educated people. In attempting to teach Salman Rushdie's story "Chekov and Zulu," I had this lesson brought home to me in a way that was particularly revealing about the perplexing dynamics of cultural prior knowledge at our historical moment.

Published in 1994, "Chekov and Zulu" is the story of two old friends who attended school together in India and who now work for the Indian diplomatic corps in England. One ("Chekov") is a Hindu and an ambitious functionary in the embassy in London, and the other ("Zulu") is a Sikh undercover operative who infiltrates potential terrorist cells in Anglo-Indian communities in England's northern industrial cities. "Chekov" and "Zulu" are their nicknames from boarding school, where they geeked out together about Star Trek stories, which they consumed not as TV reruns but through cheap novelizations of the original series. As usual for Rushdie, the story is funny, politically sharp, and heartbreaking. It traces the crack in the characters' friendship, paralleled and occasioned by the catastrophic rupture in the Indian polity that bust into violence with the assassination of Indira Gandhi by one of her Sikh guards in 1984. Zulu, loyal to but skeptical of the Indian nation, comes under suspicion because he disappears underground in Birmingham immediately after the assassination; Chekov is sent to investigate him and test his loyalty, which is ultimately shaken by the vicious and widespread state-sanctioned violence against Sikhs that follows the assassination in India. Zulu has not strayed from the cause and has in fact accumulated valuable intelligence, but the intelligence establishment back home, bent on suppression of Sikhs, cannot be convinced of his loyalty.

The story ends with the friends having separated for life. Zulu, disillusioned with government service, returns to India, where he thrives as the owner of a private security business. Chekov is killed while accompanying Rajiv Gandhi to a 1991 public appearance, where he is assassinated by a suicide bomber. At this climactic moment, Chekov realizes what is about to happen, and in his dying seconds experiences a Star Trek-themed fantasy: "The scene around him vanished, dissolving in a pool of light, and was replaced by the bridge of the Starship Enterprise. All the leading figures were in their appointed places. Zulu sat beside Chekov at the front."[8] In the fantasy, the Enterprise is out of fuel, its shields inoperative: flight and resistance are impossible; surrender to the Klingons or stoic acceptance of death are the only options. Amid caricatured dialogue embracing the show's camp appeal ("Damn it you cold-blooded, pointy-eared adding machine," McCoy says to Spock), Kirk opts for a heroic death.

> "Thank you, Mr. Chekov," said Captain Kirk. "I'm afraid that won't be necessary. On this occasion, the worst-case scenario is the one we are obliged to play out. Hold your position. Steady as she goes."
> "The Bird-of-Prey has fired, sir," said Zulu.
> Chekov took Zulu's hand and held it firmly, victoriously, as the speeding balls of deadly light approached.[9]

This story was attractive to me as a teaching text for a host of reasons: it made me laugh, even as it attacks nationalistic jingoism with lacerating irony, and I *thought* it was relatively accessible. And in the tense friendship between Chekov and Zulu, it plays out with compressed intricacy several key postcolonial themes. Chekov, despite his bitterness at the history of wealth transfer ("their fortunes and their cities, built on the loot they took," he says, gesturing to the statuary in Hyde Park), is a practiced mimic; he drinks brandy while hosting official soirees at his "modern-style official residence in a private road in Hampstead."[10] Zulu is hybrid, moving freely among his official identity and a traditional Sikhism marked by his long beard; this cultural mobility makes him an effective spy.

When I first prepared to teach the story, I succumbed to expert blind spot on several fronts, assuming that much of the needed historical context could be extracted from the story's content. A very basic grasp of the multi-sectarian nature of India, its status as a former British colony, and the fact of the partition provides the framework for grasping the significance of the assassinations and of Zulu's status as a Sikh. I would have been in better position to prepare class had I thought about whether students would have the basic framework. What I could not anticipate was that students would struggle with the element I believed would offer them a handle on the story: the Star Trek allusions. I began teaching this story in 2007—two years before the Chris Pine/Zachary Quinto film series reboot, at a rare moment of obscurity for the Star Trek universe. On my first attempt, in a class of twenty, two students had a very loose grasp of the Star Trek framework ("I used to watch them with my Dad," said a young woman). Everyone else, though they had heard of "Star Trek," was deprived of the pleasure of recognition and the sense of being in on the jokes that helped make the story fun to read.

So, my first use of the story in class produced an unredeemable fifty minutes in which a wealth of inadequate prior knowledge made the story impossible for students to engage with productively. Students mostly understood what had happened at the basic level of plot (though some faltered over the reality status of the fantasy that ends the story) but did not understand what was at stake in the differences between Chekov and Zulu. Nor did they see what was significant about Star Trek, which is not just a source of jokes and metaphors but a framework for commentary on imperialism and the paradoxes of military security and power in a modern, postcolonial nation. (In the story, intelligence commanders back in India, having adopted the Star Trek argot, refer to Sikhs as "Klingons" and fear that Zulu's "Klingon background" has caused him to go native among the terrorist cells of Birmingham.) I have taught the story subsequently and, with the relative success and visibility of the newer film series, prior knowledge (of Star Trek, at least) has increased among my students, though not, I should point out, to the degree that one might have expected from 1967 through the 1990s, when entertainment channels were less numerous and the original Star Trek series or the "Next Generation" were in seemingly perpetual syndication.

As we shall see, I have adapted my approach to this text to engage students consciously in discerning historical contexts. But first I want to note that "Chekov and Zulu" exemplifies the multiple, shifting, impermanent nature of cultural literacies, particularly in a landscape more hypersaturated with media and narratives than the one Hirsch inhabited in 1988. To his credit, Hirsch did list Star Trek (and Star Wars) in his list of 3,000 things all literate Americans must know (though I am uncertain how this would have influenced his educational reforms). But the point is that the status of Star Trek—or of any particular text as an element of "a network of information that all competent readers possess"—is temporary and unpredictable; touchstones come in and out of cultural awareness, so that deciding upon a canon of texts aimed at producing "cultural literacy" is impossible. Impossible, that is, unless you want to enshrine a narrow canon that excludes much that is contemporary, diverse, and relevant or appealing to students. It is true that reading widely will increase your stockpile of cultural information—as will watching films and TV shows, playing video games, and scores of other engagements with narratives and histories—and that this stockpile will become more robust each time its elements are reinvoked through subsequent reading, writing, conversation, and so on. And, yes, your comprehension, not only of written texts but also of water cooler conversation, will be aided by this wider net of cultural reference. Reading canonical and insurgent literatures is part of developing this net.

But my point is that if we want to assist students in the task of building up a reservoir of useful cultural information, planning a shared path of canonical texts and declarative knowledge would be considerably less effective than bringing students to consciousness of these processes, so that they can practice them deliberately. An English major who wants to pursue a PhD in Renaissance literature should be deliberately taking courses and independent studies and structuring his or her pleasure reading, from Thomas Middleton to Hillary Mantel, in a way that builds the declarative knowledge and the interpretive skills he or she needs; an English major who wants to be a music critic or work in the music industry should be reading Dave Marsh, Lester Bangs, and Chuck Closterman and spending his or her weekends listening to hundreds of hours of music. Students will need to take ownership of this process, and practice it outside and (when possible) inside the classroom. Meanwhile, I'll still be trying to get them to read Wordsworth, not as preparation for Jeopardy but for the skills of advanced reading comprehension that come from pushing yourself to comprehend sophisticated thought, rendered in lucid but complex language, and putting that understanding into words. At the same time, I will be spurring practice and metacognition on how to assemble the context necessary to understand an alien text.

Teaching Literature in Historical Context: Problems and Strategies

My ill-fated first class on "Chekov and Zulu" found me in all-too-familiar territory. Prompting students to contrast Zulu and Chekov's characters, I found them unable to say anything about the significance of Zulu's beard, which Chekov remarks upon when they meet up at the airport in London, after years apart:

> "What-ho, Zools! Years, yaar, years," Chekov said, thumping his palm into the other man's chest. "So," he added, "I see you've become a hairy fairy." The young Zulu had been a modern Sikh in the matter of hair—sporting a fine mustache at eighteen, but beardless, with a haircut instead of long tresses wound tightly under a turban. Now, however, he had reverted to tradition.[11]

I am far from an expert on India, and yet my ability to interpret this detail—and my ignorance of the challenge it would present to students—is a classic example of expert blind spot in literary interpretation. I have read not much but enough literature about India, read around in enough postcolonial theory and criticism, and been on the edges of enough discussions to recognize—despite having only surface knowledge of Sikhism—that being "modern" in matters such as hair and dress means dressing like a European, practicing mimicry; in Zulu's case, "modern" grooming would result from Western-style schooling and a desire to rise in Western-fashioned institutions. This knowledge further allows me to interpret Zulu's "reversion" to tradition: his growing of his hair and beard and adoption of the turban might signify a strengthening of his Sikh identification, or a desire to express it, or (the hypothesis arises later) a cultural fluidity/mobility that would serve a spy well.

None of this significance is legible without the prior knowledge of what "modern" and "traditional" would entail in the Indian postcolonial setting or the knowledge of Sikhs as a religious minority with a history of oppression and violent resistance. But I realized that that students could make nothing of Zulu's beard (and, in contrast, Chekov's "gray flannels, stiff-collared shirt, and double-breasted navy-blue blazer with gold buttons") only after I had already learned that students didn't understand the Star Trek framework.[12] I had spent a stumbling, improvised five minutes describing Star Trek and apologizing that the students were not enjoying the jokes about being beamed up and setting phasers on stun. Now I found myself shakily explaining what Sikhs are and why a Sikh who is in the Indian diplomatic service might or might not dress as one; I branched off into mimicry, a concept I had introduced two days ago, hoping the students would recognize it in this story. I was doing what I have for years, vowed not to do: providing students with the significance of the story, performing my own interpretive skill rather than giving them the opportunity to practice their own.

In Chapter 2, I quoted Sheridan Blau in warning about the dynamic this sort of interaction creates: you reenforce students' sense of the teacher as a highly skilled interpreter, much more skilled than the students, and thereby encourage them to treat literary interpretations as content that *you* provide rather than something that they produce. Every teacher who has students read literature that is difficult in any way—because it's embedded in an unfamiliar context, or unusually rich, or experimental, or uses the language of a previous era—has seen the following intended compliment on student evaluations: "The reading was confusing but the teacher did a good job of explaining it in class." Oof! I agree entirely with Blau's assertion that we need to demystify interpretation by breaking down its elements and shepherding students to its practice. When teachers solve interpretive problems in front of the classroom, we are liable to mystify interpretation, supporting the students' perception that literary interpretation is an esoteric talent they lack. In a story like "Chekov and Zulu," where the interpretive difficulty stems mainly from weak prior knowledge of histories and cultures, this dynamic repeats itself in a particular way: you emerge as supremely well-informed in contrast to the students' ignorance. Sure, it is true that you and I almost certainly know more about India and Pakistan and the history of colonialism than most students do: but a pedagogy that drives home students' relative ignorance is not a recipe for learning. Blau pithily describes the perception that results: "intertextual literacy, or knowledge of prior texts and background information, is crucial to producing an accurate reading of a literary work, but is also the exclusive possession of teachers and not of their students.")[13]

So, what to do? The answer depends upon what kind of class (sophomore level methods? Survey? Upper-level topics? Highly focused seminar?). Let me walk through various solutions for various settings, with their pros and cons. In the process I will be outlining how we may teach advanced literacy more effectively if we begin by conceptualizing it more thoroughly, share this conceptualization with students, and revise our curricula to make advanced literacy an explicit learning objective, taught sequentially as students move through the major.

Explanatory notes (not that great). As it happens, the version of "Chekov and Zulu" I teach appears in the Longman Anthology of British Literature, which provides moderately helpful footnotes. In cases where you are going to teach a text frequently and adequate footnotes do not exist, it would not be a terrible idea to create them and post them on Canvas or Blackboard, keyed to whatever edition you're using. The advantage of notes, of course, is that they provide targeted explanatory information that is instantly available. Toggling between the main text and footnotes is not the most pleasurable way to read, though it is more pleasurable than being confused. And some English majors will have gotten used to reading with footnotes and will use them effectively.

But there are a number of problems with explanatory notes. First, as any experienced literature teacher will attest, it is not at all uncommon for students to ignore the footnotes, especially in an anthology text that is heavily annotated (Hello, Mr. Eliot!) in agate-sized notes. We could grouse about this and call students lazy, but remember, we're teaching in the real world here, and need to start by accepting student habits for what they are. Footnotes also present two more substantive problems. They are not providing *prior knowledge*—they are providing explanation *after* the potentially confusing passage has been read; so, the reading experience is itself qualitatively different than the reading experience of someone who either (1) has the prior knowledge or (2) does not have it, and needs—in order to develop the skills of advanced literacy—to recognize their lack of adequate background, without prompting, in the moment. In other words, footnotes do not address the lack of prior knowledge: they mitigate it in the moment, in a way that does not train student readers to recognize their knowledge gaps and develop strategies for filling them.

As I have argued, confusion can be productive: student confusion caused by lack of prior knowledge is, in the long run, a good thing, *if* students can learn to work with it. Footnotes (if students read them) defuse this potentially productive confusion. Still, too much confusion, or confusion in a setting where the teacher cannot frame it productively, may discourage a student. So, in the midst of a challenging semester, it is probably better not to confuse students excessively. So, a text that requires substantial prior knowledge for basic decoding probably should be served to students with explanatory notes, at least in a lower-level class. Call them a necessary evil.

Mini-lectures. (Not terrible, if done well.) Based on my many conversations with colleagues over the years, mini-lectures seem to be the most common way that teachers introduce crucial contextual information to students. Teachers use this method to introduce major concepts, periods, movements, broad historical contexts, and so on, in addition to using smaller, precisely targeted mini-lectures to prepare students for specific texts. In the case of the Rushdie story, I used to introduce the postcolonial unit by lecturing for thirty minutes about postcoloniality/postcolonial literature/postcolonial theory, defining them, introducing the terms "hybridity" and "mimicry," and describing the language debate (writing in indigenous languages vs. English) and the phenomenon of "writing back"—all before we had read any poems or stories. And, in at least one subsequent attempt at "Chekov and Zulu," before the students read the story I gave a ten-minute lecture on the multi-sectarian nature of India, the history of independence and partition, and—more finely focused on the story—the reasons why Indian civil servants would be spying on British citizens of Indian descent in Britain (a frequent source of student confusion). Finally, a few years ago, I began showing a five-minute clip from the original Star Trek so that students would have a visual association and some exposure to the delightful cheesiness of the intertext. There is no remedy that will provide students with the pleasures of recognition and parody if they haven't experienced Star Trek in greater depth, so a few minutes and some quick discussion has to suffice.

Mini-lectures are efficient, from the teacher's perspective: you can quickly deliver contextual information that is essential to basic decoding and provide the first elements of a larger framework which, ideally, you and the students will make larger and more robust through subsequent reading and discussion. But I say "efficient from the teacher's perspective" because, from the students' perspective, who knows? (Unless you are going to test them on lecture material, which begs the question of the value of declarative knowledge.) Most students are notoriously terrible note takers. And, though the debate about lecturing as a primary method inexplicably continues, the data on lectures is overwhelming: long lectures without breaks for student activity do not work nearly as well as active-learning approaches.[14] Mini-lectures are better, mainly because student attention spans for listening seem to run between ten and fifteen minutes.[15] Anecdotally, my experience suggests that mini-lectures, delivered as a continuous stream of talk from the teacher, succeed in communicating the prior knowledge needed to comprehend a text for the small number of students who are uncommonly attentive, have unusually strong memories, or are good note takers. Declarative knowledge needs to be repeated and reactivated to stick; it also sticks when students build up conceptual frameworks to organize and contain it; and one short lecture does not make either of these things happen. For these reasons mini-lectures will work better in combination with other introductory material that you might assign; they will work better still when you enlist students in organizing the information they contain by giving them activities that work with the contents of your lecture rather than simply expecting them to take notes.

Like any broadly defined method, the mini-lecture can be done well, badly, or with middling care and success. Indeed, as Joshua Eyler has pointed out, what professors mean when they use the term "lecture" varies widely—considerably more lies behind the binary of "lecture/active learning" than tends to inform arguments about its efficacy.[16] For many years I made the mistake of designing mini-lectures as if they were pieces of writing, which meant that they were extremely rich in detail and intended in part (let's be honest!) to show off my erudition. This insufficiently strategic approach, combined with the casual contempt for lecturing that I had imbibed in graduate school, produced mini-lectures that were at once over- and underprepared—too rich in information and not carefully enough designed for clarity. They were not consciously designed for learning; they represented, in effect, short versions of the worst kinds of lectures, of the "continuous exposition" sort, which research has demonstrated to negatively influence student learning.

As with virtually every teaching method, creating effective mini-lectures begins with articulating objectives and doing design work to meet them. In cases where the mini-lecture's aim is to provide students with historical context, the objective is to have students gather declarative knowledge. Students retain declarative knowledge better when they read than when they listen, and better still when they discuss it, write about it, organize it, or otherwise activate it themselves. Mini-lectures, then, should be designed to call upon multiple ways of using declarative knowledge. Fifteen-minute mini-lectures that are punctuated with two or three minutes of reading or writing, or which integrate moments of student response or application, or enlist students in sorting information, are thus more likely to result in retention. Studies also recommend pre-lecture activities that reactivate material from prior classes or pose questions that the lecture will address, and post-lecture activities that spur immediate recall or analysis of material from the lecture, especially when we want students to be able to recall declarative knowledge.[17] James Lang suggests having students write on the same question—for instance "How would you describe the narrator in this novel?"—at the start and finish of class.[18] These activities take time, so you will have to stint a bit on detail, while still being careful to exemplify and illustrate major points with anecdotes, examples, visual images, and so forth.

I have been giving versions of one short lecture for almost twenty years in the later British literature survey and in courses on British modernism, so the ways I have adapted it may be illustrative. The lecture concerns modernity, which I define (stealing largely from Raymond Williams) as the combination of five major historical forces that have produced the modern world: industrial/imperial capitalism; Enlightenment rationalism; democratization; print culture; and the formation of the modern nation-state. For some years I performed this lecture in continuous exposition style, pausing periodically for questions while filling in the detail on each point with names of historical figures and events, dates, and statistics. This material showed my mastery of detail and (perhaps) my skill at hierarchizing information, but did little to make these forces vivid or memorable or to engage students in them. I did this amid the cognitive dissonance of my avowed opposition to lecturing. My nagging worry that students weren't getting what I was offering expressed itself in my repeating quicker versions of this lecture several times in the first few weeks of class, repeatedly sketching out the five main points at the start of class. (The repetition in later classes is, of course, not in itself a bad practice.)

Today, I weave the "continuous discourse" bits of this lecture into several activities that call on students to think from their own experience, evoke prior knowledge, and make connections across key concepts. The modernity "lecture" now takes the better part of a fifty-minute class period, but it activates students' capacities rather than treating them as vessels or note takers. I now start by asking students to write for one minute on the question, "Are you modern?" I solicit enough personal responses to illustrate that "modern" is a relational term—one is only modern in relation to something that is perceived to have come before and to be both different and "over." Some give-and-take at this stage allows me to highlight the various antonyms to "modern" (classical, traditional), and I scribble some keywords from this discussion on the board. This brings me to a transition, where I say, clearly and repeatedly, that Western people, particularly urban, educated Western people, have felt "modern"—in the sense that they felt they were living in a world that had changed dramatically in their lifetimes, for 500 or more years. Indeed, being modern, I say, might in fact inhere in this *sense of being modern*—the sense of rapid transformative change as a fact of life.

This invocation of the last 500 years gives me an opening to lay out the meat of the lecture: I posit that scholars—historians, political scientists, economists, and others—share a loose consensus that a certain set of historical changes produced the "modern world" in the West, and I quickly sketch out the five forces— Enlightenment rationalism, industrial/imperial capitalism, the modern nation-state, literacy and print culture, democratization—in chalk-talk fashion, leaving lots of space between headings for filling in later. Twenty years ago I would have talked for two or three minutes about each of these points, dropping factoids about the 1870s education act or the circulation of newspapers in fin de siècle London or the relative youth of the modern nations of Germany and Italy. Now, instead, I launch a seven-minute, in-class writing exercise in which I give students the option of answering one of the following two questions:

1. What was the Enlightenment, and how is it connected to any of the four other forces?
2. How might one or more of the five forces have been intertwined with one or more of the others? In other words, how might elements of one of these historical changes have contributed to the others?

I sit at my desk at the front of the room and write along with the students, giving a one-minute warning near the six-minute mark. When time is up, I give students thirty seconds to finish their thoughts, and then begin an open discussion on these two questions, filling in details about the enlightenment by adding keywords (such as "empiricism" or "the scientific method" or "rationalism") as they come up. I find, especially, that students are good at recognizing how these forces intertwine: how, for instance, industrialization makes it possible to print and distribute more books and newspapers, and/or how books and newspapers make it possible to start a democratic movement. This exercise has students using the concepts rather than jotting them down, and it communicates that my set of five headings is a conceptual framework that can contain historical details (such as the dates of the French and American revolutions), which I array in the available space between headings as they come up in discussion.

In a specialized class in British modernism, I would follow up by assigning W. H. Auden's "Spain" as the next reading, along with a discussion-board prompt that asks students to flag elements of modernity when they are referenced in the poem and discuss what the poem might be saying about modernity.

> Yesterday the installation of dynamos and turbines,
> The construction of railways in the colonial desert;
> Yesterday the classic lecture
> On the origin of Mankind. But to-day the struggle.

And I start the next class on this note, asking students to mine the poem for references to how elements of modernity intertwine and accelerate one another, then moving on to a discussion of the poem's attitudes toward progress in the context of the international calamity portended by the Spanish Civil War. In a survey class, where time is more limited, I still repeat the quick outline several times in the opening weeks and, more importantly, re-evoke the question of modernity frequently when the primary reading supports it, as it often does.

It is worth noting that, by integrating this "mini-lecture" into a set of activities and readings I have essentially made the actual lecturing part a relatively small part of a larger, more time-intensive method, depriving the straight, continuous-discourse lecture of its only real benefit: its time efficiency. But these are the kinds of compromises we have to make in teaching all the time.

Short supplementary readings (better!) could include the biography of Rushdie that appears above "Chekov and Zulu" in the Longman Anthology along with that anthology's rather scanty section on the decline of the empire in the "World War II and its Aftermath" section. The shorter and more to the point supplementary readings are, the better, I would say. And, crucially, I would not describe this preparatory reading to students as "supplementary": I would list it as primary reading, so that students treat it as equally important and know that they have to take equal responsibility for it as for the fiction. In the case of "Chekov and Zulu," one might assign the Wikipedia pages on the Assassinations of Indira and Rajiv Gandhi and the page on "Sikhs in India" (Yes: Wikipedia. I'm not proud. YouTube videos are also a good source of this sort of material.) You could also prepare a short handout of your own containing basic facts, but students are unlikely to view this as a primary text, and so many may not read it.

Blau has an excellent example of providing requisite prior knowledge, one that is perfect for when an important intertext is relatively short: assign the intertext as well as the "main text," and use their juxtaposition as an object lesson in the role intertextual and background knowledge plays in interpretation. He does this with Wilfred Owen's "Parable of the Old Man and the Young," which retells the story of Abraham and Isaac, with a twist at the end that makes the story a commentary on the slaughter of the First World War. At the point in the story where the angel dissuades Abraham from killing Isaac, Owen revises the ending:

But the old man would not so, and slew his son.
And half the seed of Europe, one by one.

In Blau's ingenious discussion of this lesson, he reconstructs a workshop in which student discussion uncovered the roles prior knowledge plays in comprehending this poem. Both the Abraham and Isaac story and Wilfred Owen's status as a canonical poet almost entirely associated with the First World War are key pieces of prior knowledge, as is a minimal but accurate knowledge of the First World War. And the student cohort, even in an introductory class, would likely include people who possess a range of this prior knowledge, from all to none of it. Blau's workshop began by having students read the poem and discuss it in small groups, registering their level of comprehension and naming their difficulties. A whole-class discussion followed, in which students whose prior knowledge had eased their reading talked that through. Blau followed with a debriefing that highlighted the crucial prior knowledge and underscored how it made a difference in readers' ability to interpret.[19]

In an introductory class, this lesson design would make a brilliant opening step for sensitizing students to the role prior knowledge plays in interpretation (and miscomprehension). But as to the question I am pursuing here—the issue of how to provide background knowledge—the important point is how Blau later adjusted his teaching of this text: he copied and distributed the story from Genesis, which is less than 400 words long, and assigned it alongside Owen's "Parable" and a small set of Owen's more famous poems. Assigning all these as primary texts not only makes the Owen poem more legible, it provides an opportunity to make explicit the crucial role of intertextual background knowledge in comprehension and interpretation. As I have been emphasizing throughout, I believe such consciousness of the processes of reading and interpretation—"metacognitive moments"—are essential to fomenting advanced reading comprehension and advanced literacy, but easy to ignore as we are trying to cover a long list of texts in a fourteen- or fifteen-week class.

Building Advanced Literacy Skills in a Unit on Postcolonial Literature

To regather, then, the evolution of my approaches to handling prior knowledge problems in "Chekov and Zulu": my specific objective in teaching this text was to help students recognize the concepts of mimicry and hybridity as they play out in the relationship between the two main characters; this in addition to my constant objective of giving students practice and feedback on their advanced reading comprehension and interpretive skills. After my initial fiasco, a new objective emerged: to use this text to highlight problems of background knowledge in reading literature (and specifically postcolonial literature) and give students practice in assembling the requisite background knowledge. This is a great deal to accomplish in essentially one reading assignment and one- to one-and-a-half class periods, so I have realistic expectations, but I create some efficiency by integrating the entire postcolonial unit around the content objectives concerning hybridity, mimicry, wealth transfer, the language issue, and writing back. This is how the sequence works out now: On the first day of the postcolonial unit, I assign Derek Walcott's "A Far Cry from Africa" and lead a discussion that focuses on the lines about the speaker's divided sense of self. The speaker, "divided to the vein" because of his mixed European and African origins, faces the conflict between his experience of colonial brutality, embodied in "the drunken officer of British rule," and his love of English language and literature. (You can read the full poem at https://poets.org/poem/far-cry-africa.)

Toward the end of the discussion of this poem, which has begun with an analysis of the figurative language in the earlier lines, I ask students to paraphrase the emotional conflict the lines express. From what are often accurate but shallow observations—"He's saying that both sides are bad"; "He likes the English language but he doesn't like what the British have done in Africa"—I prompt closer reading of details and discussion of further implications ("How is the speaker 'divided to the vein'? What are the implications not just 'divided' but divided 'to the vein'?" "Why might the speaker love the British tongue? What might the British tongue offer him?"). Once I am satisfied that a pretty thorough, more-or-less denotative reading is on the table, I will begin my mini-lecture on several postcolonial themes (hybridity, mimicry, the language issue, writing back), emphasizing the degree to which these themes are embedded in the lines. Note that in this introductory moment, my pedagogy here is rather old-fashioned and in fact could be said to run counter to my philosophy: I am, to a degree, advertising my expertise here: students will surely notice that I see things in this poem that they did not. In context, however, these methods are appropriate, the expert performance justified by the fact that these concepts will now become both background knowledge and interpretive frameworks for subsequent reading. In a metacognitive moment as I wrap up the mini-lecture, I make clear that this is what we've been doing: gathering some background knowledge and introducing critical concepts to look for in the literature we read for the next couple weeks.

A week later, in the class before students are assigned to read "Chekov and Zulu," I will assign as parallel texts the short biography of Rushdie in the Longman Anthology and the Wikipedia pages on the assassinations of Rajiv and Indira Gandhi and "Sikhs in India." And on the class management site, as an announcement or an all-class email, I will send the following prompt for the discussion board:

> In the reading for today, look for places where the postcolonial concepts we discussed in class are at play. In particular, look for the play of hybridity and/or mimicry in the relationship between the two protagonists.

While on a given day not everyone will take me up on this prompt—and not everyone has to write on the discussion board everyday—at least a few almost definitely will. (Classes tend to have cohorts of students who like to come up with their own questions and issues and students who like prompting; prompting is an appropriate scaffolding activity, although by the time of final essays in this class—and certainly of final projects in senior seminars—students need to be framing their own intellectual inquiries.) The prompt will spur students to think carefully about the relations between Chekov and Zulu and (I hope) to raise their own questions and recognize their perplexities about the sectarian identities and divisions in India, the significance of grooming and dress rituals, and so on. And, as I grade the discussion board, I will see who is getting a basic grasp on hybridity and mimicry, what needs to be clarified, and what other problems of background information are arising. Class discussion will then focus on these interpretive problems and, if we are efficient, go off into unpredictable directions predicated on other issues students raised on the discussion board or which arise organically in class. Meeting the basic objectives—getting students to recognize hybridity and mimicry when they see it and calling to attention the interpretive problems caused by lack of prior knowledge—will be relatively easy to meet, and we can then pursue the evergreen objective of practicing interpretive methods.

In an introductory methods class, where skill-building is paramount and developing advanced literacy secondary, or in a survey class, where you're going to give it the old college try (Har!) to have students glimpse more than 200 years of literature and culture, these small-scale methods may be the best you can do to address the problem of prior knowledge. (I'm not convinced that this is the case in the survey; I am still working on ways to place *the making of* literary history—rather than "literary history" as a purportedly stable object—at the center of the survey class.) In any case, I've conceived the activities outlined earlier as approaches for such lower-level classes.

In more specialized classes, the processes of building up advanced literacy should be foregrounded more explicitly and pursued vigorously, beginning with lessons on advanced literacy per se. In the section that follows, I outline a sequence of activities designed to introduce students to the concept of advanced literacy, prompt them to develop robust stockpiles of appropriate background information for specific settings, repeat and reemphasize the concept and reiterate the cognitive work of becoming provisionally, functionally literate on a topic. While they are drawn from a class on my specialty area (early-twentieth-century British literature), these methods and assignments can be adapted to any historical period, indeed any collection of texts that are part of a shared intertextual network or rely on a shared body of historical or contextual information. These include texts that can be seen as part of a tradition (African American literature, for instance) or a thematic or formal genre (utopian/dystopian literature, elegy, etc.).

Enlisting Students in Building Their Own Literacies

My objective in such an upper-level class is to lead students in building up provisional literacy on the theme, time period, or tradition we're focusing on and recognizing how that literacy is built. There is nothing new or radical about building up students' provisional literacy for the material on which a class will be focused—virtually all upper-level literature classes attempt this, each through its own mixture of background reading, lectures and mini-lectures, student research, primary reading, quizzes or low-stakes writing, and so on. In a Shakespeare class, for instance, we would want students to learn some background about Shakespeare's historical period, especially as it informs the texts we assign, and how the theater worked in his time; we would expect their fluency in Shakespeare's English to increase; and we would hope for increased recognition of relevant intertexts (including other Shakespearean works and classical and historical narratives). Students who succeed will have built up the provisional literacy required to do well in the class—they will become better at reading Shakespeare not only through their practice in reading his complex and period-specific language but also by steadily building up a bank of prior knowledge to bring to bear on their reading. The most effective teachers will have articulated for themselves and their students which background information is most important and strategized about the best ways to for students to get it. To these elements, I suggest that we add:

- an early lesson or two introducing the nature of cultural literacy and its role in reading comprehension;
- intermittent small activities, taking one or two class periods, that reemphasize this concept and give students repeated practice in building up their network of intertextual and background knowledge; and
- major projects that call on these developing abilities specifically. I outline each of these later.

Provisional Cultural Literacy: An Introductory Lecture/Discussion

My understanding of how such provisional cultural literacy works is simple to understand, and I start by explaining it in a simple lecture, that goes something like this. It is written as if addressed to students, with asides to you, my reader, in [brackets]:

We each have a unique body of cultural knowledge. Much of this knowledge is declarative (consisting of names, places, historical events, and words associated with broad concepts) and relatively shallow. I know that the Spanish Inquisition was an effort to enforce orthodoxy in Catholic practice and that it involved torture and execution and started in the 1400s and went on for a long time. I know that Brazil is the largest country in South America and its people speak Portuguese and that Rio and Brasilia are its largest cities. I know that Beethoven was a classical composer and that "classical" means after the baroque period and that he wrote nine symphonies, major themes of two I could hum. I don't know much else about any of these things—but that doesn't mean this information is not useful—it's quite useful. That's because any reading task—any communicative task, really—evokes and relies on elements from this store of knowledge: we would be at a loss faced with Joyce Kilmer's "Trees" if we did not know what a poem or a tree were, just as surely as Whitman's "Beat. Beat, Drums" will not make sense if we do not know that armies used to use drummers to set the pace for marching. [Here one might project the opening couplet of "Trees" and the opening lines of Whitman on a video screen. And one might follow by projecting a few lines of poetry or prose and ask students what background knowledge is necessary to interpret the lines, for instance this title and opening lines from Ruth Stone:

> Eden, then and now
> In '29 before the dust storms
> Sandblasted Indianapolis,
> We believed in the milk company.
> Milk came in glass bottles.

or the opening of Alice Munro's short story, "Material":

> I don't keep up with Hugo's writing. Sometimes I see his name, in the library, or on the cover of a literary journal that I don't open—I haven't opened a literary journal in a dozen years, praise God.]

Frequently, we encounter texts that encode cultural knowledge we do not know. In reading literature, there are two leading dynamics behind this process.

1) Writers who aspire to literary status tend to have read widely, and they refer liberally to other works they have read and which they assume their audiences have read, or at least know about. They are evoking a specific kind of cultural knowledge: intertextual knowledge.

2) When we are reading literature from a previous period and/or from another country or community, the text is addressed to an imagined audience that is different from us, which had a different set of shared knowledge than people of our time and place have. This kind of cultural knowledge is usually referred to as "contextual," but that term covers a wide array of things, including outdated slang and other vocabulary that we do not share and references to then-current events, well-known figures, and places we are not familiar with. To read texts that rely on this kind of knowledge, we have to do three things:

    a) recognize when a gap in our cultural knowledge is causing a problem;
    b) track down the missing information, and
    c) gradually build up a set of cultural knowledge that will allow us to comprehend texts of this period, place, or tradition with greater ease.

Building up cultural knowledge is a gradual and iterative process; we should take initiative in it and use our creativity. We can do background reading, including quick-and-dirty internet research: our knowledge, for the purposes of provisional cultural literacy, does not have to be deep—we're looking for broad but relatively shallow knowledge, which will let us understand references and allusions without undue labor.

When Derek Walcott writes, in his poem "A Far Cry from Africa":

Again Brutish necessity wipes its hands
Upon the napkin of a dirty cause, again
A waste of our compassion, as with Spain.

I do not need to be a historian to grasp the reference to the Spanish Civil War. All I really need to know is that Spain suffered through a terrible civil war in the late 1930s, pitting fascist and communist forces against one another, and that volunteers from Europe went to Spain to fight against the fascists; this knowledge allows me to hypothesize that the "compassion" was "wasted" not only because the fascists won but also because Communist Party rule in other countries took on a totalitarian character. (I only started studying the Spanish war in any earnest four or five years ago, but my grasp of the reference in Walcott's poem was adequate long before that.)

The bad news is that it takes a lifetime to become expert in the intertextual and background knowledge of a period, place, or tradition: indeed, literature "experts" will tell you that they never stop accumulating helpful knowledge about the fields they study, and that even they constantly feel as if they do not know enough. The good news is that you can instantly begin improving your cultural knowledge of a field. Virtually every move you make in this effort adds to your store of prior knowledge. In a fifteen-week semester, a reasonable expectation is that you build up a partial, provisional store of background knowledge that begins to increase your ability to interpret texts from the period. In doing this you are practicing an intellectual process that will be absolutely essential to your success in work and life: the process of deliberately building up the knowledge you need for specific spheres of activity.

In this class, then, I want you to take ownership of your building up of background knowledge that increases your ability to interpret the literature and culture of this period. The best part is that once you start working on this, all of your activities are mutually reinforcing. Every piece of background knowledge you gather increases your chances of reading a text of the period with ease next time around. Every text you read adds new background knowledge to your storehouse and reinforces knowledge you have gained from previous texts. Indeed, building up cultural literacy in a specific area (a historical period, a genre, etc.) is a dialogic process, in which the background knowledge feeds comprehension of new texts and the experience of new texts further builds up the background knowledge.

Let's look at how this works in the opening paragraphs of D. H. Lawrence's *Lady Chatterley's Lover*, which is on the handout I gave you at the start of class:

> Ours is essentially a tragic age, so we refuse to take it tragically. The cataclysm has happened, we are among the ruins, we start to build up new little habitats, to have new little hopes. It is rather hard work: there is now no smooth road into the future; but we go round, or scramble over obstacles. We've got to live, no matter how many skies have fallen.
>
> This was more or less Constance Chatterley's position. The war had brought the roof down over her head. And she realized that one must live and learn.
>
> She married Clifford Chatterley in 1917, when he was home for a month on leave. They had a month's honeymoon. Then he went back to Flanders: to be shipped over to England again six months later, more or less in bits. Constance, his wife, was then twenty-three years old, and he was twenty-nine.
>
> His hold on life was marvelous. He didn't die, and the bits seemed to grow together again. For two years he remained in the doctor's hands. Then he was pronounced a cure, and could return to life again, with the lower half of his body, from the hips down, paralyzed forever.

[At this point, I would give students about seven minutes to scribble some close-reading notes in the margins of the passage. I would prompt them to note any details that seem significant or striking and to begin hypothesizing significance for those details. When they are done scribbling, I would hold a two-minute debrief, asking students to share some details and the interpretations they came up with. Then I would have students read the passage again, individually, and take from five to seven minutes to highlight any places where cultural background knowledge came into play: either knowledge they had or knowledge they lacked. When this was finished, we would debrief more thoroughly, noting the many ways in which cultural background knowledge is called upon in this passage. The most obvious instances relate to the First World War, for which relevant prior knowledge includes a sense that the war was perceived at the time as an unprecedented catastrophe, which clarifies the reference to "the cataclysm" in the first paragraph; knowledge of the war's years (1914–18), which allows the date of the Chatterley marriage to place the story precisely in time; the knowledge that Flanders was a site of prolonged fighting—for some students, who are familiar with the place name, it will reinforce and specify the war context; students unfamiliar with the place name may deduce its significance based on their prior knowledge of the First World War. I might list these—and other evocations of context—on the white or blackboard as we proceed. Advanced readers may note a few other instances—the use of the word "tragedy," for instance, situating the implied author as someone who wants to situate his story in the history of literature. If you're lucky, someone in the room will have a vague sense of the novel as highly controversial, indeed quasi-pornographic, and will thus have used this knowledge to decode the significance of Chatterley being "paralyzed from the hips down"—in a novel entitled *Lady Chatterley's Lover.*]

[As this discussion winds down, the final step is to re-invoke the model of cultural literacy—the sense of cultural literacy as emerging in a dialogue between one's present reading of the text and one's storehouse of cultural knowledge. Note the traffic between the two: if anyone did not know that Flanders was a site of prolonged fighting in the First World War, that can now join the cultural stockpile. If anyone was fuzzy on the years of the war, 1917 has helped clarify that. At this moment I would project the opening lines of John McCrae's "In Flanders Fields"— "In Flanders Fields the poppies grow / Between the crosses, row on row"—and note that everyone in the room gets the reference to Flanders right now; that some may have already known the poem and knew that it was a reference to the First World War; that the likelihood that someone will recognize a subsequent reference to Flanders as a signifier of the First World War depends on that information being reactivated periodically. The entire process, in other words, is working both to make the present text legible and to build up the cultural literacy that makes it so.]

Reiteration and Practice: Cultural Literacy as Process

Once this early lecture/discussion has laid out the framework, it is easy to invoke it in passing as you are discussing individual texts and contexts. Mini-lectures on historical contexts, brief asides in class that add cultural references, and background reading are all useful as students build their storehouse of potential prior knowledge; but these learning activities will be more effective if we repeatedly cue students to recognize that they are generating new cultural knowledge, to tune in to moments of reading in which this process is playing out. I do this frequently around the margins of discussions, but it is important to bring this process back to the center of attention periodically. This next activity can take place in the middle five weeks of the semester.

It begins, for me, with a review of our previous lesson on provisional cultural literacy, mapping the process out quickly on the board again, with circles and arrows signifying the movement of information—the mind fetches information from its storehouse of contextual knowledge in order to decode a detail in the primary text; this detail, along with others, gets exported to the storehouse, reiterating or strengthening facts and little sets of facts already there. Then I introduce a short text on which we can practice our recognition of presences and gaps in our cultural knowledge as we read. The passage is the opening of Elizabeth Bowen's 1941 short story "In the Square":

> At about nine o'clock on this hot bright July evening the square looked mysterious: it was completely empty, and a whitish reflection, ghost of the glare of midday,

came from the pale-coloured facades on its four sides and seemed to brim it up to the top. The grass was parched in the middle; its shaved surface was paid for by people who had gone. The sun, now too low to enter normally, was able to enter brilliantly at a point where three of the houses had been bombed away; two or three of the may trees, dark with summer, caught on their top the illicit gold. Each side of the breach, exposed wallpapers were exaggerated into veridians, yellows, and corals that they had probably never been. Elsewhere, the painted front doors under the balconies and at the tops of steps not whitened for some time stood out in the deadness of colour with light off it. Most of the glassless windows were shuttered or boarded up, but some framed hollow inside dark.[20]

I get a volunteer to read the paragraph aloud, then set the students individually to reread it carefully, underscoring significant details and noting (1) any places where they recognize cultural knowledge coming into play in their comprehension, or (2) any elements they don't understand, indicating whether they think lack of cultural knowledge might be at play. Then as a group we talk through what students flagged when reading in this manner. By this time we will have read a set of earlier Bowen stories set in the mid-1930s, so they will recognize the London setting; from Bowen and other sources they will know about the slow-buildup to the Second World War and the German air attacks on London and other British cities. So, many students will recognize that the story is set during the blitz, inferring that the German bombing has caused one stretch of the square to be "bombed out." Sharp-eyed students will note that the steps have not been "whitened in some time," suggesting that no one is taking care of this square, and will pick up the reference to the landscaping being paid for by "people who have gone." This last detail is worth lingering over, as it references a relevant piece of cultural information that many students will not have: that many people left London during the blitz, moving to the countryside for safety. This piece of information at once lends clarity and ambiguity to the phrase "people who have gone," as it may signify people who have relocated or people who have been killed. I point this out if the detail has not come up. A last point worth drawing attention to—if none of the students raises it—is the long days that occur in England in mid-summer, with darkness not falling until 10:30 p.m. or later.

Having thus refreshed everyone and given them this metacognitive practice, I break the class into groups of four or five and set them working on passages from other Bowen stories, also from the late 1930s or early 1940s, which were assigned for homework on this day. Each group does what we did with the passage from "In the Square," adding two tasks, so that their job in groups is:

1. Read the passage, underlining any details you think seem especially significant.

2. Reread the passage, noting any place where prior knowledge is aiding your comprehension or a lack of prior knowledge is hindering your comprehension.

3. As a group, talk through your prior knowledge examples. If, after discussing them, there are still issues you don't understand, use the internet to see if you can find answers.

4. Consider how this passage might add to your knowledge of the literature, history, or culture of early-twentieth-century Britain. In other words, what might you export from this passage to your store of background knowledge?

Here is one of the passages I assign, from Bowen's "Attractive Modern Homes":

> The new town they had come to had a mellow, ancient core, but was rapidly spreading and filling up with workers. The Watsons had been edged out to this new estate, the only place where they could find a house. And how un-ideal it was. An estate is not like a village, it has no heart; even the shops are new and still finding their own feet. It has not had time to take on the prim geniality of a suburb. The dwellers are pioneers unennobled by danger. Everybody feels strange and has no time for curiosity. Nothing has had time to flower in this new place.[21]

Typically, "estate" will emerge as a crux in the group work, because the word means something different to Americans than it does to British people. A five-second internet search on the question "What does 'estate' mean in England?" reveals that an estate is a subdivision, in essence—a block of homes built at the same time as part of a single project—and that it has a negative connotation, as it frequently references drab, standardized public housing. A subsequent debriefing at the end of the class, where the groups weigh in, allows for students to register that this specialized meaning of "estate" can now become background knowledge. Similarly, the paragraph briefly illustrates how suburban development happened in the UK from the 1930s to mid-century, with estates being built in rings around older, established villages and towns. This knowledge, too, becomes part of our background knowledge. As subsequent groups weigh in, then, I can point out that we are collaboratively expanding our relevant knowledge, building for ourselves a rich historical context for the literature we are reading.

Sustained Development of Provisional Literacy: Major Projects That Build Context and Metacognition

Ultimately, I want students to construct such provisional cultural literacies over a long enough time period that they feel they are getting somewhere—not just responding to local gaps in knowledge that pertain to single texts but building up a store of knowledge that is cumulative and interrelated, and which actually helps them to interpret new texts as they read them. I spell out two such projects here, but surely there are an infinite number of possible assignments that would do the job. More important is a clear articulation of what that job is: to give students awareness of how they build up the working knowledge that allows them to comprehend and interpret texts within a specific context, and to give them practice in doing so deliberately. Any large-scale project that causes students to gather contextual information over a long period while engaging their interpretive abilities, and connecting contexts to interpretations, will suffice.

Project 1: Anthology Project. This project acts on the principle that having students construct contextual knowledge actively and consciously facilitates learning better than delivering information to them. (We almost always emphasize such active learning in interpreting primary texts—we urge, wheedle, and mentor students into producing their own interpretations. It is less common, however, for us to charge students with constructing historical context.) In short, the project calls upon students, in teams, to put together an alternative anthology of a historical period. It guides students toward resources they can mine to find relatively unknown literary texts and writers. (With the ever-expanding availability of primary texts on the internet, these resources require frequent updating.) Students justify their selections in an introductory essay, provide brief biographical information on the writers they include, and annotate the texts, providing explanatory notes that give any necessary, unfamiliar prior knowledge needed to understand textual details.

The project facilitates learning in multiple ways. It requires students to build up basic knowledge of the main, consensus traditions of the period—something they get from reading, discussion, and mini-lectures early in the semester—in order to argue successfully for "publishing" these relatively unknown writers. Justifying their selections also requires close and active reading: students must interpret and evaluate texts sufficiently to make a strong case for their inclusion. The project also activates, expands, and reinforces their store of background knowledge in several ways. To annotate the texts, students research historical facts, including people, places, events, and concepts; doing so emphasizes to students what they know and what they don't know about the period. Writing the introduction and the short biographies causes them to marshal this data in effective, concise writing. And in collaborating with each other, students encounter not only what they themselves find but what their partners in the project have unearthed. Together they need to craft the introduction that justifies their section of the anthology, which will once again show them gaps they will have to fill.

This is an ambitious project, and long experience has shown me that you have to give it ample time if students are going to do well on it. Some years ago, I sacrificed teaching James Joyce's *Ulysses* in my undergraduate, early-twentieth-century British literature class because there was not enough time to discuss the novel adequately while devoting ample class time to the anthology project. Large projects that are stretched across most of the semester, like this one, work better when students have to produce elements of it early on, at strategic moments throughout the term; at these points, students get feedback, and the class as a whole has a chance to discuss practical problems, research strategies, and successful ways of thinking about what makes a text worthy of recovery. So it's necessary to devote class periods to student performances of early work on the project. Given the realities of student lives, it also helps to set aside class periods near the end of the semester for work sessions, in which you meet with students (preferably in the library, if this is possible) and everyone spends the time working on the project. Student schedules in the real world have become complex enough that it is often difficult for groups of four or five students to find meeting times outside of class. For that reason, I like this project's mix of individual work and group work: students individually dig up and propose, to the group, writers and texts to recover; they write the short biographies and annotate the texts individually. But they share responsibility for their section of the anthology, and the introduction is a collaborative writing assignment, for which they organize information together and build consensus about how to best introduce and justify their inclusions.

Giving this project adequate space means sacrificing elements of literature teaching to which we may be quite attached: it means reading fewer primary texts and spending fewer meetings in open, interpretive discussion. It may mean that the collective understanding of a historical period (or theme, or tradition) to which you feel deep commitments emerges as less thorough or coherent than you would prefer. It may mean that you sacrifice constructing clear, coherent readings of all primary texts. But I would argue that all of this, while uncomfortable, is to the good, if we accept the notion that as literature teachers our mission is to put students in position to develop skills and dispositions and that doing so is more important than providing students with coherent interpretations of novels and well-organized notes on our (teachers') narratives of a literary tradition or period.

Here are the materials I hand out to introduce this project.

CLASS PROJECT: ANTHOLOGY

Purpose: We spend most of our class time in this course working on texts by major, canonical writers. As a result we are getting a very selective, narrow view of the extremely active, diverse publishing marketplace of the early-twentieth century. This project will put us into direct contact with lesser known, perhaps even entirely forgotten, writers and works, forcing us to reconsider (1) the cultural centrality of experimental modernism during the period and (2) the rather narrow version of modernism itself that emerges from our primary reading.

In a more practical sense, this project will sharpen and extend your research skills, requiring creativity and resourcefulness in choosing materials to collect and situating and explaining them for our audience.

Product: Our product will be an anthology of recovered poems, short works of fiction, and critical essays that—as a whole—will *challenge conventional understandings of the period's literary landscape*. The final product will consist of approximately forty works that you recover and four section introductions; explanatory footnotes where appropriate; and an appendix of short biographical notes on each author.

Teamwork: During the *recovery* portion of the project, each member will be responsible for proposing *at least* four works for inclusion. That will give a pool of sixteen to twenty works to choose from: the team will collaboratively narrow that number to about ten.

Once recovery is complete (November 18), each team will collaborate on a section introduction (six to eight pages) that discusses the works, the rationale for their inclusion, and (most importantly) the ways in which this section changes our sense of the literature of the period. The introduction should be addressed to a general audience of interested readers.

The teams will also collaborate on doing research to write explanatory footnotes for the works, where necessary, and in writing the biographical notes on each author. (Biographical notes should be signed by the team member(s) who produced them.)

At the end of the semester, each team member will also file a three-page report detailing all of his or her activities, listing and discussing the works he or she proposed, and discussing the reasons those works were or were not included.

Deadlines: Wednesday, October 5 to Friday October 9—Class presentations, in which each group presents four to five texts that they are considering for recovery, and briefly explains why they think these works are compelling.

Friday, October 23—Status report due, including a list and a short description of ten possible anthology inclusions.

Friday, November 13—Status report due, including a list and short description of twenty possible anthology inclusions.

Friday, December 4—Submit copies of all works *selected* for the anthology as a single MS word file on canvas.

Friday, December 11—*Draft* section introductions due on Blackboard.

Finals week—Complete anthology selections due, including the following:

- At least ten and no more than twelve "recovered" primary works, accurately edited in MS word files, with
  - Explanatory footnotes where appropriate
- Your final version of your section introduction, revised based on feedback from me.
- An appendix with short (one paragraph) biographies of the writers whose work you have recovered. Each biographical entry should be signed with the initials of the writer from your group who prepared it, and should indicate the sources upon which the entry was based.
- Your three-page report on your individual activities.

Grading: Forty percent (160 points) for quality of your introduction.

Is it well-written? Does it offer a vision of why the section's contents are valuable? Does it suggest ways in which the section changes, sharpens, expands, or qualifies our understanding of the literary history of the years it covers? Does it convincingly assert the value of the recovered texts? Does it show an understanding of the "standard story" of these years and how these newly found texts revise that story?

Twenty percent (80 points) for quality of your selections.

Do they genuinely expand our understanding of the period? Are they interesting or valuable in their own right? Are they accurately edited, free of editorial errors?

Fifteen percent (60 points) for your three-page explanation of your contributions.

Does it demonstrate appropriate contribution toward the project? Does it intelligently discuss the issues that went into the selection process?

Ten percent (30 points) for footnotes.

Appropriate use and number of footnotes? Accurate? Clear and concise?

Fifteen percent (40 points) for biographical notes.

Did you find information on most of your authors? Concise, informative, and well-expressed?

I have used this project five or six times; and (let's be honest, this is the real world) with varied success—I had a miraculous class where every group did superb work, and I had a class (later) where it went poorly enough that I considered dropping it. (It was after this class that I stopped teaching *Ulysses* and doing the project in the same semester.) But I stick by the project because it seems clear that almost everyone learns from it. The three-page individual reports are revealing, as students who struggled complain about the difficulty but in the process reveal the work they did and their awareness of what they needed to find out in order to justify their selections, annotate, and write bibliographies. In most of these reports, metacognition is in evidence.

The biggest challenge in leading students through this project successfully, I have found, lies in how to lay out a "conventional understanding of the period's literary landscape" that students can successfully engage as a strawman to justify their anthology selections. You know the problem: a lecture on "British modernism" will be memorable and digestible to students in direct proportion to its reductiveness; a nuanced and complicated lecture that acknowledges critical disagreements and a tortuous critical history will be difficult for students to work with; plus there are all the usual problems with lectures, student note-taking, and so on. As I write this, I am planning a version in which I will establish the groups at the start of the class and assign each group to a well-known critical explanation of modernism from a certain historical moment (Malcolm Gladwell, Edmund Wilson, etc.); they will have to present the essay's main argument to the class. This addition will present its own challenges: see my discussion of using literary criticism in Appendix 1.

Project 2: Class wiki. This project shares several objectives with the anthology project. It also puts students in charge of researching background information and invites them to identify relatively obscure writers and texts and to make a case for their significance. And it also propels students toward primary sources, including online periodicals and dusty old editions of novels and poetry anthologies, which give students exposure to literature in context in a material, embodied way that has an ineffable value. (Enthusiastic students are often blown away to find early-twentieth-century works by major writers sharing page space with patent medicine advertisements, for instance.)

What I particularly like about this assignment is that, as a semester-long project that I introduce during the first week of class, it foregrounds the process of developing a storehouse of usable, contextual knowledge from the start of the semester. This assignment works best in relatively focused classes, as the contextual information that you and the students build up collaboratively, and put up on the wiki, will constitute a tighter, more interconnected network if the semester's reading covers a relatively short period of time or another relatively focused, limited topic. (The version of the assignment I provide below was from a class in which we focused particularly on the late 1930s; I have also used the project successfully in a single-author class on Virginia Woolf.) I begin the semester by lecturing about the relations between historical background knowledge and literary comprehension and interpretation, as I described earlier in this chapter; then I introduce the project and underscore how it allows us to play out these processes consciously, identifying—individually and collaboratively—important contextual information and then seeking to clarify it deliberately. Having foregrounded the assignment and these processes in the first class meetings, I can then invoke them as we are reading the class's primary texts. For instance, when we read Christopher Isherwood's *Goodbye to Berlin*, I periodically spur students to identify contextual knowledge that would be helpful to us. The novel begins by invoking the collapse of the German economy, its "houses like shabby monumental safes crammed with the tarnished valuables and second-hand furniture of a bankrupt middle class."[22] A few students, fresh from our required core curriculum class in world history, will have a surface understanding of the economic distress in Germany after the Versailles treaty. And so here we have a set of potential wiki entries: "Weimar Germany," "Inflation in Weimar Germany," the Versailles Treaty, and so on. We could do the same with Elizabeth Bowen's story, discussed earlier: the blitz or "London during the Blitz" could become useful wiki entries.

The material I hand out to students for this assignment appears later. Here are the particulars: In teams of four or five, students are to produce a wiki that can serve as a resource for readers interested in your topic (in my case, literature and culture of Britain in the late 1930s). Each group is charged with devising and researching eight to ten topics, including a mix of noncanonical writers and texts, historical figures, events or phenomena, or keywords (in Raymond Williams's sense: important terms that show up often in discourse of the time and whose meaning is contested). I provide a short list of samples, which students can adopt, but I want them to identify more than half of the wiki topics on their own. I maintain a steadily growing list of possible wiki terms as they emerge from class discussion. (The instructions below include topics that emerged during class discussion or weekly discussion board posts when I taught this class in 2018.) I also tuck into the project a mini-assignment in which students look at primary sources (usually periodicals in online or facsimile form) and extract a set of possible wiki topics from them.

As with the anthology project, it is essential to assign early deadlines for parts of the project and to allow class time to discuss, troubleshoot, and work on the project. I write a sample wiki entry, sometimes assigned to me by the class, early in the semester, to provide a model. Drafts of half of the entries are due at midterm, so students get feedback on their research and writing and have a set of student-generated models they can read as they go forward. (All of this takes place on a simple Google Doc, which I clean up frequently to keep it easily navigable.)

English 366
Class Wiki Project

The project: Our class project will be to create a wiki that can serve as a resource on British literature and culture in the late 1930s. Its content will consist of encyclopedia-style entries of 1,500–2,000 words each on topics illuminating the cultural milieu and zeitgeist of this period.

Your learning: The project is designed to *allow you to learn in a self-directed fashion*, following your own interests and curiosity, about key cultural/historical issues, events, texts, and people in this rich and troubled period. It aims to *increase your skills and resourcefulness as a researcher.* You will seek out information in multiple ways, some of them new to you. It aims to give you *advanced practice in reading cultural texts, synthesizing source material, and writing* sharp and nuanced expository prose. And it foregrounds the process of building up a storehouse of background information that makes it possible to fully understand texts of a specific historical period.

Requirements: You will work in teams of five. Each team will produce ten encyclopedia-style entries by the end of the semester, with solid drafts of five of them completed by midterm. Your ten entries will fall into four categories: (1) writers and texts; (2) events; (3) historical figures and phenomena; and (4) keywords. Your project must include at least two from each category. Five of the ten can come from the partial list of topics below. We'll be adding to the list as the class goes along; the other five topics must be discovered by your team.

Research and citation: I want you to be as resourceful as possible in doing research, using an "everything-including-the-kitchen-sink" approach. Thus it wouldn't be a bad idea to start at Wikipedia (say, if you're writing about a reasonably well-known writer), but only to get yourself grounded and develop some general knowledge. You'll want to use academic research (books by scholars and essays found on the MLA International Bibliography) and primary materials when they're available (diaries and letters by historical figures, biographies, memoirs, etc.) It would be a mistake to try to do all of your research online: you would miss out on a surprising and eccentric wealth of primary material in the university library. It would also be a mistake to ignore the riches that good, strategic online searching can turn up, including the primary material available at sites such as www.archive.org. Since we're starting early, don't be afraid to use interlibrary loan: there are tremendous riches available in other libraries, and they get here quickly.

Your entries must be documented using footnotes written in MLA style.

Coming up with topics: Online research will help uncover potential topics. Some topics will emerge naturally from our shared reading in class (for instance the Spanish Civil War). Another wealth of sources of possible topics will be periodicals published in Britain from 1936 to 1939. A list of these—and where/how they're available in the library—appears below. You will be required to do some primary materials work on a small assignment that feeds this larger project, due at the end of week 4. You could write one or more entries on a periodical itself, and what it was up to in 1936–39.

Focusing on the period: In your research and writing, remember that we're focusing on Britain, roughly 1936–39. All entries should be focused mainly on this period. Thus if you're writing about Winston Churchill or an obscure novelist, you should be focusing on what he or she was up to in 1936–39. If you're writing about India as a British colony (which would be great!), you should focus on developments in and around these years. To some degree, each entry should address how its topic relates to or influences the period's literature.

BEGINNING TOPIC LIST

Writers and Texts (could include periodicals)

Churchill, Winston. *Step by Step: 1936–39*.
Cole, Margaret. *Books and the People*.
Greenwood, Walter. *Love on the Dole*
Macaulay, Rose.
Madge, Charles
Priestly, J. B. (John Boynton)
Wellesley, Dorothy
West, Rebecca. (Esp. *Black Lamb and Gray Falcon*)
The Oxford Book of Modern Verse (ed. W. B. Yeats)
Spender, Stephen
Nicolson, Harold

Events

The Abdication Crisis
The burning of the Crystal Palace

> The Munich agreement/"Appeasement"
> Spanish Civil War (or some smaller topic within it)
>
> **Historical figures and phenomena**
>
> Mosley, Oswald
> Penguin paperbacks
> The Left Book Club
> The Lambeth Walk
> Mass Observation
> Keynes, J. M.
>
> **Keywords**
>
> Pacifism
> Appeasement
> Eugenics/"race"
> Empire/imperialism

As with any assignment, the more times you and your students can repeat the draft-feedback-revision loop the better. I emphasize that, as the project is envisioned as an open-source resource for people interested in our historical period, not only do the terms need to be well-selected; the entries themselves must articulate the significance of the terms. (For instance, an entry on "pacifism" needs to make clear the numbers of people involved in pacifist organizations and the prominent public figures who had signed onto it as a position.) This and many other criteria appear on a rubric that I hand out to students, but the chance of students really committing to these criteria will increase every time they are discussed in class or in small groups.

Conclusion: Curriculum Design for Advanced Literacy

One could devise an infinite number of assignments like these—grounded in an understanding of cultural literacy as a process and a skill set rather than a consensus bank of knowledge. Their benefit is that they sensitize students to the vast areas of useful cultural knowledge they lack, train them to recognize when prior knowledge is hindering their interpretations, and give them instruction and practice in assembling cultural knowledge that is accurate, meaningful, and useful.

The limitation to any such assignment in a class, however, is that semesters end, and students move on to their next intellectual endeavors in individual, unpredictable ways. A student who just finished your upper-level Shakespeare class may move on to a class in modern drama, which will reactivate much of the specialized knowledge—both declarative and procedural—that you helped her assemble. Or, she may move on to a semester of core curriculum classes, or major classes in professional writing and linguistics, or literature classes in a far-flung period, in which the declarative knowledge she assembled will not be very useful. As Linkon has argued, "the structure of the English major is rarely designed to support student learning" (29). The student may also graduate to a job at Chik-Fil-A to pay the bills while she sends resumes to marketing firms. The practices of advanced reading comprehension and advanced literacy will stay with her. But the declarative knowledge about battles over royal succession, or sectarian wars, or the importance of Venice as a strategic location in Europe, which you helped her build up as essential background knowledge, are likely to disappear. Nothing will remedy this, but we can build up cultural literacy as a practice more profoundly if we design curricula that encourage students to track and monitor their own knowledge as it develops and to consciously build schema and structures for the knowledge they are accumulating. To that end I want to conclude this chapter by proposing a senior project, which could be adapted as part of a senior seminar or a portfolio-style graduation requirement, that calls on students to articulate—to themselves and others—how their cultural literacy has developed, before and after their college experience.

What I propose is that students majoring in English be prompted from the start of their education to begin assembling their personal canon of texts—texts that they feel are important, whether culturally (they think others should be familiar with them, too) or personally (they made a difference to the students' intellectual, moral, emotional, or spiritual growth). The summation of this assemblage will be a long bibliographic essay that forges links across these texts—a specialized literacy autobiography that engages specifically with the student's favored texts, constructing a narrative of the learning that has emerged in dialogue with them. Because the assignment seeks foreground, develop, and make visible cultural literacy, the assignment prompt should ask students to discuss the knowledge of history, cultures, and the wider world that their reading has helped them to assemble: to categorize this knowledge and show readers how they have organized it. The essay should be a readable, interesting account of what the student has learned—how, by engaging with his or her personal canon, the student has changed during the college experience. A student's personal canon should include texts read outside class and even before entering college. To the essay should be added an appendix listing the student's "canonical" texts and with short (two to three sentences) descriptions and explanations of each text's importance. Ideally the student should have plenty of space—fifteen to twenty pages, I would say. I would require a minimum of thirty texts but allow students to include more.

Ideally, students would begin assembling their developing canon in their freshman year and would start brainstorming on their narrative long before it's due. But—oh, right!—this book is called *Teaching Literature in the Real World*: they won't do this, without vigorous prompting from us. The assignment could be workshopped, finished, and graded as part of a senior seminar, or treated in lieu of a portfolio as a graduation requirement. (Portfolios that are submitted and graded outside of classes, of course, generate new faculty labor and are thus not ideal. On the other hand, such portfolios can be used as part of program assessments—another real-world fact of life in higher education.) The assignment should be introduced to students in a freshman- or sophomore-level introductory class—ideally an introductory class that all students in your major take. If you do not have such a class, your department can introduce students to the concept through email and social media, and you could have periodic meetings to answer questions and foreground the purpose and nature of the assignment. All of this requires work, but I think it would be very much worth doing, particularly for the metacognition the assignment requires—the schematization of knowledge and the articulation of what has been valuable in specific reading experiences. The value would lie not only in the summative experience of writing and assembling the text list, but for the formative work it could do to make students conscious of the influence of individual reading experiences on their developing knowledge, capacities, and dispositions.

A curricular feature like this, of course, would require buy-in and coordination among constituencies in your department—something you could not accomplish individually and which may not fit with your department's structure and culture. But, in more modest ways, anything we can do to make students' accumulation and organization of knowledge conscious will benefit them—activities that call on students to schematize the information they are gathering, explicit modeling of how we, as experienced professional learners, structure and hierarchize information about our fields, concept-mapping, and so on. In these ways we can help students attain the kind of cultural literacy that is possible and desirable in our age: the ability to develop the provisional, adaptable bodies of knowledge that our different lives will require.

4 ARTICULATING GOALS AND DESIGNING INTEGRATED COURSES

The Joy of Course Design

I suggested earlier that maturing as a teacher involves a series of disillusionments. Now I want to offer some solace: one teaching task whose pleasures and intensities can, in the right circumstances, stay fresh and uncompromised is the design of classes. Designing courses is among the most creative work college literature professors do—creative in the most literal and profound sense. You start with a blank page and, because of the marks you make on it, a thing happens in the world—people meet and read and think and write, in ways they would not have done had you not set pen to paper. Even within a relatively circumscribed course such as an introduction to literature or a historical survey, you devise themes to develop and questions to pursue, assign new texts and design fresh activities. In upper-level courses, you can pursue passions, problems, and perplexities of the sort that got you into this line of work in the first place, drawing on your expertise to design an intellectual journey through them. It should be clear by now that I love teaching literature, but few things about it feel as pure and uncompromised to me as coming up with an idea for a class and sitting down to work out the details. (This being the real world, the serious complications come later: when you actually try to get twenty-five or so students, most of whom do not share your passions and perplexities, to carry this intellectual ball with you for fourteen or fifteen weeks.)

This is not to suggest that the contingencies of life in the real world do not impinge on course design. We design classes within an institutional setting and—if we are to be effective—must consider local conditions, none of which is more important than the general characteristics of your students. As I have noted, if most of your students work many hours in jobs, you need to think carefully about how much reading to assign and how often, if at all, you can schedule extra activities such as study sessions or film screenings. I have shared my broad goals for teaching literature: helping students to develop advanced reading comprehension and advanced literacy. For me, every course I teach must be designed around these goals. But individual classes will do this in ways appropriate to their specific content, their level of difficulty, and any additional objectives attached to the course by its place and purpose in the larger curriculum.

Within institutions and departments, individual courses have to answer to multiple masters. At my university, our general education curriculum comes with a lengthy, highly articulated set of cognitive goals; all courses are reviewed to see that they are designed around these goals, and we are bound to plan our individual sections to meet them. For non-Gen Ed courses, our department provides much sketchier "master syllabi" that stipulate more general subject matter and objectives. Dynamics like these vary widely among institutions. So, designing an individual class often requires a pre-preparation mulling of broad and specific institutional goals, content-specific objectives, and aims that flow from your own commitments and interests.

These considerations may sound a bit square and functional—they are—but except in extreme cases or deeply dysfunctional institutions, they should not spoil the creative joy of designing courses. Indeed, creativity is empowered and channeled into productivity in part by restraint: the Dogme film movement, the sonnet, the three-minute pop song, and the seven-minute Bugs Bunny cartoon are among the many monuments to the power of working within restraints. Designing courses that meet institutional goals and are tailored to student needs and abilities does not mean becoming a functionary. Think of these constraints as pathways that will give you direction and turn your pure ideas into workable plans with the best chance of engaging students and enlisting them in the pursuit of your goals.

A course idea often starts with your teaching assignment, or with your request for a specific class. Your department has a course called "Literary History" on the books; you're intrigued by the possibilities. Or, without warning, your chairperson asks if you can cover an unexpected gap and teach sophomore-level world literature. If you're nervous or overwhelmed, the constraints—pre-articulated course content and goals—can provide a toehold and a source of ideas; so can past syllabi: never hesitate to ask colleagues you admire to share their syllabi from past courses.

Whether a new course design begins with an unexpected schedule change, a long-desired assignment, or a rare opportunity to make a new course out of whole cloth, your ideas and substantial elements of your designs should spring from your passions and preoccupations. Your ideas about subject matter—about literature, culture, society, history, philosophy, human nature, freedom, progress, and so on—should be the fuel that ignites your creativity. Once the flame is lit, it is smart to do some brainstorming, even freewriting, to articulate the issues, themes, and questions you want a course to address and the texts you want students to interpret. These two elements—texts on the one hand, and themes, questions, and issues on the other hand—are cross-pollinating and recursive; a great class may start with a set of linked texts (films about African Americans and law enforcement; island texts—*Robinson Crusoe*, *The Tempest*s of Shakespeare and Caesare, "Castaway") or with themes or problems (masculinity in twentieth-century American drama; "What happened to the 'English novel' after World War II?"). But in any event you should allow yourself space to generate a lot of ideas and possibilities before you begin to funnel this material down into specific objectives, assignments, assessments, and a schedule. In turn, this process of funneling down will allow you to identify the best and most feasible ideas and will generate new ones.

Objectives: Your Philosophy in Action

Now comes the most crucial step: formulating specific objectives for your class. Without well-articulated course objectives, a syllabus is just a list of texts and assignments. But with objectives that are clearly stated, and that your students understand, the purpose behind your choices and the educational value of your class becomes clear. In my first years as a literature professor, I made the mistake of thinking that a class consisted of a set of texts that we read and discussed and a set of papers that students wrote. While I wrote a course description that identified themes or articulated a few questions, the texts, assignments, and discussions floated somewhat freely from the description and from each other. In this I was emulating most of my undergraduate teachers, who learned their craft before the Assessment Bug infected higher education and thus were never prompted to think beyond a general faith that reading and discussing books is good for people, and that writing papers about literature improves your writing. The Assessment Bug— the imperative to specify the learning we believe is happening in our programs and to demonstrate that it is, in fact, happening—has surely generated a lot of labor for professors and administrators, work which has often been framed in vague but insistent directives, with little support from above. To my mind, though, the Assessment Bug's positive contribution has been its insistence that we articulate specific objectives. In my experience, articulating objectives at all levels—from the major as a whole to individual classes to each day's meeting—is profoundly clarifying, giving you a roadmap for when things inevitably get difficult.[1]

Good course objectives begin with your own values: they should originate in your deepest convictions about the value of teaching literature. For this reason, everyone (not just strivers on the job market) needs a well-articulated teaching philosophy. It should express and support your understanding of the value of teaching literature, articulate the changes you want students to undergo as a result of your classes, describe how you pursue these goals, and address how you know when students are meeting them. A functional philosophy will address these points in some detail but also be reducible to elevator-pitch size, to a small, clear set of goals. (You know mine: advanced reading comprehension and advanced literacy). It is important to revise your philosophy every so often, so that your growing professional wisdom can be brought to bear, to clarify and refine your aims. This philosophy then becomes your compass amid the often stormy seas of teaching literature in the real world. When you have a class full of students who don't like to participate, or when one or two difficult personalities are taking up too much of your head space, of when the vicissitudes of life have kept you from doing your best work for a time, you can go back to your statement of philosophy to reset your instruments and remind yourself of your mission and the changes you are trying to midwife in your students.

Day to day, your philosophy is the ground on which your course design stands and your guide to how to implement it. The ladder of abstraction, from philosophical tenets to daily classroom decisions, looks something like this:

FROM PHILOSOPHY AND GOALS TO DAILY CLASS PLANS

Goals of Teacher's Philosophy
+ → Course objectives → Assignments/Assessments → schedule → daily plans
Institutional/Departmental goals

All of the decisions involved in designing a syllabus and assignments are founded on the tenets of the teacher's philosophy—the goals the teacher has for all students in all classes—in tandem with whatever goals the department and the institution have for that class.

The historical literature survey class serves as an example of how these work together—or need to be reconciled. I am not personally, deeply invested in "knowledge of major writers and periods," as my department's master syllabus requires. But my department, as expressed in this document, is, and so I will do my job and allow this imperative to inform my objectives. My overarching aims and the department's imperatives can then be transformed into specific objectives for the class. Everything on the syllabus must serve those objectives: that is what makes the syllabus integrated and makes clear to everyone, students and teachers alike, what the purpose is for any specific activity, assignment, or text. Finer details, such as the sequence in which interpretive, analytical, or writing tasks and skills should be activated or the specific forms of assessments, should derive from course objectives. Linkon, drawing on the work of K–12 education experts, describes such "backward design": we work backward from objectives to all other plans: "readings are chosen based on how well they will help students understand the big ideas . . . . In backward design, readings and the course schedule are the final concerns, not the starting place."[2] In practice, this process is actually recursive: in the idea-generation stage a list of texts may help generate objectives or vice versa. But when we reach the phase of syllabus design, objectives must determine when and whether we use any text, activity, or assignment.

Objectives, Activities, and Assessments: Three Classes

The Intro Course

Course objectives should be clear, achievable (at least for a substantial percentage of your students), and observable. I say "observable" rather than "measurable" to acknowledge that some of the transformations we hope to see in our students cannot be easily turned into numerical scores or reduced to a pass/fail call; our professional judgment and interpersonal skills are involved in assessing some of our most profound goals. And, if you accept my premise that the most important things we teach students in literature classes are intellectual methods, objectives should be phrased in the language of *things students do*, and assessments should be designed for students to demonstrate their capacities to do these things.

INTRODUCTION TO LITERARY ANALYSIS: LEARNING OBJECTIVES

By the end of this class, you should be able to:

- Use multiple methods to generate multiple, analytical observations about literary texts;
- Select from these observations to make focused argumentative claims about literary texts, and support them with reasoning and evidence;
- Read interpretive essays about literature by others with comprehension and use them to place your own arguments in context;
- Use multiple methods to find useful interpretive essays and meaningful historical context about literary works;
- Write a successful, sustained interpretive argument that draws on other interpretations and integrates historical context to shed new light on a literary text.

Note that the objectives are *outcomes*, not *activities*. I used to write objectives that did not represent changes in student abilities—objectives such as "In this class, you will be exposed to major romantic, Victorian, modernist, and postmodernist texts." But exposure is not a learning outcome; as belied by my example's passive voice, this outcome is something done to students rather than something they do, and it does not necessarily entail any change in them; exposure is simply putting something in front of your students. Note also that my objectives are now expressed as action verbs, things that students will do because their growth in the class, in some interaction with their prior knowledge, has enabled them.

The Dream Course

An introduction to literary analysis class is easy to conceive in terms of learning outcomes because, like a first-year writing course, it is essentially a methods class. It requires a larger shift in pedagogical thinking to conceive of a content-oriented or thematic course in terms of objectives: here the temptation to fall back on "exposure" or coverage as objectives is strong. But students will have a greater sense of purpose if you can express to them how their work will change their capacities for the better. Here are my objectives from a specialized senior seminar:

VIRGINIA WOOLF AND EVERYDAY LIFE: COURSE OBJECTIVES

Stated simply, my hope for this class is that it will enable you to view everyday life critically; to read, understand, and enjoy the works of Virginia Woolf; and to find and articulate connections between Woolf's writing and the concept of "the everyday."

More specifically, students who are successful in this class will:

- Become adept at reading the fiction of Virginia Woolf, constructing responsive and well-supported readings of her writing and presenting them effectively, orally and in writing;
- Be able to describe and analyze the fictional techniques Woolf uses;
- Adopt an analytical view of everyday life, informed by theory;
- Become conversant in the theory of the everyday;
- Successfully analyze Woolf's engagement with the everyday, drawing on theory to enrich that analysis.

As in the literary analysis class, each of these objectives is designed so that it can be realized in sequenced reading assignments, class activities, and writing projects. The feedback I steadily give students on these activities constitutes the formative assessment that makes clear (to them and to me) who is doing well on these objectives, who needs extra attention, and where I need to make adjustments from day to day. Importantly, these activities (graded homeworks, short papers, etc.) are not only formative assessments—they are practice; the fact that they are also assessments make them incentives for busy, real-world students to keep up with their work and strive toward the cognitive transformations my class is seeking. For the semester's end I will design one or more integrative projects that constitute a summative assessment.

There is nothing revolutionary about any of this, of course: my summative assessment may simply be a long paper, though in writing up assignment guidelines, advice, and grading criteria, and in talking to students about the assignment, I will be working hard to foment metacognition—to get students to realize exactly the specific cognitive growth I want them to demonstrate in the assignment and to demonstrate to them how the final project draws on things they've learned earlier in the semester. An integrated syllabus, then, is one in which all of the readings and activities are tied to one or more specific objectives; which are sequenced so that students can move from relatively easy to relatively challenging transformations; and which can then be assessed summatively in a final project that synthesizes the objectives.

The Virginia Woolf and Everyday Life class is an ambitious, challenging upper-level class for English majors, so it is necessary to move slowly through difficult material and to sequence objectives appropriately. After a short introductory reading and an introductory mini-lecture that explains the concept of everyday life, the early calendar will stay close to the English majors' comfort zone, with the literature-specific objectives. The semester's first unit will focus on these objectives: here is how they translate into discrete activities:

VIRGINIA WOOLF AND EVERYDAY LIFE: LINKS BETWEEN LEARNING OBJECTIVES AND COURSE ACTIVITIES

- Become adept at reading the fiction of Virginia Woolf, constructing responsive and well-supported readings of her writing and presenting them effectively, orally and in writing.

  Activities:

  - Reading assignment: *To the Lighthouse*, "The Lady in the Looking Glass."

- Homework assignment: discussion-board posts (short interpretive essays).
- Close reading in class, in full-group discussion and small-group work, with emphasis on interpretive cruxes and difficulties.
- Assessment: short (four-page) essay close reading a short passage and placing it context of the work as a whole.

• Be able to describe and analyze the fictional techniques Woolf uses

Activities:

- Reading assignment: *To the Lighthouse*, "The Lady in the Looking Glass."
- Mini-lecture/discussion: point of view in fiction. Power-point showing examples of different kinds of narration from different points in literary history. Discussion of *TTL* dinner scene and Woolf's management of point of view.
- Mini-lecture/discussion: other formal elements of fiction (plot, dialogue, setting); formal experimentation. Discussion of "The Lady in the Looking Glass."
- Close reading in class, in full-group discussion and small-group work, with emphasis on fictional techniques.
- Homework assignment: discussion-board posts (short interpretive essays).
- Assessment: short (four-page) essay close reading a short passage and placing it in context of the work as a whole.

In the foregoing plan, students are working on the two Woolf-specific objectives simultaneously, in their study of *To the Lighthouse* and "The Lady in the Looking Glass." The short discussion-board essays and the four-page close-reading essay serve as practice and assessments for both objectives. (This will require that I evoke these objectives regularly and prompt students to address point of view and other formal properties on the discussion board, during class discussion, and in the short paper.) These objectives and activity-breakdowns then become the raw material for individual class plans: on appropriate days I will schedule the mini-lectures and assign group work or direct discussion to such issues as point of view in fiction. Multiple days of open discussion and group work will serve as practice and build an ongoing, collaborative dialogue about how we are reading Woolf and what the novel is saying to us. By being attentive to what is being said in class, and promptly grading discussion-board posts, I can gauge whether students are becoming adept and constructing valid meanings and defensible interpretations of Woolf and developing the vocabulary and ability to point to her formal experiments. And I can make short-term adjustments to see that the class, and individual students, are making progress.

Laying out these objectives and activities on paper may create the impression that these classes are going to be functional and joyless. But that is not the case: these activities are the skeleton of what happens in class and don't account for—or try to control—the substantive issues that form the meat of our discussions. The work of interpretation, in discussion and on the discussion board, will necessarily engage the vital questions Woolf's fiction raises. Because my teaching is method- rather than content-driven, the content we discuss in class is substantially open to student interest and the organic form our conversations take. As I discussed in Chapter 2, I decide on themes for class discussion in large part based on what students express interest in when they write on the discussion board. We are free to follow those themes, if they are feeling productive for us, as far as we like. While this class has an overarching theme of everyday life, that theme is capacious enough to allow student interests to dictate the content of our discussions and the specific topics students choose to write about.

The last time I taught this course a major theme emerged organically from the opening weeks' discussion—the question of female artistry and the obstacles to its expression in Woolf's society. We pursued this theme, placing it in the context of our later, fuller discussions of everyday life, to the mutual enrichment of both intellectual threads. When we read *A Room of One's Own* midway through the semester, one especially exciting session produced a shared "aha" moment about the ways in which, for Woolf, everyday life is the location where the politics of gender enable or hinder creativity. I still recall the intellectual sparks flying as we came across this passage:

> [Charlotte Brontë] knew, no one better, how enormously her genius would have profited if it had not spent itself in solitary visions over distant fields; if experience and intercourse and travel had been granted her. But they were not granted; they were withheld; and we must accept the fact that all those good novels, *Villette, Emma, Wuthering Heights, Middlemarch*, were written by women without more experience of life than could enter the house of a respectable clergyman; written too in the common sitting-room of that respectable house and by women so poor that they could not afford to buy more than a few quires of paper at a time upon which to write *Wuthering Heights* or *Jane Eyre*.[3]

Students observed that Woolf is explicitly tying creativity to women's everyday lives, by emphasizing the "common sitting room," the expense of paper, and the lack of variety in the life of a rural, unmarried, woman in the nineteenth century. We pursued this insight across the text, shining light on the importance of the everyday in Woolf's observation that Jane Austen must have been interrupted repeatedly while writing her novels in the sitting room, in her (at first puzzling) emphasis on the quality of the dinners in men's and women's Oxbridge colleges, in her broader claim that creative works "are not spun in mid-air by incorporeal creatures, but are the work of suffering human beings, and are attached to grossly material things, like health and money and the houses we live in."[4]

My point here is that pursing methods-based objectives does not impoverish discussion, diminish pleasure, or prevent the sorts of interpretive epiphanies whose intensity brought us to literature teaching in the first place. On the contrary, foregrounding methods greatly increases the chance that students will be able to share in these experiences. Practically, precise objectives lay out simple tracks to follow to build specific skills without limiting or predetermining the substantive insights or interpretive or philosophical questions our work might spark. Indeed, one could think of learning objectives and class plans as the constraints that enable our—and our students'—creativity.

The second set of objectives in this class is more challenging: getting students to engage successfully with the theory of everyday life. It entails some difficult reading and some mini-lectures to provide context and an overview. This will involve some intense classes where students voice frustration at their incomprehension of complex theoretical writing, and I work with them—and get them to work in groups—to identify their specific challenges and come up with strategies to address them. I will have to walk a fine line between oversimplifying complex ideas and letting students sink or swim in the theory, running the risk that they will disengage because they are too frustrated.

I talk more about teaching theory in Appendix 1, but it is worth noting here that, as with all teaching challenges, a return to objectives will clarify things when you're asking students to engage with theory. Articulate for yourself and your students what you want them to learn. The relevant objective in my Virginia Woolf class is for students to "adopt an analytical view of everyday life, informed by theory." While this sounds abstract, it's easy to concretize it. It means that you can look at some aspect of everyday life that normally does not attract attention or analysis—say, clothing, or furniture—and analyze it, asking where it came from and what it signifies, what it says about how we think and behave and how our society runs. One handy example: our culture has been awash in anxious commentary on the role of smart phones in everyday life: we wonder what effect some everyday practice is having on us, who is being enriched by it and at what expense, how it has changed our ways of thinking and being in the world. Such questions signal an analytical view and can drive analysis. So, one way to exemplify "an analytical view of everyday life" would be to share something smart from mainstream journalism that addresses concerns about smart phone use. Another would be to ask students where the clothes they are wearing were manufactured; finding (as I almost always do) that no one knows, I then lead them in a discussion of how our clothes imply a real, material relationship with people we do not know—and a relationship of which we remain ignorant. If we go on to ask how this happened and what its implications are—who benefits from it in what ways, and who does not—we have taken a step toward being analytical about everyday life.

I start at such accessible points and follow with readings in which critics analyze everyday life: such as excerpts from Luce Giard's writing about housewives and cooking, or one of Ben Highmore's brilliant chapters from *Ordinary Lives*—about the chair in his den or Indian food in British culture. These readings move us toward addressing my objectives' closing phrase, "informed by theory," which simply means that our analyses invoke, illustrate, or test generalizations previous observers have made about everyday life. Teaching students to read and "do things" with theory—though difficult because the writing is often hard to comprehend—is like teaching students to do virtually anything else: you describe how it's done; show them examples of it being done; give them practice doing it (as much as you can); and assess them on it.

I realized through trial and error that even if you can get students talking and writing in theoretical ways, and referring accurately to theoretical concepts, these practices will disappear later in the semester unless you hold students accountable for learning (even, to an extent, memorizing) key terms and concepts. Thus whenever complex theory is involved in one of my classes, I give an exam, usually a take-home but sometimes a hybrid exam that includes some in-class and some take-home. The questions are directly keyed to the objectives and specifically address what I think are the most useful theoretical concepts.

THEORY TAKE-HOME EXAM: SAMPLE QUESTIONS

1. In an essay of about 750 words, articulate *some* of the complexities of *time* as it is *experienced in everyday life*, drawing on the writing of at least two of the following: Rita Felski, Ben Highmore, Walter Benjamin, Virginia Woolf. Some questions to consider as you plan your essay: how is the experience of time in everyday life distinct from the uniform, mathematical passage of time on the clock? How do we experience different models or understandings of time at different times in our lives (or even within single days?) What forces (historical, economic, physical) influence our shifting perceptions of time? How have the historical transformations of the past 200 years influenced the perception of time? How might time be experienced differently based on class, gender, or other identity? (Do not try to address all of these questions; they're intended as stimulants to your thinking only.)

> 2. Consider two specific *objects* that have been part of your everyday life at any point in the past or present. In about 250 words each, write a short essay on each object that uses two or more of the following concepts: cathexis/the transitional object; inundations; the pedagogy of things/things as social agents (all from Highmore, "Familiar Things"); things versus objects (Bill Brown, in Highmore's "Familiar Things"); the "dialectical image" (Walter Benjamin, in the short excerpt from "On Some Motifs in Baudelaire.")

As you can see in the previous sample questions, such exams are specifically geared to get students to practice—and to enable me to assess—whether the student writers are adopting "an analytical view of everyday life, informed by theory." This exam is a formative assessment, which usually comes around the sixth week of the semester; the summative assessment will come when they write a final paper that engages with Woolf's depictions of everyday life and puts Woolf's insights (or their own) in dialogue with those of the theorists. If everything works, the midterm will raise the students' game on the theory, so that our discussions in the second half of the semester can confidently draw on the ideas covered in the exam. In a few past cases, I have asked a few students who did not do well on the exam to take it a second time, after having worked with me during office hours.

These particular activities and assessments, of course, are quite specific to a very specialized class—a dream course, really, in which I get to pursue my intellectual passions in some depth. It's fairly rare that I get to do this, and that I get to do it at all is a mark of my privileged position in the profession, despite my second-tier university and my teaching- and service-intensive job. Such an opportunity may be even rarer for you. But your take-away, I hope, should be that regardless of how specialized, unique, or ambitious your concept is for an individual class, you can (and should) design it by starting with clear, specific, observable objectives, and proceed to assignments, activities, and assessments that speak directly to them. Steering myself back firmly to the middle of the road in the real world, though, let me move on to discussing objectives in a much more common class, though one no less vexing from the standpoint of design: the historical survey.

The Survey Course

I discussed my ideas about survey classes at some length in Chapter 1 because they embody a tension between content and method that I cannot escape. As you know, I think practice and growth in intellectual methods is by far the most important thing we offer our students, and I am much less committed to an old-fashioned sense of cultural literacy founded upon knowledge of an agreed-upon canon of texts. I won't rehearse this argument here, but I re-invoke it because the survey class, in my case a course called "British Literature 1790–Present"—is where this conflict becomes most vivid. The class comes to me, pre- and partially designed around content goals—students are to be exposed to "major writers, themes, and movements" (the language is from my department's master syllabus). Again, being "exposed" is not a learning goal. If it were, it would be easy to assess: you could simply design an exam and ask students if they know who Wordsworth is, and: Bob's your uncle! (Or rather, Bill's your uncle.) I'm being deliberately absurd, of course, but as a student I have taken, and as a teacher I have designed, exams that give students passages from "major" works, ask them to identify author and text, and then—in what may be a slightly guilty acknowledgment that what the question has tested thus far has been memorization—ask students to briefly interpret the passage in context.

None of this is going to hurt anyone, of course; memorizing things is not a terrible thing to do, and it's essential in foundations courses for certain fields (such as biology or foreign languages). But we are kidding ourselves if we think that having students memorize the titles and authors of works they have read sometime in the last three months is to create knowledge students can draw from for the rest of their lives. I got perfect scores on my exams in British Literature 1 in 1993, but today, I could not differentiate a sonnet by Wyatt from one by Surrey to save my life; I could identify some poems by Shakespeare, Herrick, Herbert, and Donne because I like them and have returned to them for my own pleasure, illustrating again that declarative knowledge sticks when it is used again and again, but otherwise does not. In fact, what such exams measure is exposure and short-term memorization. Again, it's fine that students have been exposed to Donne and Herbert, Arnold and Blake and Rossetti: it raises the chance that they might love them and return to them again. But they very well may not. And exposure is not a learning goal.

And yet, here we are, in the real world, where I get paid by a university and work in an English department to teach a class whose "objectives" include familiarity with "major writers, themes, and movements"—a department, too, where one-quarter to one-third of my students are studying to be high school teachers, whose education must meet a standard of (darn it!) exposure to British literature. So, I compromise: I combine the institutional objectives with goals that are meaningful to me. I worked through these issues with some PhD students about ten years ago, when I was teaching my graduate course on pedagogy. While they were drafting objectives for hypothetical courses as part of their portfolio for my class, I worked alongside them to rejigger my objectives for British Literature 2. Here you can see how my objectives evolved from woefully nonspecific to precise and observable.

SHARPENING OBJECTIVES: BEFORE AND AFTER

OLD OBJECTIVES

This course is designed to give you a broad overview of major themes and writings of British literature since 1790 by having you read, comment on, and write about a wide variety of texts in English from the past three (but primarily the past two) centuries. The class will give you strategies for reading and analyzing texts in historical context and lots of practice in doing so. In the process you will be developing your critical thinking and oral and written communication skills.

NEW OBJECTIVES

The readings and assignments in this course are designed to help you

1. to recognize and understand the primary styles and themes of the major literary movements and periods in British literature of the last two(-ish) centuries: romanticism, Victorianism, modernism, postmodernism, postcolonialism;
2. to interpret literary texts and to situate them within these movements and periods (for instance, to take and express a position on which statements or gestures in a literary text fit in with prominent literary styles and values and which seem to resist, qualify, or undermine them);
3. to form and express ideas about the relationships between literary texts and their historical contexts (for instance, to express your sense of how a literary text might take a position in a historical controversy, or might reflect the feelings of a social movement or subculture);
4. to continue your growth as an interpreter of literature, someone who develops solid and sensible interpretations of literary texts and expresses and defends them well with evidence.

The old "objectives" are illustrative, as they show an underdeveloped attempt to work skills and methods into a class built around content goals. The first sentence dispenses with the content goals and, it pains me to say, has very little to do with learning: the content is something the course is going to "give" students; the students will read, write, and comment, but all of this seems to be in the service of being "given" a "broad overview." (When I look at that phrase I think: Was I trying to put them to sleep starting in the first week?) The second and third sentences float virtually free from the first, positing evergreen learning goals—again to be "given" to students—that could be practiced on any literature and are thus not integrally connected to the content in the class. The final sentence, containing everyone's favorite empty phrase—"critical thinking"—amounts to a statement of faith that all of this will (somehow) matter outside the classroom.

The new objectives, in contrast, show more careful thought about the particular kinds of learning—the genuine cognitive transformations—that might happen in a survey. The class is reframed as one in which, rather than being exposed to "major works," students learn to recognize styles and develop ways to talk about relations between literature and historical context. Even the more old-fashioned objectives—knowing what Romanticism is and what it looks like, for instance—is now pitched as a skill students will develop—the ability to recognize and situate—rather than as declarative knowledge. The third and fourth objectives are challenging to meet; so, embodying these objectives in assignments, activities, and assessments required some new, creative thinking and some pretty specialized design. If what I want is for students to make claims about the relations between literary texts and historical contexts, I need to give them practice doing this. This imperative has led me to in-class activities and homework assignments where, for instance, I ask students to read excerpts from parliamentary records about child labor, identify the values and beliefs about childhood that animate the testimony, and then ask them to use these insights to interpret Blake's "Chimney Sweeper" poems, or the first four chapters of *Jane Eyre*. I ask: "How would the depiction of Jane as a child have resonated with the attitudes about childhood evident in the parliamentary testimony?"

Having given students practice in this kind of activity several times, I then give them take-home midterms and finals with questions that call on students to link text and context.

EXAM QUESTIONS FOR INTERPRETING LITERARY TEXTS IN HISTORICAL CONTEXT

1. Read the excerpt from Sarah Stickney Ellis's *The Women of England* (Longman pages 1525–28), then

    1) briefly summarize Ellis's vision of the appropriate social and economic roles and behaviors of men and women, supporting your summary with examples from her text (75–100 words).

2) then select (a) a brief quote from "Goblin Market" and (b) an episode from *Great Expectations*, and, in each case, *explain how the passage or episode engages with the gender norms you identified in Ellis's text*. (In engaging with those norms, the literary text may do a number of things: reiterate them, qualify them, protest them, refute them, complicate them, raise objections, problems, contradictions, tensions). In each case, use *specific* examples from the literary text to support your sense of its engagement with Victorian gender norms (400–500 words).

2. Robert Graves's *Goodbye to All That* is often read as emblematic of a post–First World War disillusionment typical of educated men of his generation—and central to the themes and styles of British modernism. Read the excerpt from Graves's memoir in the *Longman Anthology*, and write an essay of about 750 words that (1) identifies the central conflicts in the text concerning British history, culture, attitudes, and traditions and (2) traces how a set of similar or related conflicts plays out in two of the following modernist or *fin de siecle* texts: *The Waste Land*, "The Withered Arm," the "Nausicaa" chapter of Ulysses, poems by Yeats, Auden, or Spender.

Both of these questions are built specifically on objective 3—situating literature in its historical context. For objective 2, I will likewise offer discussion-board prompts or class-discussion prompts that ask students to identify and discuss points of convergence or dissent among and between literary movements. Again, exam questions will assess the moves students practiced in class or online.

EXAM QUESTIONS ON LITERARY STYLES AND MOVEMENTS

1. Consider the following lines of Wordsworth:
   There was a time when meadow, grove and stream,
   The earth, and every common sight,
   To me did seem
   Apparelled in celestial light,
   The glory and the freshness of a dream.

> It is not now as it hath been of yore;
> Turn wheresoe'er I may
> By night or day,
> The things which I have seen I now can see no more.

    a. What elements of this stanza represent themes, questions, concerns, or problems characteristic of British Romanticism?

    b. In what ways are either the style or the content (preferably both) of this stanza characteristic of Wordsworth? How does it overlap with the concerns of other romantic poets?

2. Consider the following poem by Emily Brontë:

> **Stars**
>
> Ah! why, because the dazzling sun
> Restored our earth to joy
> Have you departed, every one,
> And left a desert sky?
>
> All through the night, your glorious eyes
> Were gazing down in mine,
> And with a full heart's thankful sighs
> I blessed that watch divine!
>
> I was at peace, and drank your beams
> As they were life to me
> And revelled in my changeful dreams
> Like petrel on the sea.
>
> Thought followed thought, star followed star
> Through boundless regions on,
> While one sweet influence, near and far,
> Thrilled through and proved us one.
>
> Why did the morning dawn to break
> So great, so pure a spell,
> And scorch with fire the tranquil cheek
> Where your cool radiance fell?
>
> Blood-red he rose, and arrow-straight
> His fierce beams struck my brow:
> The soul of Nature sprang elate,
> But mine sank sad and low!

> My lids closed down, yet through their veil
> I saw him blazing still;
> And steep in gold the misty dale
> And flash upon the hill.
>
> I turned me to the pillow then
> To call back Night, and see
> Your worlds of solemn light, again
> Throb with my heart and me!
>
> It would not do, the pillow glowed
> And glowed both roof and floor,
> And birds sang loudly in the wood,
> And fresh winds shook the door.
>
> The curtains waved, the wakened flies
> Were murmuring round my room,
> Imprisoned there, till I should rise
> And give them leave to roam.
>
> O Stars and Dreams and Gentle Night;
> O Night and Stars return!
> And hide me from the hostile light
> That does not warm, but burn
>
> That drains the blood of suffering men;
> Drinks tears, instead of dew:
> Let me sleep through his blinding reign,
> And only wake with you!
>
> While Brontë lived and wrote within the Victorian era, most critics believe her sensibility is best described as Romantic. What elements—styles, themes, problems, values, and so on—of Romanticism are visible in the poem? In contrast, what elements of the poem intersect with concerns common to Victorian literature?

In the years since I revised and integrated my British Literature 2 syllabus, I have built up a bank of such questions built around the objectives. I look through these questions periodically during the semester to make sure that I'm preparing students not only for the kind of thought that goes into answering them, but to the specific context that makes them answerable. This is tricky, because, as I've said, I want students largely to set the agenda for discussion. While it would be a rare semester if we did not spend a good hour on Wordsworth, it's conceivable that in a certain semester Question 1 would not be appropriate, and I would have to write a new one that better addresses what we talked about in class. For this reason I have to keep some rough notes on what we talk about and write new exam questions periodically.

I like these questions because they ask students to do things rather than to recall or identify things (though recollection and identifying are involved in the doing); in answering them, students practice their literature-specific skills and show me that they are taking shape. The question remains, though, of the department's content goals. As I indicated in the introduction, I believe that we should put canonical conflicts—and other historic or institutional tensions that animate our classes—before our students. As a result, a few years ago I started sharing with students on the first day of class both the department's goals and my goals, and discussing the difference between them. I project on a screen a detailed articulation of both sets, and I make the document available on Canvas for the students' reference. And at several strategic moments during the semester (i.e., before the midterm and final, or at major thematic shifts), I return to that document to remind students what we are trying to accomplish. My goals are objectives 2–4. The document lists these after breaking down more specifically how the department's goals will be addressed in the class, for example:

Departmental Objectives:
    Familiarity with major writers
    Familiarity with periods, movements, and themes
        Romanticism
        Victorian literature/culture
        Pre-Raphaelites
        Aestheticism/Decadence
        Naturalism
        Modernism
        The "Angry Young Men" and "Kitchen Sink" writers
        Postmodernism
        Postcolonialism
            Themes:
- Democratization and human rights
  (Race, class, gender)
- Imperialism and nationalism
- "Progress" and its relations to science, political history, industrialization, economics, and so on.
- The function of literature and literary writing in modern culture.

The combination of these content goals and my skill-based goals leaves us with a big job for the semester. The class remains challenging and the workload substantial, even as I have trimmed the amount of primary reading over the years to encourage quality rather than quantity of reading. I take the goal of recognizing styles and movements seriously; introduce movements and historical contexts via mini-lectures and reading (the section introductions in the anthology); and manage discussion and class activities to foreground the work of recognizing the unities and tensions within literary movements and historical moments. This class typically gets good reviews from students. As I discuss in the next chapter, student evaluations express their level of satisfaction with the class, not their learning; but the useful piece of information student surveys give me is that that, despite the workload, the class does not seem impossible to them. And a majority of the students meet my objectives, based on what I see on exams and the formal essays they write. This being the real world, only a handful do so resoundingly well; in a majority I see evidence of progress and a basic grasp of what it means to think about literature within the contexts of history and literary history. And some percentage—between 5 and 20 percent in any semester—do not meet my goals.

Conclusion

Having and communicating good objectives gives you and the students a sense of purpose that can carry you through the inevitable season of overwork and fatigue that lies ahead. During course design, as well, clear objectives simplify difficult decisions about whether to include texts to which we have personal commitments. If you've adopted good, student-centered learning goals, and you really believe in them, then all further course planning should flow from them, including choice, number, and sequence of texts. We can achieve more learning with less reading, using the space opened up to go deeper into analysis, carefully talk through intellectual skills, and give more practice and more targeted feedback. I used to have students read a substantial chunk of Wordsworth and Coleridge's *Lyrical Ballads* in the survey; I did so on the (unarticulated) belief that reading a lot is good for students; the more they read, the better, I thought. This was before I read *My Freshman Year* or really started thinking well about course objectives. "Reading a lot" is an activity, not a learning goal. And, as I have argued earlier, assigning unmanageable amounts of reading is an invitation to student disengagement and the worst sorts of corner-cutting (i.e., "Master Plots.")

Now I know exactly why I've placed everything on the syllabus exactly where it is. I start a course on Virginia Woolf not at Woolf's beginnings but with *To the Lighthouse*, because "Become adept at reading the fiction of Virginia Woolf" and "Be able to describe and analyze Woolf's fictional techniques" are my learning goals; *To the Lighthouse* best typifies her mature style and—because it is stylistically unified, unlike *Mrs. Dalloway*—is an easier text for students to manage as they are learning what Woolf is up to. In the survey, I assign Wordsworth's "My Heart Leaps Up" early on because it's simple and it neatly expresses the Romantic obsession with human somatic/intellectual/spiritual responses to nature: "My heart leaps when I behold / A rainbow in the sky." I assign "Tintern Abbey" alongside Shelley's "Mont Blanc" a bit later, so that students can apply the skills and context they're accruing in order to follow as this dynamic is played out at length, and in detail, by two poets with similar preoccupations but different views of their finer points. The simple first poem becomes an entry point to these more difficult works, which appear a week or so later. This sequencing rehearses the process of developing advanced literacy: early building blocks establish the knowledge base that enables comprehension of more complex texts.

In any class, if I have set up the sequence with learning goals in mind, I can then hold the reins lightly, leaving it up to students to let me and each other know, in discussion-board posts and in the classroom, what speaks to them, perplexes them, and riles them in the reading. We pursue the threads they choose. In real time, in the classroom, it's up to me to pull us into metacognition—to drill down on how we're making meaning—and to turn the discussion to how texts take part in dialogues and engage with the broader world. In preparing, day to day, all I need do to keep us on track is look frequently to the learning goals—and place them before students, as well—so that we can all see where we are going.

5 MANAGING RELATIONSHIPS

Against *Dead Poets Society*

Years ago, I taught a class called "Introduction to English Studies." The class was required of majors and was predicated on a curricular experiment, which predated my arrival, in integrating the subdisciplines of literature, rhetoric, English education, and linguistics into a single, coherent major. It dedicated discreet units to each subdiscipline, foregrounding the theoretical questions and social purposes they shared and introducing students to their distinct modes of inquiry. Various contingencies led to the demise of this "English Studies" model in my department, but it made for an interesting course, where one could see students envisioning themselves as different kinds of intellectuals and professionals. Once, as part of the education unit, I had students watch the film *Dead Poets Society*, intending to have us probe some of its idealistic, romantic notions about teaching literature—notions which undergird the pedagogy of John Keating, its hero-teacher character (played by Robin Williams).

This unit held two surprises for me: (1) students were quite reluctant to critique the film's romantic vision of English teaching—which is depicted as inspiring spiritual passions and a skeptical questioning of authority. Among other signs of this film's sticky ideological weight: we had just finished a unit demystifying the canon, and students claimed—vigorously and erroneously—that the Keating character is an insurgent, anti-canonical teacher, despite the fact that the literary texts he references are all mid-century warhorses, "Thoureau, Shelley, Whitman, the Biggies." (2) All but one student in this class of twenty-two had already seen the film. This was the year 2001 or 2002; *Dead Poets Society* came out in 1989, when these students were six years old, and, while it grossed $95 million, that wasn't enough to make it into the top ten in 1989. It struck me as extremely unusual that this admittedly small sample of young Hoosiers had seen this successful but less than ubiquitous film. When I suggested that there might be something profound at work in this moment—that is, that seeing this film had played a role in their becoming English majors, had helped to shape or reinforce their ideas about English teaching—they were just as reluctant to take that road as they were to problematize the film's vision of the teacher as inspirer of romantic selfhood. I will not rehearse the plot of *Dead Poets Society* (you're an English teacher! You've seen it!), but it is noteworthy how the film ends: students of the now-fired Keaton bravely stand on their chairs—reprising an exercise in "looking at things in a different way" Keating had led earlier in the film—and intone "Captain my captain" to express their solidarity with him, as stirring music swells and he leaves the classroom.

This anecdote speaks to the issues I want to address in this chapter: our visions of ourselves as teachers and the relationships with students that these visions entail. I trust I am not the only person to have sometimes indulged in idealistic fantasies about the influence I might have on students or the reverence my teaching might inspire. And part of me is tempted to say that films like *Dead Poets Society* are relatively harmless: if their cartoon visions of the hero-teacher inspire some young people to pursue English teaching as a career, perhaps that's not an entirely bad thing; in any event, the real world will cure them of their romantic visions soon enough.

Perhaps. But becoming the most effective literature teacher you can be is ultimately going to mean losing such idealistic visions and settling on a more grounded understanding of the relationships between teachers and students. This is where *Dead Poets Society* goes dangerously wrong, for in the film Keating has, in fact, taught students not to think for themselves—not to think, at all, really—but to feel and act like him, and to revere him for it. As Kevin Dettmar noted in a brilliant takedown of the film and its implications for the "crisis in the humanities":

> For all the talk of students "finding their own voice," however, Keating actually allows his students very little opportunity for original thought. It's a freedom often preached but never realized . . . . Even when the students reprise this desktop posture at the film's close, in a gesture of schoolboy disobedience (or obedience to Keating), we realize that while the boys are marching to a different drum, it's Keating's drum.[1]

While Dettmar emphasizes the anti-intellectualism of Keating's teaching (and the student's learning), which denigrates analysis in favor of passion, what troubles me most in the film, and particularly in its ending, is its cult-of-personality dynamic. To the future teacher, what *Dead Poets Society* seems to promise is a future filled with student adulation, devotion, and loyalty—gas to inflate the balloon of the teacher's ego.

Bringing this balloon back to the ground is essential precisely because our egos are unavoidably tied up in our teaching lives. If we care enough to want to be good teachers, our sense of self-efficacy will hinge on our sense of success or failure in the classroom. We will have our feet on the ground—be living in the real world—only if this sense of self-efficacy comes not from whether students like us but from the degrees to which they are meeting our learning objectives. Still, the many ways in which students respond to us are involved: education is a social event; teacher-student relationships are a series of social exchanges. Teaching is social work in this literal sense: it (re)produces society and aims at social good. Unless you are lecturing to 250 students in an auditorium (in which case you are probably not reading this book), your work entails almost daily, reasonably intense interpersonal contact with students. And we are human beings: as members of the most social of species, we want to be liked and respected, for people to think we are doing a good job. The desire for applause is human; but in the classroom, pursuing it is a subversion of the mission. Having students admire us is not a learning outcome, though it may serve as a means to the higher end of facilitating student learning. And "facilitating student learning" is the definition of teaching.

Becoming a mature and optimally effective teacher entails not ignoring our desire to be liked but subordinating it to these higher goals. To borrow a psychoanalytic phrase, the mature teacher relativizes the ego, recognizing its wants but subordinating them, day by day, to the mission. We recognize and accept the pleasure of being liked and admired by students, when it comes; we recognize and accept the sting of being disliked or dismissed by students, when *it* comes. We accept all this as part and parcel of the business we're in, which (if you accept my argument in this book) is the business of placing students in a position to acquire the skills of advanced reading comprehension and advanced literacy, coaching them in the practice of methods, and assessing their progress. Students can do well at these things and not like us or our classes; and they can do poorly at them and admire us and our classes. Successful teaching is something else, consisting in how well our students have learned, measured by how many meet the objectives we set for them. We must strive for balance, taking pleasure in our cordial relations with students, putting our more difficult interactions in perspective, but finding our deepest affirmation in the sense that we are doing all we can to put the most students in the best positions to learn.

What Am I to You?

Teacher-student dynamics *can* produce inflations of ego of the John Keating sort, and they can provoke similarly intense attachments, including those that result in sexual or romantic relationships. I started college near the end of the era in which student-professor relationships were noteworthy but not uncommon, and when professors would serve alcohol to students at celebratory end-of-semester parties. Universities have largely adopted policies that limit or ban these activities nowadays, and today I find myself very much the conservative, even the prude, on these questions. But we need not probe the most profound and cringe-inducing questions about sex and power relations in student-faculty romances to see that what is at stake, fundamentally, is an understanding of the teacher's role, and the priorities and obligations that role entails.

The teacher-student relationship is complex and multiple: it is a social and interpersonal relationship; it is a professional relationship—analogous to, though different from, those of doctors, lawyers, or accountants to patients and clients, similarly undergirded by professional regimes of credentialing and authority. And like those, it is also an economic relationship—a complicated one, not reducible to fee-for-service or (worse) pay-for-product but not innocent of the financial exchanges that make it possible. In understanding of our role we need to acknowledge all of these aspects. In the interpersonal realm, we need to be kind, to care whether our students thrive, and to show, as appropriate to the goal of student learning, strictness, flexibility, firmness, compassion, pride in their success, and many other postures. As professionals, we should be confident in both our knowledge of subject matter and our pedagogical practices—confident, in short, that we know more than the students do about these things, but willing to explain and justify our choices in order to help a student learn. As economic actors, we must recognize that our salaries and positions oblige us to bring steady energy and commitment to our work, which includes doing all we can to put all of our students in the best position to learn.

Perhaps the best way to understand the teacher-student relationship is to start with what it *is not*. And one thing a student is not is *your friend*. I know some of my colleagues will disagree. And I recognize that this is more complicated with graduate students, whom we may be appropriately mentoring not only for intellectual preparation but on the professional habitus of academic life. But the difference between a student and a friend is—or should be—that a friendship entails mutual affection and support. Friends like each other, and make that known, and give each other the help and support that the other needs within the (usually unstated) terms of the friendship. Giving and receiving flow mutually and freely and—if it's the healthiest sort of friendship—more or less equally. These are the obligations and benefits of friendship.

But this is not how the teaching relationship works. In this relationship, most of the obligation and most of the giving is on the teacher's side. We give: time preparing class, careful attention to student progress and setbacks; extra help and engagement on learning matters with those who want or need it; careful, fair evaluation of student performance. Our obligation is to do all this to the best of our ability. In return for this, we get paid. Student obligations to us are much more minimal and are simple matters of social and professional decorum; we are right to expect from them attention and respectful interaction. (We may not always get them, of course, but we can expect them and, if we are not getting them, alert students that they are not playing by the social rules of higher education.) But we have no right to look to students for affection, support, or self-affirmation: if we are seeking these from our students, we are on dangerous ground. That doesn't mean that these feelings will not sometimes flow our way from students, or that we are not allowed to enjoy them. But we cannot actively seek them out, because doing so is likely to become an obstacle to our professional obligations.

I am not at all suggesting that we should act as cold fish toward our students. I like my students (usually!). When they're in my classes or otherwise in my professional ken, I care about them, worry about them, cheer on their successes, and empathize when their lives get messy and painful. I feel affection for them. And in my interactions, I show the interest and engagement that I expect from them, and more: I show care, especially when a student is struggling and is upset and wants help. The chance of a good outcome in that situation will be low if I can't show the student that I care and that I want the student to do well. Really, it would not be going too far to say I love the students, if love is understood to be an action verb, and understood precisely as in the injunction to "Love thy neighbor." I am friendly. But I am not their friend, because being friends implies obligations on their part that are—and need to be—absent. The teacher-student relationship is already complex enough, with its a mix of the social, the professional, and the economic: we can do no good toward the educational mission by imposing, consciously or unconsciously, obligations of support or affection upon the students.

We can integrate our multiple identities as teachers in a way that mobilizes our authority without inflating our egos, getting inappropriate, or oppressing our students if we replace the model of the teacher as *hero* with that of the teacher as *helper*. Education can save lives, and it does build lives, but this saving and building is the work not of teachers but of students, making the most of the institutions in which they find themselves. On a day-to-day basis, our job is to help students to learn, and in that process to help them create the selves, lives, and futures they desire. This is a humbler remit than that of saving souls or fomenting revolution, but it is more realistic and no less noble. It also helps to reduce some of the pressure. In our teaching missions, our job is to give help—the best help we can. That is all we owe our students. If we can reframe the teaching identity around this notion of help, we can build our sense of self-efficacy on the quality of the help we give. Our personal interactions with students, with the real emotional freight they carry, become means to the end of this help. In this framework an uncomfortable conversation with a student about a low grade, or an attendance problem, or even disinterest, inattention, or disrespect ceases to be an indictment of the student or ourselves. We can recognize the seductive nature of student admiration but channel it to fuel the student's learning rather than to inflate our egos. Under the figure of the helper, we balance and orchestrate our personal, professional, and economic roles, granting precedence to the professional as the source of the unique help we offer.

This helper stance is capacious and flexible enough to accommodate a wide range of individual styles and methods, and it need not compromise our sense of authority or our desire to grant agency to the students. As I've made clear, I like to let students determine substantially the content and direction of interpretive discussions while maintaining a firm hold on—and a sharp eye on—the learning objectives toward which these discussions are leading. These dynamics are situational, depending on the exact nature of the course (students have less agency in my introduction to literary analysis, because the methods-based goals are so numerous and are the course's sole reason for being), and I am free to adapt them in mid-stream if necessary. But overall I strive for my classes to occupy a middle ground between the extremes of the banking model—where the teacher is seen as the source of knowledge—and some of the extremes of the student-centered classroom (e.g., self-grading). The construction of knowledge—both declarative content knowledge and strategic or procedural knowledge, realized in interpretive methods—is a collaborative and social process but one whose management is my responsibility. Knapp aptly expresses my understanding, a sense that

> a good teacher, like a therapist, is usually also a leader who is part of a system and who must include a necessary systemic interaction between leader and followers. By virtue of his or her credentials and institutional authority, this leader is, ideally, both insistent and nurturing, both representative of the potential level of the students' growing expertise and an outsider who occasionally must enforce norms and institutional values.[2]

My classroom is democratic in that it is a space where interests get negotiated in dialogue, and where my and students' different roles in the system that Knapp describes are made explicit. Leading a class means not constantly imposing your interests but presiding over this negotiation. My vision may posit the teacher as a more robust leader than yours, but it avoids the risk of creating a teacher-centered classroom as long as our leadership is directed toward help. The role of the helper, for me, orchestrates the social, professional, and economic relationships we have with students. The professional stance subsumes the others and is directed not toward "shaping young minds"—to evoke the Pygmalion-esque platitude—but toward helping minds shape themselves.

What Are You to Me? Student Feedback

I admit: it is relatively easy for me to say all of these things, from a tenured position and with more than twenty years in college classrooms behind me. When I started, I wanted students to like me more than is ideal; praise from students served as gas to inflate the ego. Student disinterest or rudeness stayed with me for days and kept me up at night. All of this is normal, I think, if we care enough about our work. But maturing as a teacher means putting these things in perspective. I am proud to say that I now care a good deal less whether students like me and—better still—that this emotional adjustment has allowed me to become better at articulating learning goals and keeping track of student progress.

To the career-long work of finding and maintaining this balance, the use of student surveys to evaluate teaching is generally not helpful. Different institutions and departments use student evaluations in different ways: some have heeded the research, which argues that student feedback can be used formatively to improve teaching but should not be a decisive element in personnel decisions, while others have not.[3] Individual teachers, of course, are at the mercy of their local practices. But even if student evaluations are appropriately contextualized alongside teaching portfolios, self-assessment, and peer reviews, as long as departments use them, they will weigh emotionally on teachers. There is no way to contravene the desire for praise or—more potently—the desire for respect from one's peers, so a teacher's vulnerability is understandably triggered when department chairs or personnel committees see negative student evaluations. While there is a copious and somewhat fractious literature on the usefulness of student teaching evaluations, many studies have reiterated the findings of Dowell and Neal from 1982: "student ratings are inaccurate indicators of student learning and therefore are best regarded as indicators of consumer satisfaction."[4] Consumer satisfaction is not a bad thing, and certainly, for some students, not unrelated to learning. But teachers and departments would do well to accept the seemingly obvious fact that what student evaluations measure is whether students liked a class and/or liked the teacher. It's nice when students like a class, but "liking a class" is no more a learning outcome than liking a teacher. As bell hooks wisely noted decades ago, students may not recognize the value of a course until well after it has ended and the student surveys have been filed.[5] And in classes whose learning objectives include getting students to process difficult material or reconsider long-held assumptions, "consumer satisfaction" may in fact counter-indicate learning.

I am going to be honest: getting negative student evaluations still bothers me. I got some in the last semester before this writing, with scores among the lowest I've received and a fairly blunt rejection, from about a third of the students, of a content experiment that they did not like. This was the early-twentieth-century literature course focused solely on the years 1936–9, in which I used the Wiki Project discussed in Chapter 3. Reading the course content focused on this narrow slice of time, I saw tremendous depth and detail; they saw a lot of repetition of the same issues. Fair enough, but comments like, "I don't understand why a teacher who has been teaching for all this time still has to do an 'experimental class'" prompted in me, what shall I call it? RAGE. So what I'm saying here is not "Don't let it bother you." It's more like: "Don't let it bother you *too much*." More specifically, do not fall into the trap of treating student surveys as a major indicator of your success as a teacher—even if, unfortunately, your department does fall into that trap. I have two specific suggestions for placing student evaluations in their proper perspective: (1) evaluate yourself, using your professional judgment; (2) find ways of getting more useful student feedback.

Meaningful Information on Our Performance

The first of these—self-evaluation—is absolutely essential to good teaching; we all know this, but our busy lives frequently keep us from following through on it. This is why one of the evergreen questions that committees ask of job candidates is: "Tell me something you tried in a class that didn't go well, and what you did to adjust." The committee is looking for concrete evidence that you are a so-called reflective teacher. Committees rightly view this disposition as essential. Unfortunately no one teaches us how to be reflective teachers, so we are often left stewing in scattered fashion about class periods that did not seem to go well or about stray insults on student evaluations.

Let me suggest that the means to evaluate our teaching is already at our fingertips, in the form of the learning goals we have set up for our classes. If we view our mission in any individual class as having as many students as possible meet the learning goals—and if the goals are specific and observable—our (virtual) gradebooks should indicate how well students met the goals. Indeed, if we have an integrated course design, as I explained in the last chapter, we should be able to tell how many students met our objectives in fine detail. (E.g., if the midterm exam is meant to measure whether students are understanding theory and applying theoretical concepts: how many passed it? How many had to take it a second time? How many were deploying theory in the final paper?) Tuning into these details should indicate what percentage of students met our goals—certainly the most profound measure of our success.

But this cannot be the only standard on which we evaluate ourselves because, again, we're in the real world here, and whether students meet our goals is not entirely—sometimes not even substantially—within our control. We can design lucid, achievable objectives and clear, strategically brilliant activities, prepare well for class, and grade in a timely fashion, only to find that in this particular class the race has not gone to the swift, that time and chance hath happened to us—in the form of students too overburdened or unwell or disinterested, or a thousand other things, to do their work consistently and well. Students do the learning: we do our best to put them in a position to learn. In cases where they haven't learned, our duty is to figure out where our part in it lies and what we could have done differently, if anything.

So we look back to what we have done. Is the course well-designed? Did the assignments give practice in the skills and dispositions we want students to develop? (Assignments do sometimes go wrong, and old assignments sometimes wear out their usefulness as students change.) And we recall: What did we do when things started going wrong? Did we reach out to students who weren't doing well? Did we take steps to redirect negative energies in the class dynamic? Did we clarify objectives, directions, and so on? Was the syllabus overloaded: Were we trying to do too much? Were there moments where a well-placed intervention might have made a difference, and we were too busy or otherwise unmindful to make it happen? In the real world, we are going to make mistakes, every semester, many of them. We do not have to dwell on them, but we need to do the work of recognizing them and making adjustments, where adjustments are possible. In this self-evaluation, what students say on evaluations may play a small part, but the project needs to be focused by two questions: How did my students do on my learning objectives? And what, if anything, could I have done that might have helped improve their performance?

I have the good fortune of working in a department where we are required to do this kind of self-analysis on an annual basis as part of our annual salary review. This analysis does, however, focus too much on student evaluations—the instructions ask us to summarize the evaluation scores and reflect *on the evaluations*. Early in my career, I stewed about these student surveys, dedicating space in my reflections to addressing individual negative comments from within evaluation sets that were overwhelmingly positive. I am grateful to a senior colleague who, during the promotion and tenure process, advised me to talk more, in making my case in personnel documents, about my goals and methods and why I believed I was achieving them. This advice became my formula for self-analysis, and helped me to relativize the student surveys. Now I read them, and I think a bit about every critique they contain. Some critiques are useful, as when a number of students, a few years ago, said they did not understand the point of an assignment. Regardless of the fact that this point was spelled out in documents, it hadn't gotten through to a substantial number of students. This means the document has to be changed and/or I need different strategies to communicate the purpose of this assignment. But such valuable critiques, alongside many less valuable ones, are small data points, and I do not let them unduly influence my sense of self-efficacy. Whether your department requires this kind of exercise or not, I would argue that doing it—perhaps less formally but no less thoroughly—is essential to the lifelong effort of being a truly "reflective teacher."

Still, the self-assessment I have been describing here is all summative—it takes place after the class is over and is directed toward building on strengths and adapting to problems in future courses. None of this is of any use to the students in the class which has just ended. What would have been valuable to them—and to your well-being and success during the semester—is formative self-assessment, which takes place as the semester unfolds, and in which students can play a much more useful and important part. I credit Stephen Brookfield—whose *The Skillful Teacher* has played a major role in transforming my teaching—for convincing me that we need to take steps *beyond* grading assignments and reading student social cues to determine how our teaching is landing with the students.[6] Brookfield uses something he calls (somewhat portentously) a critical incident questionnaire (CIQ) to register what has hit home with students and what hasn't. The CIQ is handed out to students at the end of each week; they immediately fill it out and return it. I have adapted Brookfield's design, and I sometimes (though not often) skip a week here or there. But I have found the surveys remarkably useful in giving me a finer-grained sense of how students are responding than I can get simply by monitoring their grades and reading their affect.

STUDENT RESPONSE QUESTIONNAIRE

1. At what point in this week have you felt most interested, engaged, or excited?
2. At what point in this week have you felt most bored or disinterested?
3. At what point this week were you most aware that you were learning?
4. At what point this week did you feel confused or frustrated?
5. What activity for this week was most useful?
6. What activity this week was least useful?
7. What do you know now that you didn't know last week?
8. What can you do now that you couldn't do last week?

If there are any terms, concepts, or ideas that you are struggling to understand, please indicate them here.

At the start of the semester, I usually provide a short summary of the week's activities at the top of the sheet to jog students' memory, as in this summary from British Literature 2 during a *Jane Eyre* week:

2/28 Mini-lecture/discussion on Jane's conflicting values and the book's structure
    Teacher-led close reading of "bed-fire" passage and "aching heart" passage
    All-group discussion of Rochester's character and Jane's choice

>   Small-group activity: identify passages to take Jane's "inventory"
>   Reading *Jane Eyre*
>   Writing discussion board post

3/2 Introduction of Midterm take-home section; brief discussion of exam
>   All-group discussion of *Jane Eyre*'s conclusion: Rochester versus St. John; is Jane really free at the end?
>   > gothic elements; symbolism
>   > Excerpt from 1844 *Jane Eyre* review
>   > Reading *Jane Eyre*
>   > Writing discussion board post.

Near the midway point of the semester I will stop providing these summaries and prompt the students to be conscious of these "critical incidents" as they happen. I do this because, once students get into the rhythm of doing these surveys week after week, their effort will diminish and they will start to treat the summaries—which are meant as memory-joggers—as a menu to pick from as they answer the questions. I give students about five minutes to fill these out, so they can't write very much. This also means that I can read them quickly and register anything that needs immediate attention. Question 4—asking when students have felt confused or frustrated, and the final question—asking students to identify areas of confusion—are particularly useful in this way. Last year, for example, I carefully designed a series of mini-lectures and handouts when several students reported that they needed some help getting a basic understanding of socialism and fascism.

But these surveys are useful in a number of other ways. Students being excited is not a learning outcome—and students being bored does not necessarily mean they are not learning—but it is nonetheless good to know when these things are happening. Again, a student's sense that an activity is useful, or not, is not the final word (that comes with more formal assessments), but these small data points can help you make decisions about revising your syllabus in the future, making small adjustments in the short term, or simply discussing learning activities and their purposes with the students—discussions that spur metacognition. Questions 7 and 8—asking specifically what knowledge or skills students believe they are picking up—are more clearly directed toward the sorts of learning objectives I value, although sometimes students rightly note that question 8 will not be applicable every week. But the overall value of these surveys is not a scientific sense of what students are learning but a real-time sense of how the class feels to them, at a point when you can still do something about it. While formal assessments should show you whether students are learning, these surveys can help point you to why they are, or aren't, meeting your objectives, or send up early warnings that you need to make adjustments. They give students a weekly opportunity to let you know if something is not working. If a majority of students raise the same flag, you now have an opportunity to respond—whether that means changing an assignment or activity or doing something to clarify your instructions.

Beyond this actionable feedback, these surveys have two practical effects that may be more profound: they communicate to my students that I care about their learning and am constantly working to monitor it; and they prompt students to be aware of their own learning, pushing them toward the holy grail of metacognition. The surveys make clear that this is not the sort of under-designed literature class I took repeatedly as a student and taught early in my career—the standard lit class where we read a bunch of books, discuss them, and write some papers, all in the vague, unarticulated faith that these activities are good for us. In tandem with my precise objectives and my (sometimes annoying, to students) insistence on revisiting them frequently, the surveys make clear that we have specific places we are trying to get as thinkers and that, as the leader in this collaborative venture, I am taking stock of whether we're getting there. Learning research suggests that students are motivated when content is appropriately challenging and they are invested in learning and doing well: they are not motivated when they are bored or when content is too difficult for them. As Ambrose et al. suggest, the three major contributors to student motivation are an expectation of success, a supportive environment, and a valued goal. The weekly questionnaires act on all of these factors, communicating your investment in students' success and giving them a chance to let you know if they are struggling or don't see the value in what they are doing.[7]

I began this book by insisting that failure is inescapable in the work we do, and that we can only survive as teachers of literature if we accept the inevitability of small failures and consciously turn them toward future learning, for ourselves and our students. By seeking regular feedback, you effectively go in search of small failures, but also small successes, that would otherwise be invisible to you. The point of these student surveys is to create an instrument that—like the seismographs in art museum galleries—registers small tremors that are indetectable without the instrument. These tremors are the sparks of student excitement or the grating of student frustration that characterize the learning experience day by day. Their use, like everything I have advocated in this book, is grounded on the indisputable consensus that learning is a positive change in students brought about by *them*; learning is something that students *do*; and our job is to do everything we can to put them in a position to do it.

APPENDIX 1
ENGAGING STUDENTS IN CRITICISM AND THEORY

"Seeing criticism (and critical debate) as a distraction from the 'primary' experience of literature itself, the standard story implies that the business of teaching is basically simple: Just put the student in front of a good book, provide teachers who are encouraging and helpful, and the rest will presumably take care of itself."
—**GERALD GRAFF,** "Disliking Books at an Early Age"[1]

In "Disliking Books at an Early Age," Gerald Graff tells the compelling story of how being given a glimpse of critical arguments made reading literature fun for him, for the first time. Graff recounts his acculturation in a tough, mixed-class neighborhood in Chicago, where being a bookworm increased one's odds of being beaten up, and his aimless drift into the liberal arts, where he could not quite see the point of reading the serious books that bored him. Then a professor suggested he write a paper about debates over the second half of *Huckleberry Finn*, which some critics find to undermine the novel's antislavery message; the professor gave him essays on the novel by Ernest Hemingway, T. S. Eliot, Lionel Trilling, and Leo Marx. From reading these essays, Graff learned that there is something at stake in books, that arguing about them is a valid intellectual exercise and is interesting, to boot. This account frames Graff's influential assertion that, though literary education has historically "protected" students from critical debates, what we have actually been teaching students in literature classes all along is "not literature but criticism, or literature as it is filtered through a grid of analysis, interpretation, and theory." Criticism, Graff writes, "is the language students are expected to speak and are punished for not speaking well."[2] We should embrace this reality, Graff argues, and engage students by "teaching the conflicts" and explicitly inviting them into critical debates.

Graff's *Beyond the Culture Wars*, which includes "Disliking Books," came out thirty years ago and was at the height of its influence while I was in graduate school. I accepted its implication that students will only be able to write viable interpretive arguments if they have read them and thus know the kinds of moves interpreters make and what is at stake in their arguments. What Graff did not address at the time was how difficult it is for students to read literary criticism or exactly how literature professors might help students to do it productively.[3] Today, while I still have a few colleagues who shelter students, especially beginners, from criticism and theory, I find that most of us are Graffites, committed to engaging students in disciplinary ways of thinking and writing.[4] And many of my colleagues do so more broadly and inventively than Graff's model imagines, given its tight focus on literary criticism. Producing criticism, after all, may be the dominant way literature experts write and think, but it is not the only way: we also write literary history, edit and annotate texts, uncover new primary works and interpret them provisionally, and read, vet, argue with, and propose new frameworks for understanding the literature and culture we study.

All of these activities are apt arenas for helping students develop advanced reading comprehension and advanced literacy—the complex of skills, dispositions, and habits of mind that this book posits as the core of a practical mission for teaching literature. Indeed: reading and understanding literary criticism and theory are powerful measures of advanced reading comprehension. And constructing a sufficient intellectual context to use criticism successfully, contextualize and annotate a primary text, or engage in literary-historical debates are measures of advanced literacy as I have defined it: a skill set that allows you to assemble the content knowledge you need to function in any setting.

Challenges and Strategies

But getting students to succeed in this complex, high-level work requires, as always, that we face realities, recognizing that many students will not enter our classes equipped to decode or interpret literary criticism or theory. We need to teach them to read it. As with other complex tasks that call on multiple skills, we need to delineate the intellectual moves involved in working with criticism and theory: first, so that *we* know what they are (rather than performing them unconsciously) and second so that students can become aware of them and can recognize and strategize about the sources of their struggles. We need to get engaged early on this challenging work, see whether they are succeeding, and intervene when they are not.

In an upper-level class, low-stakes writing is a good diagnostic. Depending on exactly how and where literary criticism or theory fits into your class, I would assign complex critical texts pretty early—certainly before midterm—using writing prompts, discussion questions, and group activities that will suss out how students are faring. I leave space and time—in the classroom, in the office, and via email or the course management platform—for instruction tailored to the whole group, to small groups, or to individual students. I personally have never had an undergraduate class where students could read complex theory without considerable difficulty; so I allow class time for struggling through essays or excerpts and use assignments that move students through the basic skills entailed in reading theory (see the "Analyzing Critical Essays Worksheet" activity and the homeworks on specific critical essays). I use problem-solving or comprehension-based questions as homework prompts and at the start and finish of class periods. And I assign students to group work in class directed toward clarifying major points in critical and theoretical texts.

For instance, a session on Walter Benjamin's "The Work of Art in the Age of Mechanical Reproduction" will begin and end with this question: "What are the positive potentials of the new media of cinema and mass newspapers for Benjamin, and what are their negative potentials?" In a prior class meeting, just before students read such a text, I will often do a mini-lecture providing a broad framework (for instance, describing the philosophical tradition or theoretical argument the essay is taking part in), and offer definitions to scaffold the reading. In the case of "The Work of Art in the Age of Mechanical Reproduction," I would speak for about ten minutes, beginning with who Benjamin was and when he was writing. I would then move on to Benjamin's fundamental questions in the essay: how had the ways Westerners consume art, narrative, and news changed in the late nineteenth and early twentieth centuries? What influence did these changes have on how we perceive the world? And what were the possible political effects of these changes—how might they advance or detract from the social purposes of art, human freedom, democratic governance, and equality? I would then provide a quick laundry list of the historic changes Benjamin is concerned with, which he generalizes under the term "Mechanical Reproduction." And I would finish with my question about Benjamin's conclusions on positive and negative potentials, so that students have a broad but clear framework for what the essay is going to be about. This is a standard scaffolding move, designed to get students to a basic level of comprehension quickly, so that they do not need to expend labor and cognitive load figuring out the essay's basic purpose but instead can go in search of its particular insights.

In the ensuing class, I would be ready to work with students in getting our hands dirty with the details of the essay—knowing that students will have made some basic comprehension errors (and that some debate about basic intentions in Benjamin's essay persists). I would enter the classroom with a pretty clear list in my head of what elements of the essay I want students to understand clearly, and we would work deliberately toward clarifying those points. Frequently, I break students into groups, with specific discussion questions designed to illuminate specific concepts, sometimes with each group given a topic or a discrete section of the essay. Given the recursivity and inductive structure of Benjamin's essay, for instance, it would work best to have students trace topics across its sections. It would be useful, then, to assign one group to follow his statements about tradition; one group to define "aura" and its importance; one group to talk about ways that Benjamin feels audiences have been empowered by mechanical reproduction; and a group to work on the binary of contemplation/distraction. I would leave a good deal of time for debriefing and airing out conclusions and problems. I would recognize that this discussion may need to stretch to a second class, or that I may have to write an email clarifying a point or two more fully.

What should be clear here is that reading a very complex essay well with students takes time and vigorous, close, collaborative work. The reward is that some students will be growing rapidly in their advanced reading comprehension. I believe the learning in such situations is real and intense; though some students will not grasp all or most of what's happening, they will—if you keep evoking their metacognition—be realizing where the problems lay and how they might change their approach. The best students often display rapid, visible, and gratifying growth through this sort of work. That is why I think it is worth doing, particularly in upper-level classes, where a greater percentage of the students will be primed to benefit. But it will only work if you give it time, which often means cutting out some primary texts or other, favored activities.

As with all pedagogical decisions, this one should flow from your objectives, which is why, if what I'm mainly interested in is providing students with a theoretical concept for application to primary texts, I'll lecture on it instead of having students read the actual theory, particularly in a lower-level class. This strategy is exemplified in my discussion of teaching postcoloniality in a British Literature Survey, discussed in Chapter 3. There, I would not assign students to read Homi Bhabha's "Of Mimicry and Man," but would rather do a mini-lecture on mimicry and hybridity, name-checking Bhabha and other critics but emphasizing simplified but applicable definitions of terms. In film class, I do ten minutes on Laura Mulvey's "Visual Pleasure and Narrative Cinema," using quotations to exemplify Mulvey's argument that women, in Hollywood cinema, are historically objects of the male gaze rather than subjects and agents; I do not force my students—many of them aspiring filmmakers, some reading-phobic to begin with—to wrestle with the Lacanian foundations of Mulvey's text.

Working with Academic Prose

When you do assign criticism or theory in lower-level classes, many students will need fundamental practice and instruction on reading academic prose. As Sherry

Lee Linkon notes, academic prose style and vocabulary are barriers to students, but so is their relative inexposure to the rhetorical strategies and structures of academic writing.[5] So teaching such fundamentals includes helping students recognize the challenges specific to these kinds of writing and introducing them to their genre conventions.

Teaching students to read academic prose is like teaching them to read anything that is initially difficult: they must learn to recognize the difficulty when it starts, discern what's causing it, and respond tactically. Obviously, if vocabulary is causing the difficulty, the answer is to look up the meaning of words; we have all, I trust, suffered through to the point of acceptance that students infrequently do this. Nonetheless we should keep trying, and homeworks or short writing prompts geared to comprehension will encourage some students to look up unfamiliar words and concepts. The length and complexity of sentences in academic prose is another barrier: as with poetry (frequently), students need to keep track of where they are in a complex, compound sentence, remain grounded in the sentence's fundamental grammar (subject/verb/object), and suspend full comprehension while key elements fall into place.

A related problem in academic prose lies in its dialogic nature: academic writers are almost constantly integrating the ideas of others into their work, to contextualize, support, qualify, build on, and argue with them. The process of integrating others' ideas produces complex sentences with lots of subordination and long, information-rich paragraphs. As a result, students frequently misrecognize an idea that the author is summarizing or paraphrasing—for the purpose of refuting it or qualifying it—as the author's own idea. Consider this paragraph from theorist and critic Rita Felski:

> Finally, women are identified with repetition via consumption. For Marxist scholars of the everyday, commodification is its paramount feature, evident in ever greater standardization and sameness. As the primary symbols and victims of consumer culture, women take on the repetitive features of the objects that they buy. Femininity is formed through mass production and mass reproduction, disseminated through endless images of female glamour and female domesticity. Women become the primary emblem of an inauthentic everyday life marked by the empty homogenous time of mass consumption.[6]

Everything Felski says in this paragraph has been flagged as the thinking of "Marxist scholars," but students new to this sort of material may not register that Felski is not expressing these ideas herself but holding them up for our review. This can be confusing, because most of Felski's sentences are declarative sentences that don't carry this framing through any explicit internal cues: the framing lies outside most of the sentences, in previous context; and building up this context, and keeping it straight, will tax a student's cognitive load. The clearest indication of the framing that makes Felski's passage legible comes four paragraphs earlier, in the essay's agenda statement:

> First . . . I would like to explore these differences [in Everyday Life theory] and . . . bring the various traditions of scholarship on everyday life into a more explicit dialogue. Second, the association of the everyday with repetition, home, and habit often involve assumptions about gender and women's relationship to the modern world. These assumptions become most explicit in Lefebvre's sociological and Marxist-oriented account of everyday life. While I have found many of his insights useful, I want to question his view that the habitual, home-centered aspects of daily life are outside, and in some sense antithetical to, the experience of an authentic modernity.[7]

As readers, if we have comprehended this agenda statement and recognized it as a major framework for the essay, we are equipped to realize that the notion of women as "primary symbols and victims of consumer culture" is not Felski's idea but, rather, one she wants to resist and qualify. But appropriately subordinating such complex ideas is a function of quite advanced reading skill that we probably struggled to build up as undergraduates and graduate students, even if we are no longer conscious of these cognitive moves today. We should not be surprised or disappointed if students come to a class having misidentified an idea the author is explicitly rejecting as that author's idea; and we should be ready to work with such errors in class and in responding to student writing, taking them as opportunities to help students develop advanced reading comprehension.

Conventions of Literary Criticism and Theory

We can thus help students learn to respond tactically to the complexities of academic prose by giving them practice, acting as a coach, and having students puzzle out problems together. When it comes to major genre conventions of criticism and theory, we will want to lay these out directly and devise prompts and activities in which students identify and recognize them. They include the following:

- Critical essays typically begin with a rich example, whose illustrative potential is then unpacked in some detail; this often takes place before the writer reveals the purpose of the essay (unless an abstract precedes the main text).

- An essay's purpose is almost always revealed explicitly, often in a statement beginning, "In this essay I . . ." or "This essay + action verb." This statement of purpose often does not come in the essay's first paragraph and sometimes is embedded in the middle of a long paragraph near the end of the introduction. In a lengthy critical essay, the introduction can be four or five densely printed pages long, so the agenda statement can come this late, or later.

- An essay's thesis may be contained within or adjacent to the statement of purpose. Or it may not: it may not appear in fully articulated form until the end of the essay. More commonly, the thesis comes near the end of the introduction and is repeated multiple times, with further developments, turns, and articulations, as the essay proceeds. Sometimes, in lieu of a thesis, the agenda statement contains a central question, which is returned to, partially answered, and reformulated as the essay progresses.

- Many essays are divided into clear sections that carry forward discrete, identifiable pieces of the argument. Sometimes, the writer will helpfully spell out these stages at or near the agenda statement. The sections themselves often contain a subthesis.

- As noted earlier, essays virtually always name their interlocutors and situate themselves within an existing discussion. In rare cases this work happens in footnotes; more commonly, the main text sketches out the existing discussion in some detail, with footnotes offering greater detail or lists of other relevant texts.

Getting students to recognize these moves aids in the comprehension of the essay at hand, helps acculturate students to the dialogic and constructed nature of literary knowledge, and introduces them to key conventions in academic writing. Graff and Birkenstein's *They Say, I Say: The Moves that Matter in Academic Writing*, a superb undergraduate handbook, builds out from this central insight, providing templates for students to use in making such characteristic rhetorical moves in their writing. As readers, students can learn to recognize all of these conventions through low-stakes writing prompts and class activities that highlight them.

Indeed, there are countless ways to get students to recognize and begin practicing these moves, including Graff and Birkenstein's templates and Linkon's compelling "literary inquiry project," in which a conventional research paper is broken down into all of its component performances (framing questions, finding primary evidence, searching for sources, reading sources, constructing a critical framework, etc.).[8] In Linkon's courses, each of these stages is introduced in class or through course materials, and students practice, receive feedback, and complete graded assignments for each step before completing the actual essay. Linkon also sometimes has students complete the parts but not the finished whole of the research project, and I have colleagues who use similar "everything but the paper" assignments to help students learn literary-critical practices. But while these approaches remain wedded to the research essay, the elements of advanced reading comprehension and advanced literacy can also be taught and learned through non-essay-driven assignments—ones that draw on other scholarly practices such as editing, curation, and the writing of literary history. In the following I offer a set of lower-stakes and homework-ish assignments designed to help students work productively with criticism and theory.

WORKSHEET ON ANALYZING CRITICAL ESSAYS[9]

1. Identify any information borrowed from other critics in the text and note its function. What does it provide and how does it help the author of your essay make his/her/their argument? Does it provide an alternate interpretation of the text for your author to respond to? Does it agree with one of your author's points (and thus lend it credibility)? Does it offer a critical, theoretical, or philosophical concept that your author wants to use as an analytical tool? Does it provide historical background? Does it offer a point to sharpen, qualify, build upon, and disagree with?
2. Formulate the central question or questions the essay responds to.
3. List any important binary oppositions central to the argument.
4. What are the essay's most important analytical and/or interpretive claims? (i.e., What is the thesis, and what secondary claims support it?)
5. Describe the *kinds* of evidence the critic uses, pointing to specific examples.

DEFINING MODERNISM, GROUP HOMEWORK

Your team's job in this assignment is to read carefully an essay that defines literary modernism, to comprehend the definition that the essay offers, and to present that definition to the class in a ten- to fifteen-minute presentation.

The format of the presentation appears later. Be sure that it addresses these questions: How does the writer define modernism? According to the author, what are its characteristics, in terms of form and content? How is it different from the literature that came before? What caused modernism to happen when it did? (Historical, philosophical, economic, social changes?)

Use these questions to brainstorm and gather material for the presentation, but *do not* mechanically address them one by one. Organize your presentation around the specific tasks laid out below.

TEAMWORK BUILDING EXERCISE /"READING CIRCLE"

Once everyone has read the essay, each person should reread the essay taking a slightly different tack.

- Have one person (or two people, if you have five in your group) in charge of articulating the essay's main argument (which in this case will be either its definition of modernism or its explanation of its roots, causes, and sources.) The questions above should be very helpful to this person.
- Have one person in charge of finding the best examples from the essay that support and exemplify the argument's main thrust.
- Have one person attempt to represent the article's main ideas graphically (as creatively as you like: in a flow chart, a continuum, a table that lists binary oppositions, a set of drawings or pictures, etc.). It might make sense for this person to be in charge of handouts, PowerPoint, etc. (see the following).
- Have one person in charge of raising objections: Does this definition have any logical problems? Any overgeneralizations? Does it leave anything important out? Does it leave anything unexplained? Does it mention other critics with whom its author disagrees?

Everyone should read the essay for Wednesday's class. In class, we will have a workshop session, where you can assign the roles and brainstorm together about the essay and the presentation. You will probably have to meet sometime between Wednesday and Friday in order to finish preparing your presentation, though you may be able to work together online or break into subgroups.

You're welcome to use handouts, to project a visual (e.g., Vizi or PowerPoint) presentation, or to simply write on the blackboard.

HOMEWORK ASSIGNMENTS ON SPECIFIC CRITICAL ESSAYS

English 230
Homework # 7

A. In R. W. Dent's essay "Imagination in *A Midsummer Night's Dream*,"
   1. Identify four places where Dent states the opinions of previous critics. (Note: in many cases Dent does not name these critics, but instead summarizes a large set of critics' responses generally.)
   2. Briefly summarize what the critics have said (or the approaches the critics have taken).
   3. Explain how Dent's arguments relate to the critics' ideas (i.e., Does he agree? Disagree? Partially agree? Use the critics' ideas to build his own? etc.)

B. How would you summarize Dent's main argument? What are some of his secondary interpretive claims?

English 230/Homework #12

1. *Find the conversation* in this essay. What ideas of previous critics is this writer responding to? Briefly sketch out the previous critics' ideas that are most important to this essay.
2. What is Ganz's response? What is her argument, and how does it differ from those of the previous critics?
3. What kinds of evidence does Ganz use in this essay? Divide the evidence into types and give a few examples of each type.
4. The essay is helpfully divided into three sections, with a little squiggle at the end of each section. What is the purpose of each section? (This is also a way of asking: how is the essay organized?)

APPENDIX 2

GRADING AND FEEDBACK IN LITERATURE CLASSES

When we prepare for a new semester, grading enters our thinking only in terms of how best to keep it from interfering in the courses themselves, for in no way can grading be said to be an integral part of the process of writing. Grading is something we must participate in because it is the currency of schools. And it seems to be a currency that is particularly alien to the discipline of writing.

—**CHERYL SMITH AND ANGUS DUNSTAN,** "Grade the Learning, Not the Writing"[1]

Problems of Grading

I have said earlier that becoming a teacher involves a series of disillusionments, and few are as powerful as those brought about by our early experiences of grading. Most of us become college literature teachers in part because we thrived under the culture of grading—because good grades felt like strong incentives to us and because we reached or exceeded the standards they represented. As naïve, beginning graduate students, we may have looked forward to the chance to deploy grades as incentives to learning and growth. Stepping into classrooms in the role of teacher, though, we face some sobering realities. Most students are neither as motivated nor as evidently skilled as us. Few have our mastery of standard English, such that, in some student writing, merely understanding what they are trying to say is laborious. Grades frequently seem to create not growth but conflict: students want to be given precise and specific tasks that they can accomplish, akin to boxes that they can check, in order to receive the grade they want; they disagree with our evaluations and grow frustrated. Or, students seem more concerned about grades than their learning or the ideas and intellectual questions that excite us. Or they return revisions to us that have ignored what we saw as constructive feedback.

Add to all this that grading in literature and humanities classes—which focuses heavily on the assessment of writing—is time consuming and draining, drawing heavily on our stores of concentration and patience and accumulating in daunting amounts at midterm and at the end of the semester. When a semester is ending, grading stands between us and a break from the intensities of engaging with students, a chance to allow our creative and scholarly selves to come forward. It is no wonder that for many of us, grading is our least favorite routine task. Many of us, I expect, share the sentiment voiced in the epigraph above—the notion that grading is "something we must participate in because it is the currency of schools" but that it is incidental or obscurely connected to the learning that happens in our classrooms.

More profoundly, as some scholars of rhetoric and composition have been arguing for several decades, and with increasing nuance and urgency more recently, grading reinforces social inequalities by enshrining narrow, socially normative standards, putting poor, working-class, first-generation, and nonwhite students at acute disadvantage. English classes, where writing is the main medium for performances and assessments, must particularly grapple with the problem of Standard English: students raised in communities whose local languages are further from standard English are apt to struggle or fail to meet standards of grammatical correctness or style, which we can no longer realistically view as race-neutral. As Asao B. Inouye writes, the problems of grades are intricately tied up with, but not limited to, Standard English:

> Raciolinguistically diverse students come to our classrooms with *habitus* (or linguistic, bodily, and performative dispositions) that do not match the White racial *habitus* embodied in the standard of the classroom. In short, the traditional purposes and methods used for grading writing turn out to be *de facto* racist and White supremacist. Grading by a standard, thus, is how White language supremacy is perpetuated in schools.[2]

In my experience, "grading to a standard" not only disadvantages students of color or the "raciolinguistically diverse"; it also sets an often-insuperable barrier to students whose previous schooling simply hasn't brought them to facility with Standard English. In literature classes, an unquestioned or excessive reliance on mastery of grammar and usage means, effectively, that we are as interested in sorting students by their proficiency in Standard English as in teaching them to become better readers and interpreters of literature or equipping them with the means to developing supple and fertile advanced literacy.

In the rhetoric and composition world, so-called contract grading has emerged as a popular antidote to the problems of grading. Such approaches vary widely but share a commitment to negotiating types and weights of assignments with students and establishing "contracts" stipulating that students who complete an agreed-upon set of tasks and assignments are guaranteed a certain grade. Some contract grading schemes are entirely labor-based: if you complete the full list of tasks, you get an A, and, while teachers still give substantial feedback on writing and other performances, this feedback is disconnected from grading. Others leave room for evaluative "bonuses" for distinguished work, guaranteeing a "B" to all students who stick to the contract but allowing for A's for students who surpass others in meeting course goals.[3]

The Approach: Start with Objectives and Grade the Learning

I see no reason why contract grading would not work in a literature class, and some of my colleagues have used it or adapted some of its elements. But I strive toward an approach that preserves the evaluative nature of grades but assesses student work based on their learning, rewarding them for development and improvement in the methods my classes emphasize rather than holding them to a preexisting ideal. A student in my classes whose final paper falls well short of perfection in grammar and usage, but which shows facility and substantial improvement in the course's procedural knowledge, may get an A; a student who brought superior language skills into the room but has not improved in his/her/their ability to interpret or contextualize texts, or in other course objectives of a specific class, will not. This approach embraces the degree to which students are motivated by grades: if I am clear enough about the course objectives, and return to them frequently, and give students frequent feedback on their growth along those lines, students who work successfully toward the objectives should get the best grades. (For instance, as you will see in the samples I provide later, I frequently refer to interpretive skills in commenting on student writing. In more advanced classes, I might suggest primary research strategies or ways of precisely stating claims about a text's involvement in historical controversies.)

What about writing? Improving student writing remains an overarching goal in my classes, and I include it in my published objectives for almost every class I teach. But "improving writing" does not have to emphasize a student's proximity to Standard English. If I notice in early, low-stakes writing that a student struggles with Standard English, or has trouble making their meaning clear, I will give specific feedback to this student to help their writing improve and will invite them to office hours, so we can work together on specific expression problems or error patterns. In the process I will talk to them about my attitude about Standard English: since it is the lingua franca of many professional settings, students would do well to improve in their mastery of it; but my grading will focus not on their writing's correctness but on its clarity, the richness of its insights and evidence, and the skill with which the student uses methods of interpretation and the tools for building advanced literacy.

This approach requires tracking individual student progress, which is undeniably difficult in larger classes or for teachers with larger teaching loads. The ubiquity of course management systems has made tracking student progress easier, since these platforms retain all previous student work and your grades and feedback. When you are grading a major assignment, it does not take long to look back at your previous comments on informal and formal student writing and to key your responses to the elements you've asked the student to work on. If your teaching load is such that even this is not feasible, you might have students do frequent self-evaluation on objectives and attach self-evaluation check sheets to formal assignments, so that you can gauge whether their self-evaluation is accurate and give them targeted feedback. Portfolio grading, in which student writing from the start to the finish of the semester is submitted together, does potentially streamline grading time, and it allows for your final grades to substantively reflect student growth on objectives. But it is summative rather than formative feedback—it does not respond to student work in time for them to put your feedback into action in your class. That is why I spend much more effort on timely, efficient formative feedback that emphasizes my course objectives.

I recognize that this approach would not satisfy the aims of advocates for contract grading. I do not, at present, give students a lot of say over the kinds of assignments I use or the texts I assign (although, as I made clear in Chapters 2 and 3, I give them substantial influence on the content of our discussions, and I create assignments that require students to discover texts that are relevant to the historical periods my courses focus on). I believe I am better-positioned to know what sorts of assignments will advance my objectives, and I do not believe most of my students know enough about the content in most of my classes to have well-informed commitments about it. (I do frequently workshop assignment instructions and make small adjustments based on student feedback.) My courses are also deeply logocentric, with virtually all assessed student performances coming in verbal or written form.

I will keep working and keep adapting my classes, and in the future I plan to draw on student enthusiasms and skills for multimedia creations. Nonetheless, I remain committed to helping students increase their verbal skills—an emphasis that I think is appropriate for this discipline. There is no complete escape from the norming function of universities; I hope that when a student brings a nondominant habitus to my class, my teaching will not devalue that habitus but expose the student to the possibility of developing new capacities—the possibility, ultimately, of having a code-switching repertoire of ways of being and carrying oneself intellectually. I am committed to working individually with students whenever they are willing and able. And I have faith that clinging tightly to an ethos of teaching students, not sorting them, will guide me in the thousands of micro-interactions in which these issues come into play.

The problems I have set out here are unlikely to disappear: they are structural to higher education and involve tensions that we simply have to navigate. But rather than viewing grades solely as a necessary evil, we should work with them to the best of our ability to serve our objectives, recognizing that managing these tensions day to day is part of our jobs.

Here is my advice for grading in literature classes, drawn from experience, consultation with colleagues, and engagement with various sources from this book's bibliography, most centrally Walvoord and Anderson's classic *Effective Grading*.[4]

Effective Grading and Feedback in Literature Classes: Guidelines

1. **Start with an integrated syllabus, and grade on your objectives.** Chapter 4 discusses integrated course design, in which all assignments, activities, and assessments are clearly and explicitly keyed to course objectives. In short, you should not be spending time writing commentary that does not speak to your objectives. As Walvoord and Anderson pithily put it: "Why spend time grading student work that does not address your most important goals?"[5] Think about how you will be grading—on which objectives, what specifically you'll be looking for, and how you'll respond—at the earliest design stage of syllabi and assignments. Think through specifically how assignments speak to objectives and make their relevance clear to students. Otherwise, you will find yourself improvising objectives and standards as you're grading; the purpose of the assignment was not clear to you, so there is no chance it will be clear to your students.

2. **Emphasize timely, formative feedback.** When you provide feedback on low-stakes assignments such as homework and weekly writing, you are giving students actionable information, guiding them to practices or improvements they can practice on higher-stakes assessments. In my literature classes, I have found that the most effective feedback is frequent, targeted commentary on low-stakes writing. When clearly tied to learning goals, such commentary is generally more effective than

feedback on higher-stakes writing (i.e., the two or three formal essays or presentations in a typical semester). Likewise feedback on drafts is more actionable than feedback on "final" versions of essays. Commentary on major assignments early in the semester is useful if you allow for post-submission revisions; grade-motivated students will often revise and will engage carefully with your commentary. (Student lives being as they are, however, a substantial number of my students frequently plan to revise but never get it done.) The later in the semester and the more high-stakes an assignment—that is, the more it feels and functions as a formal assessment rather than a coaching situation—the less effective the feedback will be. I learned this early in my career, when I told students that I was not going to write comments on finals unless students asked me to in advance. None did so. None! I can think of no greater waste of time than writing extensive feedback on undergraduate final exams or final essays.

Timely feedback means feedback that gets to students at a time when they can still act on it.[6] A lengthy postmortem on a paper that a student is never going to return to is a waste of your time, and many students will not even read it carefully. Offer feedback that students can put into action, and make clear to them how they can do so. See my examples of feedback on low-stakes student writing, later.

3. **Make commentary concise and targeted**. Based on the student's performance on the activity, select the two or (at most) three learning areas that you want the student to work on. Even when students need a lot of work on multiple areas, they cannot work on everything at once or, often, even successfully process all the feedback we want to give them. And few things are more dispiriting to students than a paper that is excessively scrawled on in red ink or, nowadays, tagged with multiple layers of marginal comment bubbles. Offer a concise paragraph that speaks the language of your course objectives and points to specific moments in the performance to illustrate the need for improvement. Use comment bubbles or margin scribbles sparingly, and mainly to illustrate the points in your final comment.

4. **Track the individual student's progress**. Go back to your previous comments on student assignments and take note of what you've been asking the student to work on. Note improvement (or its lack). Register improvement in words of praise; offer specific ideas for further improvement; or, if the student has made major strides, move on to other, more advanced skills and practices for students to work on. If the student has not made progress on the issues you've cited, point that out and offer help.

If you do not use a course management system, you will need to keep separate notes on student progress. (This should be a powerful incentive to use a course management system, if your institution makes one available). But if your course objectives are clear enough, you should be able to keep records of areas for improvement on them, or error patterns in their prose, in concise phrases or fragments.

5. **Make effective use of student conferences**. Though time-consuming, one-on-one conferences are remarkably effective in helping students learn to do things, and they signal your commitment to their learning and build rapport. In some cases, students will want mainly to talk through ideas for a project; listen well and ask questions to complicate the ideas; ask them where their evidence will come from, and push them on it. For students who are visiting because they are struggling with your course goals, model the cognitive moves you're trying to get students to make; then give them a tiny assignment to work on while you wait. For instance, if a student is struggling to make basic interpretive moves, work through a short poem with them, leaving half the lines for them to work on; give the student five minutes to mark up the second half, then talk through the results. If a student's prose is wordy and indirect, overreliant on weak verbs and passive structures, rewrite one or two of their sentences, talking through what you do while they watch. Then give them a chunky one to rewrite. Reconvene, point out marks of improvement, clarify, or rearticulate advice.

6. **Frontload feedback**. We all know the emotional and physical rhythms of a semester. We and our students start out with a sense of openness and possibility and a commitment to do everything better this time around; as schoolwork and other commitments ramp up, so do anxiety and fatigue. Students are in the best position to make good use of your feedback earlier in the semester; which is why I design most courses to include a great deal of low-stakes assessment in the first four to six weeks. As the semester goes along, my written feedback gets shorter and more pointed, focused, and strategic. A graph of the time I spend responding to student writing would show a steady decline from start to finish of a semester (or at least this is what I strive for), because the degree to which feedback is actionable, for most students, decreases along a similar slope. (It is noteworthy that this is virtually the opposite of what most of my undergraduate teachers did three decades ago—assigning two or three formal essays as the only writing, giving no feedback in the first month, providing summative feedback only, and grading themselves blind with final papers and exams in December and May).

As with all of my advice in this book, you will need to tailor your assessments to individual classes and students. Extremely motivated students will want more feedback and be in a better position to do something with it, even late into the semester. Students with poor language skills will need intensive extra help early on; you will have to do your best to work with them amid your many time commitments; some of them, unfortunately, will not follow through with you.

7. **Avoid grading binges, if possible**. Your brain was not built to respond sensitively to ten or twenty student essays in a single day. While we all will likely get into situations where we have to spend hours or days grading heavily, it is wise to minimize these. Use your calendar and your basic math skills: divide the stack of artifacts by the number of days left until you want to have them finished. (I think a week between assignment deadline and grade is ideal; two weeks is fine; longer than that probably erodes the likelihood that a student will revise and the actionability of your feedback.) Then grade two or four or six or eight papers a day, in relatively short sessions. Research shows that feedback is more effective the shorter the time between the performance and the grade; and that even minimal, early feedback on drafts is effective.[7] Stand up, walk, breathe, and stretch at least once an hour. After a couple hours give your mind something else to work on, or to tune out to: listen to music, exercise, watch TV. Freshen up for your next session.

SAMPLE COMMENTS ON LOW-STAKES WRITING

- "Really good noticing and sorting of details into patterns. You also do a good job of paraphrasing the main messages of poems. Note, though, that your sentences on the first page of the homework aren't interpretive claims: they're paraphrases of the poem's literal meaning. An interpretive claim would make a claim about the specific significance of a detail—how it contributes to the effects and meanings of the poem. Better still, interpretive claims would show specific insights about how the poem works (not just what it means, but how its meaning and effects are achieved). Your best interpretive moves here are in noting the repetition of questions."
- "Very strong effort, and you're making good progress in attempting & refining interpretive claims. I think the claims on Dickey and Stallings are both quite good. The Dickey one is a bit more concise and to the point. The Stallings point could use a half-turn so that it's considering the effect the poem wants to have (not just the

preferences of the speaker, Hades). What might you get if you asked, 'What effect is Stallings going for by emphasizing the tenderness of Hades towards his bride?'"

- "Excellent interpretive claim about the play. You could (even in this short exercise) have pointed to a bit more evidence, and especially to some details, that support it. The first sentence of the first ¶ is off to a great start till you interrupt it with 'what Hale stated.' Content very good; sentence is getting over-complicated and the connections aren't made clearly."'

- "You have a strong interpretation of the play sketched out very nicely in that ¶. Really, the outline of a good essay on this play is already in there in the major points you raise in the ¶. That said, the ¶ uses the phrase 'gendered language' but is really talking about what the men say, not the gendered nature of how they're saying it. So maybe you need some different terminology. I would expect an analysis of 'gendered language' to focus on *how* things are said—word choices, modes of address (command vs. statement vs. question); implied tone of voice., etc. You're reporting and interpreting (very well) what's being said but not the language in which it's said. We can discuss this if you want to pursue this as paper #2, which could be the basis of a very strong essay about what the play says about power relations between the genders."

- "While this paragraph makes good claims and has good evidence, as your reader I don't understand how the evidence supports the claims. The writing needs an intermediate step where you point to the evidence and make clear to us how it supports the point you're arguing. For instance, how does Rankine's *repetition* of 'it's not untrue' 'make the speaker sound reasonable?' (The phrase itself, as you say, is a concession, but how/why does the *repetition* enhance this effect)? See me if you want to discuss further."

NOTES

Chapter 1

1 The most thorough working out of this question, to my mind, is Sherry Lee Linkon's, *Literary Learning: Teaching the English Major* (Bloomington: Indiana UP, 2011). Subsequent references in parentheses.

2 See Linkon, *Literary Learning*, 108; Sheridan Blau, *The Literature Workshop: Teaching Texts and Their Readers* (Portsmouth: NCTE, 2003), 203–16; Robert Scholes, *Textual Power: Literary Theory and the Teaching of English* (New Haven: Yale University Press, 1985); Susan A. Ambrose et al., *How Learning Works: 7 Researched Principles for Smart Teaching* (San Francisco: Jossey-Bass, 2010), 18–19.

3 Linkon, *Literary Learning*, 2.

4 While the late Harold Bloom got a good deal of coverage (and sold a good number of books) with his cantankerous defense of the canon, the most influential and compelling defense is still probably E. D. Hirsch's *Cultural Literacy: What Every American Needs to Know* (New York: Vintage, 1988), discussed below. For a recent attempt to recapitulate an old-fashioned humanism that is committed to content if not exactly to the canon, see Mark Edmundson's advocacy for "soul-making education" in *Why Teach: In Defense of a Real Education* (New York: Bloomsbury USA, 2013), a book much at odds with my unapologetic pragmatism in this book.

5 This definition is adapted from Ambrose et al. *How Learning Works*, 3.

6 The most prominent study on literature and compassion is David Comer Kidd and Emmanuelle Castano's "Reading Literary Fiction Improves Theory of Mind." *Science* 342, no. 6156 (October 2013): 377–80.

7 Stanley Fish, *Save the World on Your Own Time* (Oxford and New York: Oxford University Press, 2008).

8 Scholes, *The Rise and Fall of English: Reconstructing English as a Discipline* (New Haven: Yale University Press, 1999); *English After the Fall: From Literature to Textuality* (Iowa City: University of Iowa Press, 2011).

9 "The Necessity of Critical Pedagogy in Dark Times." [Interview]. *Truthout.Org* blog, February 6, 2013. https://truthout.org/articles/a-critical-interview-with-henry-giroux/. Accessed August 1, 2018. My methods-obsessed approach is vulnerable to Giroux's critique of "cognitive developmental" approaches to literacy. See his chapter "Literacy, Ideology, and the Politics of Schooling," in which Giroux argues that cognitive development teaching seems to position the student as "agent in the

literary process" (218) but ignores "students' life experiences or the class, racial, and gender histories of the different students exposed to this approach." Content becomes abstract in a methods-based approach, so that students engage with political problems but within the "structured debates of the classroom" in forms "devoid of even the hint of social and class conflict" (218). As I hope will become clear, it is possible to teach from a foundation of methodology but in ways that both acknowledge and situate the conflicting interests in the classroom and make visible the power dynamics in texts—and their analogous relation to contemporary dynamics. Henry Giroux, *Theory and Resistance in Education: Towards a Pedagogy for the Opposition* (Westport: Bergin and Garvey): 205–32.

10 Paolo Friere, *The Pedagogy of the Oppressed* (1970; New York and London: Continuum Press, 2000), 71–86.

11 Marshall Gregory, "Do We Teach Disciplines or Do We Teach Students? What Difference Does It Make?" *Profession* (2008): 125.

12 John V. Knapp limns this process archly: "1) teacher asks a question to which he or she already knows the answer; 2) student responds with what the student thinks the teacher wants; 3) the teacher evaluates the response, and if the teacher approves, moves on to the next question or the next student. If incorrect, the teacher either works on the first student respondent until the correct answer is forthcoming or again attends to another member of the class for the 'right' answer." "Current Conversations in the Teaching of College-Level Literature." *Style* 38, no. 1 (Spring 2004): 50–92.

13 Blau, *Literature Workshop*, 75, 77–8. For a thorough discussion of dispositions of expert versus nonexpert readers, see Linkon, *Literary Learning*, 28–32.

14 The most extensive working out of an argument in favor of a coherent tradition remains E. D. Hirsch's *Cultural Literacy*. It is telling that one of Hirsch's key illustrations of the power of cultural literacy comes from his father's experience as a business executive, where he was able to communicate urgency to his colleagues by using the phrase, "There is a tide"—an allusion to Shakespeare's *Julius Caesar* (9–10). Hirsch is drawing on a framework of mid-twentieth-century elite schools feeding talent to large US corporations—a relatively homogenous culture that would inevitably have its own cultural codes and happened to be able to draw on canonical literary knowledge as a source of material for them. Though Hirsch sincerely seems to believe that minorities and other marginalized populations will have greater social mobility if they become conversant in the canon, he fails to address the cultural homogeneity and exclusiveness of the mid-century, elite school milieu—or the role of higher education in sustaining and reproducing it (110–11).

15 See Gerald Graff, *Professing Literature: An Institutional History* (Chicago: University of Chicago Press, 1987).

16 Zadie Smith, *White Teeth* (New York: Vintage, 2000), 227.

17 The centrality of symptomatic reading has come under pressure in recent years, most powerfully in Rita Felski's *The Limits of Critique* (Chicago and London: University of Chicago Press, 2015) and the special "Surface Reading" issue of *Representations*, edited by Stephen Best and Sharon Marcus. As Felski notes, even while symptomatic reading and the "hermeneutics of suspicion" have dominated literary criticism, the classroom has consistently been an arena for a more diverse set of approaches (4).

18 This may sound flippant, but, as Graff has shown, the study of English was a central element of higher education in the first 150 years of US history, during which college was very much finishing school for the children of the very wealthy. Graff, *Professing Literature*, 55–145. Elite schools, including Ivy League universities and liberal arts schools, continued to have larger numbers of English majors—both as a percentage of enrollment and in pure numbers—into the twenty-first century and until the Great Recession and the current "crisis in the humanities."

19 See *Textual Power; The Rise and Fall of English*, and *English After the Fall*.

20 Ambrose et al., *How Learning Works*, Chapter 2.

21 On the importance of narrative in learning, see Josuah R. Eyler, *How Humans Learn: The Science and Stories Behind Effective College Teaching* (Morgantown: West Virginia University Press, 2018), 54–5, 76, 99–100.

22 Linkon, *Literary Learning*, 5.

23 In this I depart from Linkon; while it is true that students build declarative knowledge and methods (which Linkon refers to as "content knowledge" and "strategic knowledge") in a mutually reinforcing fashion, Linkon has more faith in the ability of students and curricula—in a short and overcrowded four years in school—to construct stable body of content knowledge for students. Linkon suggests that students cannot develop strategic knowledge in the absence of a stable body of content knowledge, as suggested when she writes: "The content of literary studies seems obvious . . . we study major texts, movements, and genres; the core ideas of various schools of literary theory; and some basic tools and terms of literary analysis" (2). In practice, few majors are designed to offer students shared and stable bodies of declarative knowledge. As I argue here and in Chapter 3, we will serve students better if we focus on cultural literacy as local and provisional—as something students will build, now and in the future, out of distinct canons of material appropriate to their changing intellectual and professional contexts.

24 Scholes, *Rise and Fall*, 145–55.

Chapter 2

1 The term "zone of proximal development" was coined by L. S. Vygotsky in *Mind in Society: The Development of the Higher Psychological Processes* (New York: Oxford University Press, 1930). For a discussion of recent work building on Vygotsky and its application to classrooms, see Ambrose et al., *How Learning Works*, 132.

2 Diepeveen economically synthesizes some useful science on emotional/physiological reactions to difficulty in *The Difficulties of Modernism* (New York and London: Routledge, 2003), 64–81.

3 Francois Meltzer, "Unconscious," in *Critical Terms for Literary Study*, eds. Frank Lentricchia and Thomas McLaughlin (Chicago: University of Chicago Press, 1995), 147–62.

4 A similar understanding informs Gerald Graff's brilliant work on teaching students the analytical moves of critical writing on literature. See his eminently useful textbook *They Say, I Say: The Moves That Matter in Academic Writing* and, for the

philosophical grounding of his approach *Teaching the Conflicts*, particularly the chapter entitled, "Disliking Books at an Early Age."

5   See Ambrose et al., *How Learning Works*, 99, 111–12.

6   According to studies of the connection between aesthetic pleasure and difficulty, tolerance for difficulty increases with increased expertise in a field; see Diepeveen, *The Difficulties of Modernism*, 77. For a vision of literary pedagogy founded on theories of expertise, see Linkon, *Literary Learning*.

7   Stephen D. Brookfield, *Becoming a Critically Reflective Teacher* (San Francisco: Jossey-Bass, 2017), 153–70. Likewise, Linkon's *Learning Literature* analyzes how literature professors, as "expert readers" think and urges that we design our pedagogy to nurture those same skills and dispositions in students. To elucidate this point she quotes educational psychologist Sam Wineburg's findings on the teaching of history: "Only by making our footsteps visible can we expect students to follow in them" (20).

8   See Blau, *Literature Workshop*, 144–6.

9   Special issue of the effect of fear and stress on memory. *Learning and Memory* 24 (2017).

10 Rebekah Nathan, *My Freshman Year: What a Professor Learned by Becoming a Student* (Ithaca: Cornell University Press, 2005), 22.

11 Ibid., 137–8.

12 Ibid., 138.

13 In 2003, Nathan reports, the percentage of students who reported doing ten or fewer hours of class preparation per week was 41 percent, compared with 37 percent in 2018; the percentage of students who reported never coming to class unprepared was 22 percent in 2003, 27 percent in 2018. NSSE 2018 Summary Frequencies. National Survey of Student Engagement. http://nsse.indiana.edu/2018_institutional_report/pdf/Frequencies/Freq%20-%20SR%20by%20Carn.pdf. Accessed August 21, 2018.

14 Brian Gallagher, "'I Love You Too': Sexual Warfare and Homoeroticism in Billy Wilder's 'Double Indemnity.'" *Literature/Film Quarterly* 15, no. 4 (1987): 237–246.

15 David Rosenwasser and Jill Stephen, *Writing Analytically*. Seventh edition (Boston: Cengage, 2012), Chapter 3.

16 Ibid., 211.

17 Blau, *Literature Workshop*, Chapter 5.

Chapter 3

1   See Ambrose et al., *How Learning Works*, Chapter 1, for learning research on prior knowledge; Blau, Chapter 4, for problems with prior knowledge specific to literature teaching, and for Blau's approaches. I substantially share Blau's formulation of the problem. But Blau's focus in *Literature Workshop* is mainly on introductory settings, where it is harder to get students to build up contextual knowledge in a sustained way. The projects I outline at the end of this chapter constitute my strategies for getting English majors and more seasoned students to attack the problem of background knowledge more thoroughly and at greater scale.

2   Hirsch, *Cultural Literacy*, Chapter 3.

3   Cognitive learning research has even suggested that declarative knowledge is not a distinct kind of learning but a function of procedural knowledge: in other words, what makes a fact or concept stick in our minds is the cognitive procedure through which it is processed—an item of declarative knowledge is "learned" when our brain's learning procedures have placed it in relation to other stimuli. See Hezewijk and Berg, "Declarative and Procedural Knowledge: An Evolutionary Perspective." *Theory and Psychology* 9, no. 5 (October 1999): 605–24.

4   See Ambrose et al., *How Learning Works*; 180–216. E. D. Hirsch, *The Schools We Need: And Why We Don't Have Them* (New York: Random House, 1997), 141.

5   The canon wars played out in books such as Allan Bloom's *The Closing of the American Mind* (New York: Simon and Schuster, 1987) and Harold Bloom's *The Western Canon* (New York: Riverhead Books, 1994) as well as Hirsch's *Cultural Literacy*, with ripostes coming from John Guillory in *Cultural Capital* (Chicago: University of Chicago Press), and Gerald Graff in *Beyond the Culture Wars: How Teaching the Conflicts Can Revitalize American Education* (New York and London: Norton, 1992).

6   In making this argument I differ with Linkon, whose model of developing student expertise through understanding of the "habits of mind" of expert readers I otherwise sanction wholly. While Linkon's strategies for course and curriculum design, like mine, heavily emphasize intellectual methods (which she calls "strategic knowledge"), she implies a more stable shared set of texts for students, asserting that "Without content knowledge, strategy is useless" (2).

7   Scholes, *Rise and Fall*, 148.

8   Salman Rushdie, "Chekov and Zulu," in *East, West* (New York: Vintage International, 1994), 170.

9   Ibid., 171.

10 Ibid., 156, 163.

11 Ibid., 154.

12 Ibid., 154.

13 Blau, *Literature Workshop*, 92.

14 Though it focuses on math and science teaching, Freeman et al.'s 2014 meta-study is the most comprehensive study of the effects of lecturing to date. It finds that failure rates in STEM classes increase by 55 percent as compared with active-learning approaches. Freeman et al., "Active Learning Increases Student Performance in Science, Engineering, and Mathematics." *Proceedings of the National Academy of Science* 111 (June 10, 2014): 8410–15 and https://www.pnas.org/content/111/23/8410. Accessed January 27, 2019.

15 Eyler, *How Humans Learn*, 167 and 238, n. 27.

16 Joshua R. Eyler, "What We Mean When We Talk About Lectures." *Inside Higher Ed*, October 16, 2018. https://www.insidehighered.com/advice/2018/10/16/examining-wide-range-views-about-what-classroom-lecture-actually-opinion. Accessed January 7, 2019.

17 See James Lang, *Small Teaching: Everyday Lessons from the Science of Learning* (San Francisco: Jossey-Bass, 2016), 19–40.

18 Ibid., 32.

19 Blau, *Literature Workshop*, 85–8.
20 Elizabeth Bowen, *Collected Stories of Elizabeth Bowen* (New York: Random House, 1981), 608.
21 Ibid., 522.
22 Christopher Isherwood, *Goodbye to Berlin* (New York: New Directions, 2012), 3–4.

Chapter 4

1 As this book focuses on practical advice for individual teachers, a thorough account of how the imperative for learning objectives emerged, in parallel form, in K–12 learning and policy debates and in initiatives for higher education assessment, is beyond my scope. The language of "learning outcomes" emerged with the rise of, and resulting controversies over, so-called outcomes-based education for K–12 in the 1970s. State governments and higher education accrediting agencies have been moving colleges and universities toward formalized assessment requirements, usually involving locally generated objectives (or student learning outcomes), since the late 1970s, with momentum for such programs picking up decidedly in the early 2000s and still more in response to public debates about the value of higher education in the wake of the Great Recession of 2008–9. The literature of assessment is copious, but a good overview of the history and current thinking can be gleaned from Richard J. Shaveson, *A Brief History of Student Learning Assessment* (Washington, DC: Association of American Colleges and Universities, 2007) and Richard Arum, Josipa Roska and Amanda Cook, *Improving Quality in American Higher Education: Learning Outcomes and Assessments for the 21st Century* (San Francisco: Jossey-Bass, 2016).
2 Linkon, *Literary Learning*, 72–3. The most thorough and practical explanation of Backward Design in education is Grant Wiggins and Jay McTighe, *Understanding by Design* (Alexandria: Association for Supervision and Curriculum Development, 2005).
3 Woolf, *A Room of One's Own* (New York: Harcourt, 1928).
4 Ibid., 42.

Chapter 5

1 "Dead Poets Society Is a Terrible Defense of the Humanities." *The Atlantic*, February 19, 2014. Online. https://www.theatlantic.com/education/archive/2014/02/-em-dead-poets-society-em-is-a-terrible-defense-of-the-humanities/283853/. Accessed November 28, 2018.
2 Knapp, "Current Conversations in the Teaching of College-Level Literature," 59–60.
3 See for instance Francisco Zabaleta, "The Use and Misuse of Student Evaluations of Teaching." *Teaching in Higher Education* 12, no. 1 (2007). Online. https://srhe.tandfonline.com/doi/full/10.1080/13562510601102131?scroll=top&needAccess=true#.W_1D1S2ZPq0. Accessed November 29, 2018.

4   David A. Dowell and James A. Neal, "A Selective Review of the Validity of Student Ratings of Teaching." *Journal of Higher Education* 51 (1982): 51–62. The research data about the influence of gender and race on teaching evaluation scores is equivocal, but anecdotal evidence, and an internal study conducted at my university, suggest that students frequently write discursive comments that focus inappropriately on gender- or race-specific traits.

5   bell hooks, *Teaching to Transgress: Education as the Practice of Freedom* (New York: Routledge, 1994): 52–3.

6   Stephen D. Brookfield, *The Skillful Teacher: On Technique, Trust, and Responsiveness in the Classroom*, Third edition (San Francisco: Jossey-Bass, 2015), 35–9.

7   Ambrose et al., *How Learning Works*, Chapter 3, 129–32.

Appendix 1

1   Graff, *Beyond the Culture Wars*, 71–2.

2   Ibid., 64–8, 74–5.

3   Graff and Cathy Birkenstein's *They Say, I Say: The Moves that Matter in Academic Writing* offers a very useful guide for students to reading and producing academic prose. Though it is not written specifically for literature majors and is equally useful in other humanities and social sciences, its exercises will be suggestive for literature teachers about detailed ways of helping students interpret and work with criticism. I have used it with a lot of success in my introduction to literary analysis; students frequently comment on its usefulness. Gerald Graff and Cathy Birkenstein, *They Say, I Say: The Moves that Matter in Academic Writing* (London and New York: Norton), 2009.

4   Blau—whose methods I otherwise so admire and emulate—more or less punts on this issue, recognizing that student writing needs to have an audience and take part in a larger discussion, but creating peer communities and conversations instead of inviting students into professional debates. Students struggle to read criticism, and professional articles "are not models" for student writing or learning, he argues. Blau, *Literature Workshop*, 174–8.

5   Linkon, *Literary Learning*, 24.

6   Rita Felski, "The Invention of Everyday Life," *New Formations* 39 (2000): 15–31.

7   Ibid., 18.

8   Linkon, *Literary Learning*, 78–98.

9   This worksheet is liberally adapted from one devised and shared with me by James Phelan. For a version of it and a discussion of his pedagogical aims, see James Phelan, "On Teaching Critical Arguments: A Matrix of Understanding." *Pedagogy* 1, no. 3 (2001): 527–37.

Appendix 2

1   In Christopher Weaver and Frances Zak, eds., *The Theory and Practice of Grading Writing: Problems and Possibilities* (Albany: State University of New York Press, 1998), 163–70.

2 Asao B. Inouye, *Labor-Based Grading Contracts: Building Equity and Inclusion in the Compassionate Writing Classroom* (Boulder: University Press of Colorado, 2019), 5.

3 There are many other variations. See, among other sources, Inouye, *Labor-Based Grading*, Weaver and Zak, *Grading Writing*; Jane Danielewicz and Peter Elbow, "A Unilateral Grading Contract to Improve Learning and Teaching." *College Composition and Communication* 61, no. 2 (2009): 244–68.

4 Barbara Walvoord and Virginia Johnson Anderson, *Effective Grading: A Tool for Learning and Assessment in College* (San Francisco: Jossey-Bass, 2010).

5 Ibid., 9.

6 See Ambrose et al., *How Learning Works*, 142–6.

7 Ibid., 142.

BIBLIOGRAPHY

Ambrose, Susan A., Michael W. Bridges, Michele DiPietro, Marsha C. Lovett, and Marie K. Norman, *How Learning Works: Seven Research-Based Principles for Better Teaching*. San Francisco: Jossey-Bass, 2010.

Arum, Richard, Josipa Roska, and Amanda Cook, *Improving Quality in American Higher Education: Learning Outcomes and Assessments for the 21st Century*. San Francisco: Jossey-Bass, 2016.

ten Berge, T. and R. van Hezewijk, "Procedural and Declarative Knowledge: An Evolutionary Perspective." *Theory and Psychology* 9, no. 5 (October 1999): 605–24.

Blau, Sheridan, *The Literature Workshop: Teaching Texts and Their Readers*. New York: Heinemann, 2003.

Bowen, Elizabeth, *Collected Stories of Elizabeth Bowen*. New York: Random House, 1981.

Brookfield, Stephen D., *Becoming a Critically Reflective Teacher*. San Francisco: Jossey-Bass, 2017.

Brookfield, Stephen D., *The Skillful Teacher: On Technique, Trust, and Responsiveness in the Classroom*. Third Edition. San Francisco: Jossey-Bass, 2015.

Comer Kidd, David and Emmanuelle Castano, "Reading Literary Fiction Improves Theory of Mind." *Science* 342, no. 6156 (October 2013): 377–80.

Dettmar, Kevin, "Dead Poets Society Is a Terrible Defense of the Humanities." *The Atlantic*, February 19, 2014. Online. https://www.theatlantic.com/education/archive/2014/02/-em-dead-poets-society-em-is-a-terrible-defense-of-the-humanities/283853/. Accessed November 28, 2018.

Diepeveen, Leonard, *The Difficulties of Modernism*. London and New York: Routledge, 2002.

Dowell, David A. and James A. Neal, "A Selective Review of the Validity of Student Ratings of Teaching." *Journal of Higher Education* 51 (1982): 51–62.

Eyler, Joshua R., *How Humans Learn: The Science and Stories Behind Effective College Teaching*. Morgantown: West Virginia University Press, 2018.

Eyler, Joshua R., "What We Mean When We Talk About Lectures." *Inside Higher Ed*, October 16, 2018. https://www.insidehighered.com/advice/2018/10/16/examining-wide-range-views-about-what-classroom-lecture-actually-opinion. Accessed January 7, 2019.

Felski, Rita, "The Invention of Everyday Life." *New Formations* 39 (2000): 19–20.

Felski, Rita, *The Limits of Critique*. Chicago and London: University of Chicago Press, 2015.

Fish, Stanley, *Save the World on Your Own Time*. Oxford and New York: Oxford University Press, 2008.

Freeman, Scott, Sarah L. Eddy, Miles McDonough, Michelle K. Smith, Nnadozie Okoroafor, Hannah Jordt, and Mary Pat Wenderoth, "Active Learning Increases Student Performance in Science, Engineering, and Mathematics." *Proceedings of the National Academy of Science* 111 (June 10, 2014): 8410–15 and https://www.pnas.org/content/111/23/8410. Accessed January 27, 2019.

Friere, Paolo, *The Pedagogy of the Oppressed*. New York and London: Continuum Press, 2000 [1970].

Giroux, Henry, "The Necessity of Critical Pedagogy in Dark Times." [Interview]. *Truthout. Org* blog, February 6, 2013. https://truthout.org/articles/a-critical-interview-with-henry-giroux/. Accessed August 1, 2018.

Giroux, Henry, *Theory and Resistance in Education: Towards a Pedagogy for the Opposition*. Second Edition. Westport: Bergin and Garvey: 2001.

Graff, Gerald, *Beyond the Culture Wars: How Teaching the Conflicts Can Revitalize American Education*. New York and London: Norton, 1992.

Graff, Gerald, *Professing Literature: An Institutional History*. Chicago and London: University of Chicago Press, 1987.

Graff, Gerald and Cathy Brikenstein, *They Say, I Say: The Moves that Matter in Academic Writing*. London and New York: Norton, 2009.

Gregory, Marshall, "Do We Teach Disciplines or Do We Teach Students? What Difference Does It Make?" *Profession* (2008): 117–29.

Hirsch, E. D., *Cultural Literacy: What Every American Needs to Know*. New York: Vintage, 1988.

hooks, bell, *Teaching to Transgress: Education as the Practice of Freedom*. New York: Routledge, 1994.

Inouye, Asao B., *Labor-Based Grading Contracts: Building Equity and Inclusion in the Compassionate Writing Classroom*. Boulder: University Press of Colorado, 2019.

Isherwood, Christopher, *Goodbye to Berlin*. New York: New Directions, 1996 [1939].

Knapp, John V., "Current Conversations in the Teaching of College-Level Literature." *Style* 38, no. 1 (Spring 2004): 50–92.

Lang, James, *Small Teaching: Everyday Lessons from the Science of Learning*. San Francisco: Jossey-Bass, 2016.

Linkon, Sherry Lee, *Literary Learning: Teaching the English Major*. Bloomington and Indianapolis: Indiana University Press, 2011.

Nathan, Rebekah, *My Freshman Year: What a Professor Learned by Becoming a Student*. Ithaca: Cornell University Press, 2005.

Rosenwasser, David and Jill Stephen, *Writing Analytically*. Seventh Edition. Boston: Cengage, 2017.

Rushdie, Salman, "Checkov and Zulu." In *East, West*, 147–71. New York: Vintage International, 1994.

Scholes, Robert, *English After the Fall: From Literature to Textuality*. Iowa City: University of Iowa Press, 2011.

Scholes, Robert, *The Rise and Fall of English*. New Haven and London: Yale University Press, 1998.

Scholes, Robert, *Textual Power*. New Haven: Yale University Press, 1986.

Shaveson, Richard J., *A Brief History of Student Learning Assessment*. Washington, DC: Association of American Colleges and Universities, 2007.

Smith, Cheryl and Angus Dunstan, "Grade the Learning, Not the Writing." In Christopher Weaver and Frances Zak (eds.), *The Theory and Practice of Grading Writing: Problems and Possibilities*, 163–70. Albany: State University of New York Press, 1998.

Smith, Zadie, *White Teeth*. New York: Vintage, 2000.
Walvoord, Barbara and Virginia Johnson Anderson, *Effective Grading: A Tool for Learning and Assessment in College*. San Francisco: Jossey-Bass, 2010.
Wiggins, Grant and Jay McTighe, *Understanding by Design*. Alexandria: Association for Supervision and Curriculum Development, 2005.
Woolf, Virginia, *A Room of One's Own*. New York: Harcourt, 1928.
Zabaleta, Francisco, "The Use and Misuse of Student Evaluations of Teaching." *Teaching in Higher Education* 12, no. 1 (2007). Online. Accessed November 29, 2018.

INDEX

Note: Page numbers followed by "n" refer to notes.

absorbed knowledge *vs.* stored knowledge   12
academic prose   28, 30, 134–6, 156 n.3
Achebe, Chinua
   Things Fall Apart   65
advanced literacy   xi, 9, 22–4, 36, 37, 58–96, 117, 121, 132, 138, 142, 144
   clueless   59–65
   curriculum design   94–6
   enlisting of students, in own literacy   78–9
   prior knowledge in literature classes   65–8 (*see also* background knowledge)
   problems and strategies   68–76
   provisional cultural literacy   79–83
   skills, building   76–8
   sustained development of provisional literacy   85–94
advanced reading comprehension   xi, 9, 16, 23–58, 64, 68, 76, 95, 98, 99, 121, 132, 134, 136, 138
   creating incentives to read   31–41
   homework and   41–2
   homework assignments   46–8
   interpretation, demystifying   48–54
   interpretive methods   46–8
   low-stakes writing   54–8
   metacognition   48–54
   need for reading   31–4
   reading schedule   34–7
   take-home quizzes   42–6
aestheticism   8
"Analyzing Critical Essays Worksheet" activity   138

Anderson, Virginia Johnson
   Effective Grading: A Tool for Learning and Assessment in College   145
anthology project   86–90
Arnold, Matthew   39
   Culture and Anarchy   37, 38
assessment   6, 14, 15, 50, 96, 99, 100, 104, 107–9, 111, 112, 121, 142–4, 155 n.1
   formal   129, 146
   formative   42, 54, 103, 108
   high-stakes   145
   low-stakes   147
   self-assessment   125, 127
   summative   42, 103, 108
Auden, W. H.
   "Spain"   74

background knowledge   75–7, 79–82, 85, 86, 90–1, 95, 153 n.1, *see also* advanced literacy, prior knowledge in literature classes
backward design   100–1
Baishya, Amit   21
Baldwin, James   18
Bangs, Lester   68
banking model of education   12
Benjamin, Walter
   "Work of Art in the Age of Mechanical Reproduction, The"   107–8, 133–4
Bhabha, Homi
   "Of Mimicry and Man"   134
Birkenstein, Cathy
   They Say, I Say: The Moves that Matter in Academic Writing   137, 156 n.3

Bishop, Elizabeth
    "Fish, The"   42
Blake, William
    "Chimney Sweeper"   111
    "Clod and the Pebble, The"   49
Blau, Sheridan   16, 26, 27, 70, 75, 156 n.4
    Literature Workshop, The   38, 153 n.1
Bowen, Elizabeth   91
    "Attractive Modern Homes"   85
    "In the Square"   83–5
Brookfield, Stephen D.   28
    Skillfull Teacher, The   31, 128

canon   xii, 5, 7, 8, 11, 12, 17, 18, 21–3, 60, 62–5, 67, 68, 75, 95, 96, 109, 115, 119, 151 n.14, 152 nn.4, 23, 154 n.5
Casablanca (film)   19
class discussion   11, 13–15, 18, 32, 49, 56, 77–8, 91, 104, 105, 112
class participation   15
close reading   17–19, 23, 42, 50, 52, 58, 82, 104, 128
Closterman, Chuck   68
clueless   59–65
cognitive learning research   154 n.3
Coleridge, Samuel Taylor   20
    "Eolian Harp"   4
    Lyrical Ballads   116
collaboration   8, 32
commentary, concise and targeted   146
confusion   45, 70, 71, 129
    praise of   26–8
    textual   28–31
content knowledge   5, 20, 124, 132, 152 n.23
contextual knowledge   80, 83, 86, 90, 91, 153 n.1
contract grading   143, 144
Conversation Poem   4
course design   16, 24, 97–100, 116, 126, 145
    integrated   126–45
creativity   23, 81, 88, 98, 105, 106
Crime and Punishment   22
critical pedagogy   11
cultural knowledge   64, 65, 79–81, 83–4, 94
cultural literacy   6, 8, 20, 60–4, 67, 95, 96, 109, 151 n.14, 152 n.23

definition of   60
inadequate   61
as process   83–5
provisional   79–83, 85
curriculum design   94–6

Dead Poets Society (film)   119–21
declarative knowledge   12, 15, 22, 37, 43, 54, 60–4, 68, 71, 72, 95, 109, 111, 124, 152 n.23, 154 n.3
Dickens, Charles   34
discipline   xi, 14, 16–17, 63, 144
discussion (and discussion-based)   xii, 8, 11–15, 17, 21, 24, 27, 36, 38–40, 43, 50, 52, 54, 58, 59, 61, 63, 69, 71, 73–83, 86, 87, 90, 99, 104, 106, 108, 114, 116, 117, 124, 129, 134, 137, 144, 156 n.4
    class   11, 13–15, 18, 32, 49, 56, 77–8, 91, 104, 105, 112
    cultural   26
    group   4, 104
discussion board(s)   4, 41, 42, 54–8, 74, 77, 78, 91, 104, 105, 112, 117
    notes   56–7
    weekly posts   55
Divine Comedy, The   62
dream course
    activities of   103–5
    assessment of   103, 104, 108
    objectives of   102–8
Dryden, John
    Annus Mirabilis   27

economic functions of higher education   10
Eliot, George   34
Eliot, T. S.   131
    "Love Song of J. Alfred Prufrock, The"   20, 22, 59
    Waste Land, The   62
Ellison, Ralph   18
emotional/intellectual transitions   32
empirical knowledge   xii
enlisting of students, in own literacy   78–9
expert blind spot   30, 66, 68
explanatory notes   70–1

fact-based quizzes   32
Fauset, Jesse   18
feedback   xii, 4, 14, 24, 46, 76, 87, 91, 94,
    103, 124–6, 130, 138, 142–8
  formative   145–6
  frequent   6, 41, 42, 58, 143
  frontload   147–8
  guidelines for   145–8
  student   124–6
  targeted   41, 42, 116, 144
  timely   145–6
Felski, Rita   135–6
Fish, Stanley
  Save the World on Your Own Time   8
formal assessment   129, 146
formative assessment   42, 54, 103, 108
Foucault, Michel   16
Friere, Paolo   12

Gallagher, Brian
  "Double Indemnity"   45
Giard, Luce   107
Giroux, Henry   11
grading   4, 24, 32, 41, 42, 56, 58, 89, 104,
    128, 141–9
  binges, avoidance of   148
  contract   143, 144
  criteria   103
  guidelines for   145–8
  objectives and   143–5
  portfolio   144
  problems of   141–3
  self-grading   124
Graff, Gerald   152 n.18
  Beyond the Culture Wars   132,
    154 n.5, 156 n.1
  "Disliking Books at an Early
    Age"   131–2
  Professing Literature   152 n.18
  *They Say, I Say: The Moves that Matter
    in Academic Writing*   137, 152 n.4,
    156 n.3
Great Expectations   35–6
Gregory, Marshall   12
group discussion   4, 104
group homework   139
group projects   86–90, 90–4

Hemans, Felicia   20

Hemingway, Ernest   131
hermeneutic circle   53
Highmore, Ben   107
high-stakes writing   145
Hirsch, E. D.   60–3, 67
  *Cultural Literacy: What Every
    American Needs to Know*   60,
    151 n.14
historical context   7, 12, 15, 58, 59,
    66–76, 83, 85, 86, 101, 110–12, 116
historical reading   26
homework   84, 133, 135, 145, 148
  and advanced reading
    comprehension   41–2
  assignments   46–9, 53, 54, 104, 111,
    138, 140
  graded   103
  group   139
Horowitz, David
  Front Page   10
Huckleberry Finn   131
hybridity   71, 76–8
hypothesis testing   23, 24

individual student's progress,
    tracking   146–7
Inouye, Asao B.   142
integrated course design   15, 24, 100,
    103, 97–114, 126, 145
interpretation, demystifying   48–54
interpretive methods   46–8
intertextual knowledge   80, 81
intro class   46–8, 49–54, 101–2
Isherwood, Christopher
  Goodbye to Berlin   91

James, Henry   34
Jew of Malta, The   22
Joyce, James
  Finnegans Wake   34
  "Sisters, The"   47
  Ulysses   86, 89

Kilmer, Joyce
  "Trees"   79–80
Knapp, John V.   151 n.12
knowledge   3, 4, 6, 7, 9, 14, 16, 24, 28,
    30, 32, 34, 40, 96, 100, 117, 137,
    151 n.14

absorbed   12
background   75–7, 79–82, 85, 86, 90–1, 95, 153 n.1
content   5, 20, 124, 132, 152 n.23
contextual   80, 83, 86, 90, 91, 153 n.1
cultural   64, 65, 79–81, 83–4, 94
declarative   12, 15, 22, 37, 43, 54, 60–4, 68, 71, 72, 95, 109, 111, 124, 152 n.23, 154 n.3
empirical   xii
hierarchy of   21
intertextual   80, 81
prior   22, 59, 62, 65–71, 73, 75–6, 78, 79, 81–6, 94, 102, 153 n.1
procedural   5, 95, 124, 143, 154 n.3
schematization of   24, 96
self-knowledge   x
shared   80
stored   12
strategic   5, 62, 124, 152 n.23, 154 n.6

Lacan, Jacques   30
 "Mirror Stage, The"   29
Lawrence, D. H.
 Lady Chatterley's Lover   82–3
Law School Admission Test (LSAT)   25
Learning and Memory (journal)   32
learning, definition of   6
learning theory   14
lecture   xii, 5, 11–13, 20, 33, 38, 50, 75, 79–83, 90, 104, 134
 mini-lecture   53, 61, 71–2, 74, 77, 78, 83, 86, 103, 104, 106, 116, 128, 129, 133, 134
 short   72, 73
Lentricchia, Frank
 Critical Terms for Literary Study   29
liberatory pedagogy   9
Linkon, Sherry Lee   5, 21, 95, 100–1, 134–5, 137–8, 152 n.23
literary criticism   24, 31, 90, 132, 133, 136–8, 151 n.17
literary history   5, 6, 12, 14, 20, 21, 37, 40, 78, 89, 98, 104, 116, 132, 138
literary inquiry project   137–8
literary pedagogy   11, 30
literary styles and movements   112–14
literary texts in historical context, interpretation of   111–12
literary theory   29, 33–4, 152 n.23
literature professors, as expert readers   153 n.7
low-stakes writing   42, 54–8, 78, 133, 137, 143, 145, 148–9
LSAT, *see* Law School Admission Test (LSAT)

McLaughlin, Thomas
 Critical Terms for Literary Study   29
Mantel, Hillary   68
Marsh, Dave   68
Marvell, Andrew   62
 "To His Coy Mistress"   59
Marx, Leo   131
Meltzer, Francoise   29, 31
metacognition   22–4, 26, 30, 48–54, 58, 61, 64, 68, 76, 77, 84–94, 96, 103, 117, 129, 130, 134
method   4–9, 11–17, 19, 22–4, 37, 40, 54, 55, 58, 64, 75, 77, 102, 105, 106, 110, 121, 127, 143, 144, 152 n.23
 analytical   xi, 46
 critical   7
 intellectual   6, 14, 101, 108, 154 n.6
 interpretive   xi, 7, 14, 38, 46–8, 50, 78, 124
Middleton, Thomas   68
mimicry   71, 76
mini-lecture   53, 61, 71–2, 74, 77, 78, 83, 86, 103, 104, 106, 116, 128, 129, 133, 134
modernity/modernism   37–8, 73–4, 77, 78, 139
Moore, Marianne
 "Baseball and Writing"   61
Morrison, Toni   18
motivation   30, 32, 130, 141, 143, 146, 147
Mrs. Dalloway   117
Mulvey, Laura
 "Visual Pleasure and Narrative Cinema"   134

Nathan, Rebekah   33–4
 My Freshman Year: What a Professor Learned by Becoming a Student   32–3, 116
national culture   62

National Survey on Student Engagement (NSSE)   33–4
New Criticism   17–18, 23
"Notice and Focus" exercise   49
NSSE, *see* National Survey on Student Engagement (NSSE)

objectives   4–6, 10, 11, 13–15, 24, 30, 36–8, 40, 41, 46, 50, 54–6, 72, 76, 78, 90, 98–112, 114, 116, 124–7, 130, 143–7
  departmental   115
  dream course   102–8
  intro course   101–2
  learning   13, 70, 101, 103–4, 106, 121, 124, 125, 127, 129, 155 n.1
  philosophy in action   99–101
  sharpening   110
Odyssey, The   22
Owen, Wilfred
  "Parable of the Old Man and the Young"   75, 76

parallel structure problems   42
pedagogy/pedagogical   7, 8, 22, 26, 28, 31, 59, 61, 70, 77, 102, 109, 119, 122, 134, 153 n.7
  critical   11
  discussion-based   13
  liberatory   9
  literary   11, 30
  methods-based   64
  questions   10
philosophy in action   99–101
poetry reading   2–3, 4, 45, 46, 50–4, 135
political reading   26
politics   xii, 5, 7–11, 13, 25, 26, 34, 54, 105
pop quizzes   32, 55
portfolio grading   144
postcanonical   17–23
practice   6, 8, 9, 14–18, 22–5, 28, 29, 32, 33, 36, 38, 39, 41, 42, 44, 46, 48–58, 63, 65, 66, 68, 69, 73, 76, 79, 83–6, 94, 95, 101, 103, 104, 106–8, 111, 112, 115, 116, 121, 122, 125, 127, 134, 136, 138, 145, 146, 152 n.23

prior knowledge   22, 59, 62, 65–71, 73, 75–6, 78, 79, 81–6, 94, 102, 153 n.1, *see also* background knowledge
procedural knowledge   5, 95, 124, 143, 154 n.3
professor–student relationship   119–24
projects   10, 38, 61, 77, 80, 83, 85–95, 103, 115, 125, 127, 147
  anthology project   86–90
  class wiki   90–4
  literary inquiry project   137–8
prompting   4, 31, 37, 41–50, 53–5, 58, 68, 70, 74, 77, 78, 82, 95, 96, 99, 104, 112, 125, 129, 130, 133, 135–7
provisional literacy, sustained development of   85–94

quiz/quizzes   31, 78
  fact-based   32
  pop   32, 55
  questions   3, 44, 45
  take-home   2, 41–6, 54

reading
  close   17–19, 23, 42, 50, 52, 58, 82, 104, 128
  comprehension, advanced   xi, 9, 16, 23–58, 64, 68, 76, 95, 98, 99, 121, 132, 134, 136, 138
  historical   26
  lack of, strategies against   37–41
  need for   31–4
  political   26
  schedule   34–7
  symptomatic   18–19, 151 n.17
reiteration   19, 51, 78, 83–5, 125
relationship/relationships   24, 41, 76, 106–7
  Dead Poets Society   119–21
  management   119–30
  teacher–student   119–24
resourcefulness   23, 30, 88, 92
Robinson Crusoe   99
Rosenblatt, Louise   32
Rosenwasser, David
  "Five Analytical Moves, the"   47
  "Notice and Focus"   47
  "10-on-1" exercise   48, 50
  Writing Analytically   46–8, 51

Rosetti, Christina
    "Goblin Market"   56–7
Rushdie, Salman
    "Chekov and Zulu"   65–71, 75–7
Rutter, Emily   10

Scarlet Letter, The   20
schematization of knowledge   24, 96
Scholes, Robert   7, 19, 20, 22, 23, 64,
    150 n.2, 150 n.8, 152 n.24, 154 n.7
self-assessment   125, 127
self-grading   124
self-knowledge   x
Shakespeare, William   16, 62, 79
    Hamlet   5, 32
    Julius Caesar   151 n.14
    Othello   25–6, 60
    Tempest, The   20, 62, 99
shared knowledge   80
Shelley, Percy Bysshe
    "Mont Blanc"   4, 117
short supplementary readings   75–6
Smith, Zadie
    White Teeth   18
social justice   7, 9, 23
Song of Solomon   62
Southey, Robert   20
Stephen, Jill
    "Five Analytical Moves, the"   47
    "Notice and Focus"   47
    "10-on-1" exercise   48, 50
    Writing Analytically   46–8, 51
Stevens, Wallace
    "Anecdote of the Jar"   50–4
stored knowledge *vs.* absorbed
    knowledge   12
Stowe, Harriet Beecher   18
strategic knowledge   5, 62, 124, 152 n.23,
    154 n.6
student-centered classroom   6, 124
student conferences, effective use of   147
student response questionnaire   128
student's engagement, in criticism and
    theory   131–40
    challenges to   132–4
    conventions of   136–8
    strategies for   132–4
    working with academic prose   134–6
summative assessment   42, 103, 108

survey course   108–16
    activities of   111
    assessment of   111, 112
    objectives of   109–12, 114–16
Survey of Student Engagement   10
sustained development of provisional
    literacy   85–94
symptomatic reading   18–19, 151 n.17

take-home exam   107–8
take-home quizzes   2, 41–6, 54
teacher–student relationship   119–24
teaching, definition of   6
teamwork building exercise   139–40
Tennyson, Alfred
    "Lady of Shalott, The"   56, 58
textual literacy   5
textual power   5, 19, 64
theory   2, 8, 14, 24, 31, 106, 107, 126
    conventions of literary criticism
        and   136–8
    cultural   45
    literary   29, 152 n.23
    postcolonial   69, 71
    revolution   16
    student engagement   131–40
    take-home exam   107–8
To the Lighthouse   103, 104, 116–17
Trilling, Lionel   131

unconscious competence   30

Walcott, Derek
    "Far Cry from Africa, A"   76, 81
Walvoord, Barbara
    *Effective Grading: A Tool for Learning
        and Assessment in College*   145
weekly discussion board posts   55
Whitehead, Alfred North   61–2
Whitman, Walt
    "Beat. Beat, Drums"   79
wiki project   90–4
    learning   92
    period   93
    requirements   92
    research and citation   92–3
    topics   93
Wilde, Oscar   8
Williams, Raymond   73, 91

Woolf, Virginia   10, 20, 90
   "the everyday" concept   102–8
Wordsworth, William   116
   "Lines Written a Few Miles above Tintern Abbey"   1–5, 11–12, 14, 117
working knowledge   86
writing   xi, xii, 4–6, 10, 15, 17, 18, 24, 29, 30, 41, 68, 72, 74, 86, 87, 91, 96, 99, 106, 107, 132, 141, 144, 147
   assessment of   142
   expository   48
   feedback   143, 146
   high-stakes   145
   improvement of   143
   in indigenous languages *vs.* Standard English   71
   low-stakes   42, 54–8, 78, 133, 137, 143, 145, 148–9
   professional   95
   rhetorical strategies and structures of   135
   short   41, 135
   skill   42, 100
   tasks   100

zone of proximal development   26

www.ingramcontent.com/pod-product-compliance
Lightning Source LLC
Chambersburg PA
CBHW071847230426
43671CB00012B/2094